MEDIEVAL HUNTING

RICHARD ALMOND

SUTTON PUBLISHING

First published in 2003 by
Sutton Publishing Limited · Phoenix Mill
Thrupp · Stroud · Gloucestershire · GL5 2BU

British Library Cataloguing in Publication Data.
A catalogue record for this book is available from the British Library.

ISBN 0 7509 2162 5

To Anne, Rosamunde and Rohan

Typeset in 11/14.5pt Sabon.
Typesetting and origination by
Sutton Publishing Ltd.
Printed and bound in England by
J.H. Haynes & Co. Ltd, Sparkford.

Contents

List of Illustrations

List of Ilustrations

Acknowledgements

In my research for this book, I have consulted hundreds of manuscripts and printed sources over a period of more than eleven years. Many of these sources feature in this publication. Obviously, over such a long period, I have received help, advice and comment from a large number of people: I wish to thank you all collectively. In addition, I owe a special debt of gratitude to Professor Tony Pollard for reading this typescript and for his constant interest, sage advice and invaluable discussion on 'things medieval'. Finally, but not least, I wish to thank my family for their encouragement, tolerance and unfailing belief in me as an author.

Foreword

Late-twentieth century historians, as a whole, disapproved of hunting. As a result they tended to underrate its significance in the medieval centuries. They would note its popularity, especially with the aristocracy, and pass on, regretting the frivolity (or the cruelty), to other weightier and worthier matters. Or, in the case of the common man hounded for poaching, highlight only his struggle against repression. Both focuses were misleading, for hunting was central to the lives of all classes, and enjoyed by all three estates and both sexes. In this splendid new examination of the subject, Richard Almond brings manuscript illustration, documentary sources and literary evidence together to lay bare the purposes, methods, customs and rituals of the pursuit of wild game as a shared culture.

Most of what writing there has been on hunting has focused on the aristocracy, understandably because the surviving sources were generated for their use and pleasure. Besides throwing new light on aristocratic hunting, especially the under-researched participation of women, Almond here does full justice to the hunting practised by the common man, which had its own skills and rituals. Inevitably, since aristocrats sought to preserve a monopoly of the best sport, hunting could be a source of social conflict. However, in the later Middle Ages, from which centuries the greater quantity of evidence survives, hunting was less divisive than either before or after. Broadly speaking, in an era of low population, there was enough game to go around. Social barriers were crossed not just in the organisation of the hunt, but also, as illustrations show, in the aristocratic knowledge and appreciation of general practice.

Nevertheless the boar and especially the deer, were the noble quarry. The aristocratic rituals and ceremonies developed in pursuit of the hart, the mature, male red deer, were of deep cultural significance on several levels. The chase was seen as a preparation for war, not only because it made men fit and hardy, but also because the hunter put himself at risk. Going over the tusks or the antlers for the kill was a moment of supreme danger. It was also a moment, as poets knew, erotically charged. Hunting was thus more than a pastime, a preparation for war, or part of the struggle for existence; it ritually re-enacted male domination. To be learned in venery was as essential an attribute of nobility as to be well-versed in chivalry.

What sets the book apart from earlier works on the subject is the skilled reading of the visual evidence, set against the poetic treatment of the topic and the information provided in the instructional manuals which guided aristocratic hunting. Almond is too good a cultural historian to assume that what illustrators were commissioned to show, poets composed for their audiences, or even instructors set down for the learner, can unquestioningly be taken as representations of reality, of what actually happened. It is one of the great strengths of this work that he continually probes into what might be a representation of the actuality and what of the ideal. What we know of medieval hunting is thus as much how men wanted it to be perceived as what it in practice entailed. But in itself the very representation is highly revealing of the medieval world view. This is a book that both redresses a gap in our understanding and, through its analysis of the evidence, especially the visual, opens up a new window on the medieval mind.

Professor Tony Pollard, 2003

Introduction

Hunting. One of the oldest activities of man and linked from the earliest times with gathering. Today, however, it is one of most emotive words in the British Isles, immediately conjuring up stereotypical images of fox-hunting, regularly thrust at the public by the British media, hunt-supporters and the anti-hunting lobby. At the outset, therefore, it must be stated that this book is a scholarly study of hunting in the Middle Ages and of its place and functions in late medieval society. In the time-span with which this book primarily deals, the later medieval period and Renaissance (roughly from the early thirteenth to the end of the sixteenth centuries), there were numerous methods of hunting and a wide variety of beasts and birds to hunt, many of which are no longer legitimate quarry species.

Hunting and hawking are an integral part of European culture and they have provided an immense wealth of written and illustrative material, much of it instructive, some humorous, some ludicrous and not a little of it ambiguous and requiring reading on several levels. All of this evidence, however, is interesting, whatever one's views on modern hunting, and assists in recreating a picture of medieval life and society. Because it was an important part of everyday life, hunting was a feature of some schoolboy songs in the Middle Ages.[1] Hunting still survives in a few children's rhymes, notably 'Bye Baby Bunting, Daddy's gone a' hunting, / Gone to get a rabbit skin, to wrap a Baby Bunting in'. On wider and higher literary levels, the works of Boccaccio, Chaucer and Shakespeare all include passages about, and clear allusions to, hunting and hawking, as do those of many other writers of the period. This is not surprising; these pastimes were part of their culture and everybody else's, whatever their class or status. For those fortunate enough to

1

be able to participate in the formal chase on horseback and in falconry, which was also pursued on horseback, there were a number of well-known instruction texts on quarry species, methodology, dress and correct behaviour. These didactic manuals and treatises make fascinating reading for anybody remotely interested in what country life was like and how the aristocracy and gentry behaved and even thought, many centuries ago. The illustrated heritage of hunting and hawking is, perhaps, by its very nature, more immediately fascinating. The evidence is overwhelming in variety and amount and includes fabulous illuminated manuscripts such as Books of Hours and psalters, panel paintings, altar pieces, paintings by famous artists, tapestries, wall-paintings, frescoes, stained and painted glass, tomb sculpture and wood-carvings such as misericords. It has the advantage of being virtually all in colour too, so in that respect alone is more empathic to the mind-picture of the period than black-and-white photographs of the nineteenth and twentieth centuries which inevitably conjure up images of a dull, drab, monochrome world. The medieval world was none of these things; the pictorial evidence grabs the imagination and presents a colourful and intensely romantic slice of history. Is this image accurate? It is not, but it does nevertheless form some part of the whole picture and all the evidence of hunting is vitally important in the clarification, assemblage and creation of a holistic image of the medieval world.

Confusions of terminology need to be clarified at this point. What was 'hunting' in the late medieval period and early Renaissance? From the 1750s in England, when a Leicestershire landowner called Hugo Meynell began to raise faster breeds of foxhound,[2] the term hunting has referred specifically to hunting live quarry with foxhounds, basset hounds, beagles, harriers, otter hounds or staghounds. With the invention of personal firearms which were capable of hitting moving or flying quarry, shooting evolved as a separate field sport in the British Isles. The ancient pastime (not occupation) of angling was already considered a separate sport. This is not so in continental Europe, North America or most of the rest of the world, where hunting is used as a much more generic term which covers all varieties of hunting and shooting. A working definition of what I regard as medieval hunting is therefore necessary at this point. In order to try and accommodate the great wealth and variety of evidence from the Middle Ages and early Renaissance, my parameters are necessarily wide: *Hunting is the pursuit and taking of wild quarry, whether animal or bird, using any method or technique.* Wilhelm Schlag, the author of the Summary and Commentary accompanying *The Hunting Book of Gaston Phébus*, a recent translation of Manuscrit français 616, the best version of *Livre de chasse*, defines hunting as follows:

> Hunting in this context, and throughout the book, denotes all methods of taking game employed at the time, i.e. by shooting with bow and crossbow, trapping, etc., and not merely chasing it on horseback with a pack of hounds.[3]

His definition, too, is wider than the general historical notion of medieval hunting, embracing as it does methods other than the aristocratic chase. Even so, his study is of one particular treatise which necessarily constrains his parameters.

What was considered 'game' in the Middle Ages? It certainly did not include all 'fur and feather', but, equally, the term covered more than the modern, legally defined game birds and animals. It was to some extent, therefore, a more generic term than it is today or has been for several centuries. The aristocratic medieval hunter's division of quarry into the categories of 'beasts of the chase', 'beasts of venery' and 'vermin' is discussed in chapter three.

Anglers will immediately note that fishing is excluded from my definition of hunting. This is not because I am anti-fishing. The very reverse, as I was brought up by my father to be a fly fisherman. There is a very good reason for omitting fishing and it is that 'fishing with an angle' has its own fascinating history and there are scholarly historians of angling who research and write about it. One of the latest historical works to be published is *Dame Juliana – The Angling Treatyse and its Mysteries*, by Fred Buller and Hugh Falkus. Some anglers protest that fly fishing is true hunting and I agree that it contains many of the essential elements of hunting: the quest, the stalk, the pursuit, the fight and the death. However, it was, and is, treated as a separate subject by authors and there I must leave the matter. Disappointed anglers may be interested to find a short discussion on the status of angling in the Middle Ages in chapter six.

Having defined hunting, a further question needs some consideration at this early stage. Where did hunting take place? The parameters of hunting are so wide that depending upon the scale and method, it could have occurred just about anywhere, ranging from woodland, through heath and waste to pond, field and orchard. Throughout this book I have used several terms which refer to where hunting took place and these need to be clarified now to avoid confusion. A Forest belonged to the monarch and was a legal term for an area subject to the Forest Laws which were codified by the king. Each forest was administered by a hierarchy of appointed officials who were accountable to the king. An area such as the New Forest was originally a preserve for hunting deer, reserved for the king and to whomever he granted licence. The inhabitants of a forest usually retained long-established use-rights (*usufruct*) within the area, unlike the situation in a park.[4] A chase was a free liberty; hence the Forest Laws did not apply to such an area. However, in practice this distinction was usually lost for many of the chases were granted to favoured nobles and prelates by the king, who retained jurisdiction and required the Forest Laws to be observed and enforced through seigneurial courts. In addition, when the Crown acquired chases from subjects, whether through confiscation, lack of an heir or by gift, then the Forest laws automatically became applicable to those areas.[5] A park or deer-park was an area completely enclosed from the common waste by a permanent fence of wooden pales, constructed to hold breeding populations of red, fallow or roe deer for the purpose of hunting by the owner. A park was usually situated close to the main residence from which the progress of the hunt could be viewed. A park could belong to the king, an aristocrat, a prelate or an ecclesiastical body and was usually administered by a parker or keeper. The right of imparking could be granted or purchased and the number of parks increased

4

enormously during the later Middle Ages and Tudor period.[6] As well as creating chases and licensing imparkment to favoured persons such as tenants-in-chief, the Crown could also grant rights of free warren, the entitlement to hunt for lesser game (not red deer) on the demesne land of the grantee. Parks and free warrens only had the protection of Common Law.[7]

As the habitat suitable for red deer diminished, the necessity to impark and hunt captive populations became more urgent. Between 1500 and 1640 there were forty-four game reserves in England which were still regarded as Forests; over the same period there were twenty-three areas designated as chases, of which thirteen were in, or had passed into, private hands.[8] Outside the forest boundaries, chases, imparked areas, free warrens and conygers (garrenas), freeholders were allowed to hunt on unenclosed land.[9] For the common man who was not a freeholder, areas where he could hunt using his own methods were usually severely curtailed by law and often necessitated a clandestine approach. Hence, although there was a great deal of commonalty hunting, much was discreet or unlawful. However, poaching on royal and other men's land was by no means restricted to rustic peasants and other humble folk.

The main purpose of this book is to demonstrate incontrovertibly that in the late medieval world hunting was a universal activity. It must follow, therefore, that I believe that most of the population either hunted in some way or at least had some knowledge of hunting and its vocabulary. My book presents a considerable corpus of evidence which strongly supports this belief. The available material indicates that rank and status were the deciding factors in how one hunted and what was hunted. In other words, different levels of society hunted in markedly different ways using methods and techniques peculiar to, and indicative of, their own class. Scholars studying the later Middle Ages should be aware of this and acknowledge hunting as one of the most important activities in the medieval world. These are considerable assertions, largely for two reasons. Firstly, almost all recent British historians, with a very few notable exceptions, either ignore hunting as if it did not exist or simply dismiss it in a few lines, relegating the art of venery to the level of an élitist sport confined to the nobility. Secondly, again with the same exceptions, very little scholarly research has been conducted into hunting. It is not that a corpus of evidence does not exist or is unavailable in both textual and pictorial form. Rather it is that over the course of the twentieth century, the great majority of British historians have tended to disregard hunting and its important place within the social and economic fabric of the medieval world. William Baillie-Grohman and his wife Florence, joint editors of *The Master of Game* (1904 and 1909), were the great exceptions to this lack of interest. A select few modern historians of the medieval period have acknowledged the importance of hunting in their overall considerations of late medieval society; these include Maurice Keen, Nicholas Orme, Anthony J. Pollard and Oliver Rackham. However, almost no specialist or single-study books on medieval hunting were published by English authors and very few scholarly articles appeared in the academic press until the late 1980s. The great exception to this general neglect was *Lexicon of the Mediaeval German Hunt*, by David Dalby, published in 1965, a fastidiously researched work on Germanic hunting methodology and vocabulary. Thus, as less and less was researched and written on the subject in the twentieth century, so hunting really did lose its significance. Interest was not to be revived in this country until John Cummins published *The Hound and the Hawk, the Art of Medieval Hunting*, in 1988, later reinforced at a literary level by Anne Rooney's *Hunting in Middle English Literature*, in 1993. Roger Manning's scholarly *Hunters and Poachers, A Cultural and Social History of Unlawful Hunting in England 1485–1640*, appeared in the same year. Jean Birrell made a valuable contribution to our understanding of peasant deer poaching in royal forests in her chapter in *Progress and Problems in Medieval England*, published in 1996.

Although hunting and hawking are acknowledged to be recurrent themes in late medieval English and European literature,[10] for the majority of modern readers the many references to these activities are undetected and remain hidden, and are thus without any contextual significance. However, if one is versed in medieval hunting vocabulary and, in addition, possesses a theoretical and pragmatic widely based knowledge of modern hunting methodology, the numerous references to hunting and hawking in imaginative and romantic medieval works are very significant. Recent work on the identification and usage of hunting language within the fifteenth-century ballads of Robin Hood demonstrates this point. The authors have used hunting and woodsman's language to try and establish the outlaw's possible occupation, and the universal audience for whom the ballads were written.[11] The original ballads have been analysed by scholars *ad infinitum* yet the significance of this vocabulary has been almost completely ignored. This in itself is puzzling as all the Middle English words can be found in the hunting manuals and treatises and the rhymes can only be fully understood when the language is properly clarified.

Man's atavistic traits and the need to be 'at one with nature' were inevitably experienced far more strongly by medieval man, whatever his class, than by his modern counterpart. This is understandable as most of the population lived and were employed in the countryside. Perhaps 95 per cent were peasants, the majority of them unfree, living and working in village communities. The nobles and gentry tended to live in the countryside, visiting and administering their estates and manors. Many of the great monasteries and abbeys were situated in great rural estates. There were few towns and cities, and in England, with the exception of London, these were small in size. Norwich was probably the wealthiest and most populous town after London by 1520, and Bristol, Canterbury, Gloucester and Lincoln were all important centres of trade and commerce. Lay poll tax returns for 1377 indicate that the population of York, the so-called capital of the north, may have numbered some eleven thousand at the end of the fourteenth century,[12] slightly larger than a small modern market town such as Richmond in North Yorkshire. However, as trade developed in the later Middle Ages, so too did towns and and ports, particularly those connected with England's premier export industry, the wool trade, later to be overtaken by the trade in cloth. But in spite of this increasing urbanisation, even townsmen remained in touch with the countryside. Land was owned and cultivated just outside the city walls, farmers living within the town but walking without the walls each day to work. Animals were kept in yards and gardens within the town. Townsmen of all levels hunted and poached in the fields and woods surrounding the town, using the same methods as their rural brethren. Wealthy townsmen, particularly the merchant class, who were ambitious and anxious to rise in status, imitated their social superiors and took up the mounted chase. Thus the links between town and country remained unbroken for centuries, only to be severed, but even then not completely, with enclosures and the mass movement of labour to the industrial cities for employment from the mid-eighteenth century onwards. Two and a half centuries later, that break is almost complete. Politics, investment, planning and development are very largely orientated towards urban areas and their communication links. Even British agriculture, the provider of at least some of our food and guardian of the land, is misunderstood, neglected, misused and abused by the authorities and many of the general public. Hatred of hunting by some Members of Parliament is but one unfortunate facet of this loss of ease with nature and our countryside heritage.

The atavistic urge or need to hunt, described by John Cummins as

the fulfilment of an enduring compulsion to retain a link with nature in a period barely emerging from the primitive, when immersing oneself in the forests of Europe could still create the illusion of being amid a limitless wilderness with infinitely renewable sources of game,[13]

was, and to some extent still is, a powerful psychological impetus to hunters. Although it seems unlikely that the hungry peasant out poaching would have been aware of these emotions, educated nobles certainly were, and Gaston Fébus, in particular, writes of the satisfaction of simple pastoral delights in his manual of hunting *Livre de chasse*,[14] as does the anonymous author of *The Parlement of the Thre Ages*,[15] although this poem belongs to a tradition of didactic literature rather than that of hunting treatises. My point here is that the fundamental desire to hunt was common to all men (and of course, to many women) and that to associate hunting

8

exclusively with the upper levels of medieval society is not only inaccurate but completely unrealistic. This bias in favour of hunting as a purely élitist pastime was initiated by the authors of the manuals, particularly the English writers, who largely ignored the hunting methods of the commonalty and in their writings concentrated on upper-class hunting techniques. Secondary sources appear to have perpetuated this trend and so the inaccuracy gained credence becoming an accepted 'well-known fact'. However, the main purpose of the hunting manual was to present the knowledge of venery from an aristocratic viewpoint to an aristocratic audience; hence bias was inevitable.

Certainly, a great deal of the ancient lore of hunting and woodcraft has been lost as society has increasingly moved away from the land and into towns and cities; this must be to the detriment of the many variants of hunting and shooting which still flourish today. Fortunately, much hunting and hawking methodology and wisdom was written down in what can be termed how-to-do-it books, the late medieval hunting texts. In spite of their frequent disorder and fragmentary structure, the most outstanding features of these fourteenth- and fifteenth-century hunting manuals and treatises is the vast accumulated knowledge they contain and the expertise which is indicated and expected of the true hunter. These early books of instruction were compiled and written by aristocratic authors for the education of aristocratic or 'gentle' hunters, young and old.

To authors of works on hunting such as Gaston III, compte de Foix, and Edward, Duke of York, hunting was not just a sport or pastime; it was the essence of life itself, the very reason for existence. In the Prologue to his *Livre de chasse*, probably the most informative and technically useful text on medieval hunting, Gaston Fébus writes of the three delights of his life – arms, love and hunting, but claims to be an expert only in the last.[16] However, even for the nobility, there was more to hunting than mere pleasure and its various functions are clarified and examined in chapter one.

In his love of hunting, the medieval noble usually had the example of his monarch. Famous royal hunters included Holy Roman

9

Emperors Frederick II of Hohenstaufen and Maximilian I, Kings Edward III and Henry IV of England and Philip II of France. Royalty and the upper classes hunted as part of their heritage; it was expected of them; it was part of being a gentleman. William Langland commented in *Piers Plowman* that it was proper for 'lewede men to labory, lordes to honte',[17] and this view of the formal chase as élitist and the prerogative of the ruling classes is undoubtedly accurate. Aristocratic hunting is both well documented and profusely illustrated. My approach to sorting this somewhat unwieldy corpus of evidence into a useable and coherent structure was to divide the material into two chapters: in chapter two, the elements of aristocratic prerogative, dress and equipment are considered; in chapter three, quarry type, language, methodology and techniques are examined.

In contrast, commonalty hunting lacks direct evidence and even indirect evidence is in short supply. Both textual and pictorial information on lesser men hunting tends to be marginal to the aristocratic chase. A few medieval authors acknowledge commonalty hunting methods and techniques, others ignore them completely. Much of the official evidence recording commonalty hunting refers specifically to deer poaching; whereas the frequency with which other quarry was hunted is more difficult to assess. The threads of evidence showing that people from other classes hunted in their own ways constitute chapter four. As the amount of evidence is relatively small compared to that for aristocratic hunting, the systematic approach combines the structures of chapters two and three, providing some measure of comparison for the reader.

However, even the mounted aristocratic chase and its success depended upon the administration, organisation and expertise of the king's, or great magnate's, hunt establishment. This organisation consisted of a hierarchy of officials and salaried professional huntsmen, most of whom were not of gentle birth but originated in the commonalty. These men were 'lerned' but not 'gentle', as William Baillie-Grohman's compilation of hunt officials and their salaries in *The Master of Game* clearly indicates.[18] In *The Stag of Love*, Marcelle Thiébaux comments that 'there is no lack of medieval evidence of the hunt's widespread practice'[19] and this can reasonably be interpreted to include the participation of those other than the nobility, that is, the employed hunt officials. Furthermore, in certain methods of hunting, the professionals employed beaters from the locality to drive game, principally deer, towards the gentle hunters waiting at their stands or trysts, bows in hand. Were these peasant beaters participators in the hunt? I think that they were and undoubtedly their experience made them knowledgeable of aristocratic hunting practices, just as modern beaters are *au fait* with every aspect of grouse- or pheasant-shooting, although they are not actually shooting the game themselves. Then there is poaching, the grey area of hunting. All classes were doing it, including nobles, gentry, ecclesiastics and townsmen, even women, and being prosecuted and fined by the Forest courts. Where do poachers fit into the structure of medieval society? Both occupational hunting and poaching are explored in chapter five.

Then there is the conundrum and ambiguity of medieval women hunting. Were they active participants with a true 'lernedness' of venery or merely decorative audience on the sidelines? Why were they apparently marginalised by men and why do modern historians remain silent on this subject? What other roles did women play within the wide parameters of hunting? This complex subject is analysed in chapter six.

The traditional picture of medieval hunting is thus not as clear cut as most historians would have us believe. We need to assess a wide variety of evidence, searching in particular for three elements, participation, quarry species and methodology, in order to appreciate the universality of hunting and its essential contribution towards a better understanding of our medieval forebears. Chapter seven is thus necessarily a brief summary of the eclectic collection of evidence and my own thoughts on the interpretation of this material, together with some examples of composite pictorial evidence which support my notion of the universality of hunting.

Finally, I must make two points relating to the analysis and interpretation of the source material used in the compilation of this book. Firstly, throughout the book I have used both textual and illustrated sources and have endeavoured, wherever possible, to read them together in order to produce clear and plausible results. Secondly, the precise interpretation of any evidence, particularly illustrated material from hundreds of years ago, presents particular problems and challenges to the historian attempting to elucidate what actually happened and what constituted 'reality'. There are almost always several levels of meaning to a medieval or Renaissance hunting illustration, whether it be from a manuscript, painting, misericord or tapestry. This multiplicity of possible meanings also often applies to medieval literature, especially romantic and imaginative texts. Although this methodological difficulty provokes issues, sometimes of an ambiguous or conflicting nature, it is also immensely stimulating to the historian and helps make the interpretation of medieval and Renaissance sources an utterly fascinating pursuit.

ONE

'Delite' and Other Functions

In *Livre de chasse*, a canonical manuscript begun on 1 May 1387 and completed in 1389,[1] Gaston Fébus remarks: 'tout mon temps me suis delite par espical en trois choses, l'une est en armes, l'autre est en amours, et l'autre si est en chasce . . . .'[2] This illustrates the importance that hunting held in the life and mind of one medieval French noble, a self-confessed hunting enthusiast and former mercenary captain who had retired from his profession to his vast estates in south-west France. However, it can be applied to a greater or lesser extent to the educated European upper classes as a genre and as a class. The Second Estate, the nobility and knights, hunted and were expected to do so. Not everybody in the establishment automatically approved, however; in his satirical work *Policraticus*, John of Salisbury derides hunting as one of the diversions and frivolities of courtiers and adopts a hostile, even socialistic, attitude towards aristocratic hunters.[3] In addition, he acidly remarks, 'Rarely is one found to be modest or dignified, rarely self-controlled, and in my opinion never temperate.'[4] Harsh words, although he admits his criticisms are partially for amusement's sake.

Yet in spite of the apparent monopoly of this pastime by the upper classes, hunting in its widest sense was not the preserve of the courtiers and educated élites. Owing to the various and disparate needs of medieval society, the functions of hunting ensured that it was widely engaged in throughout every community.

For the ruling classes, avoiding idleness, and therefore sin, was important and hunting provided the ideal anodyne of healthy, violent and enjoyable exercise. Edward, Duke of York, using the words of Gaston Fébus, comments on this function of venery:

13

The first resouns is for the game causeth oft a man to eschewe þe vii deedly synnes. Secoundly men byn bettir ryding, and more just and more vndyrstondyng, and more appert, and more esye and more vndirtakyng, and bettir knowyng of all contrees and of all passages . . . and helthe of man and of his sowle for ho that fleeth þe vii dedly synnes . . . shal be saued, than a good huntere shal be saued, and in this world haue joye ynow, and of gladnesse and of solace . . . .[5]

He continues in the same manner, emphasising the dreadful possibilities idleness afforded for dwelling on the sins of the flesh:

for whan a man is ydul and rechless without travayle and men ben occupyed to be doyng somme þinges, and abideth ther in here oiþer in here Chambre it is a thyng which draweth men to ymaginacioun of fleishly lust an plaisire. . . .[6]

Gentle hunters were instructed in the art of hunting from an early age and *The Master of Game* advises, 'It wilt tech a man to be a good huntere, first þe must be a childe passid vii. or viii. yere of age or litel elder . . .'.[7] According to Nicholas Orme, the tradition of including hunting in the curriculum of young nobles, particularly heroes, dates back to the epics of the twelfth century.[8] Gottfried von Strassburg's *Tristan*, written in about 1210, provides the earliest available full account of education for a young noble; its requirements include knowledge of tracking and hunting, riding, the military arts and athletics as well as the study of reading, languages and proficiency in music and chess.[9] Horn, a king's son and the hero of a French poem written between 1150 and 1175, learns 'to play all the instruments under heaven, to hunt in wood and by river, to manage a horse and defend himself'.[10] In *Guy of Warwick*, a slightly later French poem of about 1235, Guy, the son of the Earl of Warwick's steward, the Lord of Wallingford, has a Master to teach him and is given experience in handling dogs and falcons.[11] The education of these fictional young heroes is reflected in that of many historical figures of the late medieval period. Thus, Alexander III of Scotland, aged ten, hunted in Galtres Forest near York in 1251[12] and Henry VI coursed hares and foxes at Bury St Edmunds in 1433/4 when he was twelve.[13] This royal tradition of formalising the subjects included in the educational system was quickly adopted by all ranks of the aristocracy eager to produce educated offspring who would make their way successfully in the world. Thus Geoffrey Chaucer, son of a London vintner, received the education of a gentleman, beginning as a page in the household of Prince Lionel, second son of Edward III.[14] This education inevitably included instruction in hunting and hawking, and his poems, such as The Booke of the Duchesse and The Assembly of Foules contain many references and allusions to both aristocratic activities. Several illustrations in *Livre de chasse* show Gaston Fébus as Master, instructing young nobles in the arts of hunting.[15] This gentlemanly ideal of educating one's sons in the correct way continued into the Tudor period and beyond. Henry VIII's archbishop, Thomas Cranmer, was an active and enthusiastic athlete in his youth and his father

was very desirous to have him learned, yet would he not that he should be ignorant in civil and gentleman-like exercises, insomuch that he used him to shoot and many times permitted him to hunt and hawk and to exercise and to ride rough horses . . . after study, he would both hawk and hunt . . . and would sometimes shoot the long bow.[16]

The curriculum for girls was necessarily different in several respects, but in *Medieval Children*, Nicholas Orme comments that, 'noble and gentle girls needed to learn table manners like those of their brothers, and some of them took part in hunting of a less exacting kind'.[17]

For young men of the upper classes, the three basic accomplishments – facility of address, the practice of religion and mastery of etiquette – were acquired early in life, and were followed by knowledge of literature, music and the visual arts and competence at dancing plus training for war, hunting, archery and indoor games. From hunting children learned several essential skills, including horsemanship and the management of weapons, and gained knowledge of terrain, woodcraft and strategy.[18] For the future ruling classes, the warriors and leaders in war, hunting provided invaluable lessons and practical experience. This formal education also produced a class which spoke its own technical language of venery and understood the hunters' catechism of specialised vocabulary, indicating they were 'lerned' both by birth and training.[19] Because of this early instruction, the upper classes took hunting and hawking as part of their existence for granted and, in addition, the rest of society expected them to participate in these activities. In *Piers Plowman* William Langland makes this latter point very clearly. Peris, the farmer, agrees to labour, having been told, 'Y shal swynke and swete and sowe for vs bothe',[20] then says to the knight that in return he must guard the Church, protect Peris from wasters and wicked men

> And go hunte hardelyche to hares and to foxes, To bores and to bokkes þat breketh adoun myn hegges, And afayte thy faucones to culle þe wylde foules For þey cometh to my croft my corn to diffoule.[21]

Other texts reinforce the knightly function of hunting. The fourteenth-century French treatise *Le Livre de l'ordre de chevalerie*, arguably the most important chivalric manual of the late Middle Ages and probably translated from the lost *Le libre del Orde de cauayleria* written in about 1276 by Ramon Lull, advises that the knight 'exercise upon his horse either by hunting or in other ways that may please him'.[22] In his *War in the Middle Ages*, Philippe Contamine refers to the warrior element in hunting, commenting that 'Because of its role in contemporary armies, all exercise on horseback [by the knightly classes], notably hunting, could be considered as preparation for war'.[23] King Alfonso XI, who ruled Castile between 1312 and 1350, echoed the ideas of Xenophon and wrote of the similarities between war and hunting:

> For a knight should always engage in anything to do with arms or chivalry and, if he cannot do so in war, he should do so in activities which resemble war. And the chase is most similar to

16

war for these reasons: war demands expense met without complaint; one must be well horsed and well armed; one must be vigorous, and do without sleep, suffer lack of good food and drink, rise early, sometimes have a poor bed, undergo heat and cold, and conceal one's fear.[24]

Piers Plowman highlights another important function of the hunt. Forests, chases and parks covered much of the British Isles so virtually every town and village was near to woodland and wasteland which harboured an abundance of game and other birds and animals. Many of these creatures were regarded as enemies by a society based upon agriculture,[25] particularly by the peasants whose fields, orchards and animals were plundered. Langland refers to this problem when he comments, 'Thy shep ben ner al shabbede, the wolf shyt þe wolle'.[26] Foxes were a particular problem, taking lambs in the spring and geese, ducks and hens throughout the year. A marginal picture in *The Luttrell Psalter* shows a fox carrying off a fat goose, a considerable economic blow to its owner.[27] Hunting thus helped in protecting and preserving the food stocks and was seen as the responsibility of the Second Estate whose duty it was to protect the Church and the rest of society.

Hunting had another immediate practical use in that it provided fresh meat, especially at times when there was no other to be had. Owing to the lack of winter feed, much domestic stock was probably slaughtered in the autumn and the meat salted down for use during the cold season,[28] although this long-held theory is now in dispute. No doubt by the spring, salted meat tasted foul and fresh game held attractions for both legitimate hunters and poachers alike.

Much of the need for fresh meat was supplied by venison, the flesh of deer. In this respect, the most important species was the largest and heaviest, the red deer. As regards numbers and commercial significance fallow deer were secondary, although they became increasingly important during the period as red deer stocks declined. The smallest species, the roe deer, was very much less prized, common though they were in English forests and parks.[29] Deer were required in large quantities, particularly during the lean months of winter and in late summer when they were in prime condition with plenty of fat. This constant demand for venison is clearly shown in *The Master of Game* which relates that Edward II moved his huntsmen with their packs of hounds around the country in order to obtain fat venison. For example, on 27 July 1313, John Lovel, Master of the King's Buckhounds, was sent to various specified forests and chases in Wiltshire, Southampton and Berkshire to take a total of 24 harts (male red deer over six years) and 54 bucks (male fallow deer). On the same day, William de Balliolo, Master (probably) of the Greyhounds, and Robert Lesquier, Master of Harriers, were despatched to various forests and chases in Nottinghamshire, Derbyshire, Huntingdon, Northampton and Essex to take a total of 34 harts, 58 bucks and 40 hinds (female red deer). On the 14 and 15 July 1315, orders were given by the king for 322 harts, 302 bucks and 24 does (female fallow deer) to be taken in thirty-three forests, parks and chases in the kingdom.[30]

The quantity of game required by the king appears phenomenal. Hunting a single hart for sport on horseback, using a pack of hounds, could take all day and although 'sporting', only produced one carcass. Other methods had to be employed and the most effective was driving several, or sometimes many, deer at a time into fixed nets, thus producing large quantities of much-needed protein. A miniature in the Calendar of MS Egerton 1146, an early sixteenth-century German Book of Hours, shows a mounted noble engaged in such an activity.[31] However, this type of hunting was not regarded as 'sport' by the nobility but rather as food collection, an occupation for the trained professionals working in the great hunting establishments of the king and his premier magnates. Gaston Fébus considered the use of nets unsporting, but includes a chapter and illustrations on their manufacture and application in his treatise.[32] He is at pains to make clear to his audience the vast difference between gentlemanly sport, with its lack of necessity, and the mere provision of meat, a point reiterated by Edward of York:

Men take them with hounds, with greyhounds and with nets and with cords, and with other harness, with pits and with shot and with other gins and with strength, as I shall say hereafter. But in England they are not slain except with hounds or with shot or with strength of running hounds.[33]

Their point is clear: red deer are taken in specific accepted sporting ways; other methods exist but do not concern the noble or gentle hunter. Anne Rooney's research shows that Middle English literature concentrates upon the courtliness of hunting rather than the obvious element of the chase: 'This is what marks it as a noble sport, rather than the simple and ignominious pursuit of animals for food or fur'.[34] For the upper classes, methodology and courtly practice were inextricably connected and dictated the functions of sport and provision of fresh meat, particularly venison.

The dates of the royal orders to obtain venison are interesting in that they point to the high value of fresh fat venison, even in the summer months when agricultural food production should have been approaching its maximum. Venison clearly formed an important part of the high-protein diet of the ruling classes. Significantly, it also represented status, wealth, power and privilege; the common people did not eat venison as they were not allowed to take deer. Presents of venison to relatives, friends and acquaintances were customary and well received. Such gifts were sometimes recorded in household accounts or letters, as in the Stonor letters of 1480 which twice mention gifts of fallow buck meat from their parks.[35] Newly made gentlemen were thus imitating the traditional generosity of their social betters. Framlingham was a large park of fallow deer belonging to the Duke of Norfolk. The 1515–19 game-roll of Richard Chambyr, the keeper or parker, shows the duke's largesse as regards his gifts of venison (buck and doe meat) to his aristocratic friends and neighbours, churchmen and their institutions, the local parson (as tithe), and even nearby towns and villages.[36] As Lord Treasurer, the Marquess of Winchester was entitled to a 'fee-buck of the season' from the Great Park of Nonsuch Palace. In 1556 he generously gave this privilege to the Company of Grocers.[37] These town worthies no doubt used their expertise to produce a splendid annual venison feast for the guild members, presumably including the Marquess.

The fat of game is termed 'grease' in the hunting books whether the animal was hunted for sport or to replenish the larder, and this word was a familiar one in even the highest of household economies. The fat of red and fallow deer was usually referred to as 'suet', occasionally as 'tallow', whereas that of the roe buck was termed 'bevy-grease' and the fat of other beasts 'grease'.[38] In *Sir Gawain and the Green Knight* Sir Bertilak summons Gawain and 'Shewes him the schyre grece schorne upon rybbes'[39] of probably red, or possibly fallow, deer. The anonymous author of *The Tretyse off Huntyng*, calls the white or silvery fat of the hare 'argent',[40] and William Twiti, Huntsman to Edward II, comments in *The Art of Hunting* that the hare is 'þe most merveylous beste þat is in þis lond. . . . For as miche as he beriþe grese and crotyth and rongith.'[41] Twiti further explains, 'And the tyme of grece begynneth alle way atte the fest of the Natiuyte of Saynt John Baptist [24 June]'.[42] However, Twiti may have been referring to the 'time of grace', meaning the 'fence month'. Summer was the season of good grazing during which both game and livestock accumulated a layer of fat, but in England June was also traditionally the fence month for red deer when the hinds dropped their calves and the herds of deer were left undisturbed by hunting or any other interference.[43] This period was the English medieval equivalent of a close season and is discussed in more detail in chapter three.

Hawking was very much an upper-class sport, largely because of the huge cost of birds and equipment, and the inordinate amount of time necessary to train the falcon or hawk. However, falconers were providers of fresh meat for the aristocratic table, although on a small scale. In the days before effective guns were invented, the only real alternative to trapping avian prey, apart from a lucky bow-shot, was to fly falcons and hawks at game birds and other edible birds. The peregrine falcon was the preferred bird of prey for nobles. The female peregrine or falcon was favoured over the male or tiercel by aristocratic falconers because of her greater size and fierceness; she would take cock and hen pheasant, partridge, wild duck of all species, wild geese and bustard, as well as large sporting prey such as herons and cranes which, surprisingly to modern palates, were also deemed edible.[44] *The Parlement of the Thre Ages* describes various types of falcon taking mallard and herons:

> Laners and lanerettis lighten to thes endes, Metyn with the maulerdes and many doun striken; Fawkons pay founden freely to lighte, With hoo and hawghe to the heron pay hitten hym full ofte, Buffetyn hym, betyn hym, and brynges hym to sege, And saylen hym full serely and sesyn hym there-aftire.[45]

The larger falcons would take hares as well as the larger quarry birds while the smaller hunting birds were mostly used for partridge. The tiny merlin was particularly useful against rising larks,[46] larks' tongues being a delicacy much in demand by the upper classes and more prosperous and sophisticated townsfolk. Obviously, the quantities provided by hawking were insignificant compared to those furnished by any form of deer hunting with hounds, by driving deer towards hunters waiting at stations or by driving deer into fixed nets. However, the results of a successful hawking foray ended up on the high table and provided a much appreciated tasty supplement to any feast.

So far the importance of hunting for food, particularly deer, has been discussed primarily in relation to the upper and educated classes. The rest of society probably did not have much opportunity to eat venison, unless it had been poached. However, it must be emphasised that in the short term, acquiring fresh meat of any variety was probably more important to the peasants than to the aristocracy who had access to other sources of meat. The methods used by the common folk had to be far more catholic, and ranged from trapping wild boar to liming sticks on branches to catch songbirds and netting sparrows. Supplementing and varying the basic diet of vegetables and bread was the function of these practical forms of hunting; nor did peasants limit themselves to catching small animals and birds. In *Livre de chasse*, Gaston Fébus is one of the few authors to include a number of commonalty hunting methods such as how to trap a wild boar. He tells how a wild boar raided a farmer's orchard and was trapped in a pit, the entrance to which had been concealed with brushwood. As John Cummins comments: 'When one thinks that many a peasant spent much of the year fattening a domestic pig in preparation for winter, an autumn windfall such as this in one's orchard was probably as welcome as the apples themselves.'[47] Gaston Fébus also relates that French peasants used various trapping techniques to guard their stock and crops against wolves, bears and other beasts.[48]

At the other end of the quarry scale, peasants caught small birds such as thrushes, sparrows, finches and songbirds, using nets, nooses, decoys and bird-lime. These scraps of protein were taken not only for their food value but also because, unless kept down in numbers, they seriously damaged crops. The main quarry species of professional wildfowlers were wild duck and geese, but they took songbirds too, selling them in the towns as food.[49] Any type of fresh protein was welcome and, with the exception of foxes and wolves, just about every animal and bird was considered edible.

Rabbits, usually referred to in the medieval texts as conies, a term derived from the Latin *coningus*,[50] were in a category of their own for several reasons. They are praised in Proverbs where they are included in the 'four things which are little upon the earth, but they are exceeding wise' and then specifically, 'The conies are but a feeble folk, yet make they their houses in the rocks'.[51] Conies were introduced to the British Isles by the Normans and for several centuries total numbers remained small. They did not do well in the damp British climate and were not natural burrowers. However, both their meat and fur were highly marketable and so conies were husbanded in artificial burrows, in warrens, areas of land preserved for the domestic or commercial rearing of game, rather than allowed to breed in the wild and be hunted. These medieval warrens represented almost the sole source of rabbits in England and it was not until the eighteenth century that the animals spread successfully in the wild, notably in the easily excavated sandy soils of East Anglia.[52]

Rabbits were regarded with contempt by true or gentle hunters as they were hunted for their fur, not for sport.[53] The Duke of York remarks, 'Of conyges speke I not for no man hunteth far hem but zit be bisshunters . . .' meaning fur-hunters belonging to the commonalty.[54] He is, of course, quoting Fébus who was familiar with the animal as his vast lands lay in southern France, the natural habitat of the rabbit. However, landowners were eager enough to be granted rights of warren and husbanded conies because of the considerable revenue which their meat and fur generated. Not surprisingly, the element of hunting snobbery was not seen to be at odds with the opportunity to profit from farming these small creatures. Not only is the status of rabbit hunters in question, so is their gender, and *Queen Mary's Psalter* shows peasant women taking rabbits at an artificial warren using ferrets and nets.[55] Although rabbits were thus unusual as a quarry species in medieval England, doubtless some escaped and bred in small numbers in the wild. Presumably these feral bunnies were poached and hunted by common hunters, and thus changed their status from a husbanded to a hunted species.

An ancillary function of hunting for meat was the production of raw materials for the processing industries supplying domestic and commercial markets. Furs, hides, skins, antlers, horns, teeth and bones were all used in huge quantities for a wide range of products. Hides were made into leather by two distinct processes, tanning and tawing (tawers produced white leather).[56] The most valuable fur, with royal and noble status, was ermine, produced from the winter pelage of the stoat. The stoat's tail retains its black tip and when used on robes, these were arranged at regular intervals. Hence, the heraldic description of the fur Ermine is black spots, which can be of various patterns, set on a white ground.[57] Following close behind in status was lettice, made from the white winter coat of the weasel.[58] Both these furs were used for whole robes and trimming robes, and under the various sumptuary laws were restricted to royalty and the nobility. Even knights and ladies with annual incomes of between 400 marks (£266 13s 4d) and £1,000 were forbidden to wear ermine and lettice.[59] Rabbit fur was much sought after by the lower classes, especially in the fifteenth century as prosperity increased in the towns and ports.[60] The white belly-fur from conies resembled the higher status ermine and was used as an imitation trimming by socially ambitious people wanting to make the 'right' impression. Non-specific white fur was known as miniver and was also in much demand.

Under the 1363 statute, the womenfolk of esquires with an income of over 200 marks (£133 6s 8d) could wear 'fur turned up of miniver, without ermine or lettice'.[61] *Vair* is another heraldic fur and was red squirrel skin, said to be the fur from which Cinderella's slippers were made, mistranslated as *verre*, meaning 'glass'.[62] Wolves provided valuable warm fur, used especially for hoods, capes and cloaks, and wolfskins were also processed by tawers. Between 1394 and 1396 the monks of Whitby were paid 10s 9d 'for tawing 14 wolf skins'.[63] Fox pelts were much sought after too, but *The Master of Game* cautions, 'The foxes' skins be wonderfully warm to make cuffs and furs, but they stink evermore if they are not well tawed'.[64] The 1363 statute allowed the wives and daughters of craftsmen and yeomen to wear the furs of fox, lamb, cat or coney.[65] Badgers were trapped not only for food (smoked 'badger ham' long remained a country delicacy) but also for their hide which provided poor men with the most durable material for footwear.[66] Imported beaver fur was used to make hats for the wealthy in the later Middle Ages, but the late twelfth-century writer Giraldus Cambrensis mentions that beavers were still to be found on the River Teifi in Wales and on an unnamed river in Scotland.[67] Deer of all three species furnished a great variety of useful raw materials. Deerskin was soft yet tough, ideal material for many types of clothing, including the so-called 'buff' coats favoured by soldiers and hunters.[68] The hide of a deer was valuable, even from a rotting carcass; thus, the skin of a 'putrid' hind found in Sherwood Forest was valued by the Forest court in 1334 at 2s.[69] According to Forest Law, tawers were forbidden to live within the Forest, 'for they are the common dressers of skins of stolen deer'. If apprehended, they were removed and had to pay a fine at the Forest eyre.[70]

Various medicines were made up by apothecaries from antler, and the heart and penis of male deer, those of the hart being considered particularly efficacious. These included antidotes for the plague and poison, and remedies for the bloody flux, colic, gout and birth pains.[71] Antler had many other uses including as knife handles, sword grips, picks, buttons and combs. The recent excavations at Jorvik, Viking York, show that comb-making from antler was an ancient industry. Bones were ground up and made into glue. Teeth were made into tools, such as the burnishers used by illuminators to polish gold leaf in manuscripts; and into ornaments, especially the eye-teeth of red deer hinds which were popular with hunters' ladies. On the continent, *charivaris* were made from the mounted teeth, claws, tusks, horns and antlers of quarry. These elaborate pieces of hunting jewellery not only adorned the wearer but were also believed to protect them from sickness and danger.[72]

Even feathers had their uses. The primary feathers of large birds, particularly the goose, were cut and made into writing quills, and also used to fletch arrows. Long decorative feathers, such as the tail-feathers from the cock pheasant, were used to ornament hats and caps. The two tiny first primaries, or 'pin-feathers', from woodcock wings were used by medieval artists as paint brushes in the production of manuscript miniatures and marginalia. French shooters still call the pin-feather *la plume du peintre*.[73]

The final, and in some ways most important, function of hunting and hawking was that of providing pleasure, and this surely applied at all levels of society. However, under the Roman Catholic regime of the later Middle Ages, any kind of pleasure was regarded with suspicion and could be linked with sin, particularly lust. This attitude was so entrenched in the medieval mind that pleasure often engendered a sense of guilt in the psyche of believers. In *The Testament*, François Villon repeats an old warning on the theme of upper-class pleasures:

> 'In hawks and hounds, in love and war,'
> everyone says the melancholy:
> 'One joy per hundred pains or more.'[74]

However, this is the cynicism of a ruined gentleman-playboy. Gaston Fébus, who delighted in hunting above all else, even love and war, tried to increase the enjoyment of his fellow-men by instruction through his treatise. He found great pleasure in the pastoral way of life and being at one with nature, a feeling experienced by all genuine hunters. Gaston's monologue from *Livre de chasse* clearly communicates this aesthetic appreciation.[75]

The unknown author of the alliterative poem *The Parlement of the Thre Ages* also expresses his delight in the pastoral scene when the lawless hunter and dreamer enters the wood to seek a deer to poach:

> Als I habade one a banke be a bryme syde,
> There the gryse was grene growen with floures–
> The primrose, the pervynke, and piliolepe riche–
> The dewe appon dayses donkede full faire,
> Burgons & blossoms & braunches full swete,
> And the mery mystes full myldely gane falle:
> The cukkowe, the cowschote, ken were pay bothen,
> And the throstils full throly threpen in the bankes.[76]

He then describes the habitats where game may be lying-up at this time of day, those creatures with the potential to supply the further pleasures of the hunt, even though in this case the hunting is of the illegal variety.[77]

Fébus also immensely enjoyed the more obvious excitement of the chase itself and the accompanying rituals and ceremonies. His description of hunting the hart overflows with enthusiasm, every aspect being described as 'good'.[78] In short, everything connected with hunting gave pleasure and satisfaction to Fébus, and by extension to all other hunters. Edward of York echoes Fébus's sentiments and maintains that hunters were happier than other men because of their appreciation of the beauties of nature and their pleasure in the thrills of the chase.[79] Gaston Fébus sums it up neatly, even including a piece of reassurance for those concerned about the after-life, 'Good hunters live long and happily, and when they die, they go to Paradise'.[80]

Fébus thus returned to one of his original points, and one repeatedly emphasised in other medieval treatises and manuals, that of the moral nature of hunting. This was an essential function to the educated élite as it balanced the nagging guilt created by the pleasures of the chase. Hunting would make a better man during this life, save his mortal soul from sin and guarantee his speedy passage to paradise. Hunting was the obvious anodyne to the most worrying of medieval man's problems, or rather to those which concerned the ruling classes, and a place in heaven was perhaps the most pressing as it was uncertain. Whether the peasant poacher, or noble or ecclesiastical poacher for that matter, felt morally improved by a spot of illegal hunting is open to question and the sources are not clear on this delicate point. Perhaps like the opportunities for pre- or post-hunt sexual dalliance, the moral sin of poaching was best kept locked away in a dark corner of the hunter's conscience. Certainly, the pleasure of poaching game must then, as now, have been part of the attraction of illicit hunting. Sometimes the pleasure of poaching local venison had a very sound and understandable human basis for those villagers surrounded by vulnerable herds of red or fallow deer. Recent research into the thirteenth- and fourteenth-century records of the Forest courts reveals that peasants poached deer not only for immediate consumption but for future pleasures too, such as a family wedding feast or Christmas dinner. There is also evidence of peasants making gifts of venison and undoubtedly deriving a very human enjoyment from their unusual opportunity to provide largesse.[81]

In addition to providing pleasure at all levels, sporting leisure activities like hunting and hawking were an important part of making connections; medieval aristocratic 'networking'. As Maurice Keen points out:

the acquaintanceships and friendships formed through them, played an important part in the social life of the landed classes. An invitation to hunt offered the prospect of pleasure . . . and also of encounters in which all sorts of matters could be discussed usefully and informally – local and national politics, family affairs, marriage and giving in marriage.[82]

Standing around at covert-side, waiting for game to be flushed or received, was not perhaps a time for conversation, though doubtless it occurred and was frowned upon, as now ('coffee-shopping'), by the more dedicated hunters. It was the pre- and post-hunt festivities which were particularly valuable times for these political and familial conversations, as well as for less serious gossip and flirtation.

TWO

'Lordes to Honte'

Hunting rights have been a bone of contention and division in European society for at least twelve hundred years. Hunting was regarded as a privilege of the ruling classes and restrictions on gratuitous hunting were initiated by European monarchs in the early medieval period. On the continent, the hunting rights of free men began to be replaced by extended imperial and royal rights during the Carolingian period. Large areas were declared royal forest, essentially hunting preserves, within which the local population was not allowed to hunt or trap game. The local nobility progressively obtained or assumed the right of setting up and administering such preserves. In Germany, from the eleventh century onwards, the free peasantry increasingly lost their hunting rights to local overlords. This development marked the beginning of new social divisions within medieval society based on privileges, leisure and pastimes.[1] The privilege to hunt denoted status and was an expression of leisure, a mark of the ruling élite. This entitlement was therefore much sought after by those with any pretensions to gentility. The well-bred author of *Tristan*, Gottfried von Strassburg, commented in 1210 that this occurred in German lands 'at a time when the petty nobility were acquiring social refinement with an *élan* of which only upstarts are capable'.[2] He wittily made the distinction between 'those who were skilled in the chase' and 'those who wished to pass the time hunting',[3] thus comparing the established nobility with the newly arrived parvenus, always an easy target for aristocratic commentators. Hunting was therefore already well established as an indicator of rank and status in European society by the early thirteenth century. By the time of the Renaissance in northern Italy, hunting was regarded as a noble activity throughout the Italian peninsula and very much 'the privilege of the patrician and signorial classes.'[4] These Italian self-made princes and nobles, whose favoured pastimes were hunting and hawking, accorded very well to von Strassburg's earlier sarcastic description of 'upstarts'. They had, largely, made their fortunes and acquired power through the practice of arms, usually as hired mercenaries or *condottieri*. Now they were determined to demonstrate their power, wealth and status. As Neil MacGregor remarks:

> But these were no simple action men. They tempered the brutalities of *Realpolitik* and the chase with the chivalric culture of Arthurian romance, emulated the refined opulence of Franco-Burgundian courts and, while professing Christian values, sought the *virtu* of pagan Greeks and Romans.[5]

These were the new hard-headed nobility who were going to take the opportunity of acquiring any and every ancient aristocratic privilege and making it very much their own inclusive right, thus reinforcing their power and dominance. The same motive, but perhaps on a lesser scale of real social power, applies to the English Tudor nobles and gentry. Relatively few of them were descended from feudal lords and knights; many were newly arrived, but all wished to present an authentic public face of aristocratic values in order to legitimise their place in society.[6] Naturally, as occurred in the fourteenth century with the Edwardian revival of chivalry, these ambitious men turned to the past for appropriate symbols and pastimes, enthusiastically embracing the martial skill of jousting with its attendant noble element of visual 'badging', heraldry, and the aristocratic arts of hunting and hawking; The English Paston family provide a good case in point. This family emerged from obscure origins in Norfolk, the result of the efforts of William Paston (1378–1444) who, thanks to a good education, rose to be a judge by 1429. His sons and grandsons attained prominent positions, acquiring both wealth and property, thus confirming themselves as landed gentry. The Pastons became one of the most influential families in East Anglia from about 1485 to the outbreak of the Civil War.[7] As members of the ruling élite, they naturally participated in gentle pursuits including hawking, as is shown in their family letters. Thus in October 1472, John Paston III wrote to his brother John Paston II: 'Item, as for a goshawk or a tercel, I weened to have had one of yours in keeping ere this time; but far fro eye, far fro heart. By my troth, I die for default of labour.' Bored on his estate in Norfolk, he had in fact asked his brother several times for a hawk to fly.[8] His brother replied three weeks later: 'I sent you word of an hawk; I heard not from you since. I do and shall do that is possible in such a need.'[9]

Although there is much persuasive evidence of commonalty hunting in England and Europe, the late medieval manuals and treatises make it clear that the pursuit of certain quarry using particular methods was the preserve of the nobility and gentry, the so-called upper classes. This rather loose generic term must be qualified and clarified at this point as it covers a wide social range of men and women. Within 'upper class' all ranks of society are included from royalty and the greatest nobles down to the esquire and gentleman. However, Marcelle Thiébaux comments that 'authorised hunters covered a range of men from barons and honoured clerics to tenants and freemen'.[10] This is rather ambiguous as it might include men who were all upper class (many men of gentle birth were tenants) but equally it could be interpreted to include some who were not strictly of gentle birth.

The most highly regarded and informative authors of hunting and hawking books were aristocratic, sometimes royal, and often closely connected to a royal or noble court. Frederick II of Hohenstaufen, the author of *De Arte Venandi cum Avibus*, possibly the most practical book ever written on falconry, was Holy Roman Emperor from 1215 to 1250 and the maternal grandson of Frederick Barbarossa.[11] Henri de Ferrieres, the late fourteenth-century writer of *Les Livres du roy Modus et de la royne Ratio*, was a member of a famous noble Norman family.[12] Gaston Fébus, the late fourteenth-century author of probably the most influential hunting text, *Livre de chasse*, held the titles of Comte de Foix and Vicomte de Bearn.[13] Edward of Norwich, who translated and adapted Fébus' book for

an English audience as *The Master of Game*, was Duke of York.[14]
Maximilian I, *Der gross Weidmann* and the author of many books
including the *Jagd und Fischereibücher*, was Emperor of Germany
and later Holy Roman Emperor.[15] In addition, the authors of
medieval romance and other imaginative literature containing
passages on hunting reveal their own gentle origins by
demonstrating their personal knowledge of hunting. Gottfried von
Strassburg, the author of *Tristan*, was probably a member of the
urban patriciate of Strassburg, a very cultured man who was also
'deeply versed in hunting lore and no doubt a keen hunter'.[16] From
their familiarity with courtly practice, the anonymous authors of
The Parlement of the Thre Ages and *Sir Gawain and the Green
Knight* were clearly gently born, and Geoffrey Chaucer, although of
London middle-class origins, was educated as a gentleman with all
that that implies. These and other aristocratic authors had enormous
influence on the education, mores and social attitudes of the gently-
born for generations to come.

The dedications and introductions in medieval hunting manuals
distinctly reveal the exclusive class nature of the chase. Gaston
Fébus dedicated his *Livre de chasse* to Philip the Bold, Duke of
Burgundy, another noted hunter and one of the uncles of the young
king Charles VI.[17] Edward, Duke of York, dedicated *The Master of
Game* to King Henry IV's eldest son, Henry of Monmouth, Prince of
Wales, Duke of Cornwall and Earl of Chester.[18] The Shirley
manuscript of *The Master of Game* concludes that 'þis lytell tretys'
should be 'alwey to be submitted under þe correccoun of gentyle
hunters', and the craft and terms are given 'openly to þe knowledge
of alle lordes, ladyes, gentylmen and wymmen'.[19] In the Prologue of
The Master of Game, Edward praises both hunting and hawking as
noble pursuits: 'this book shall be all of hunting, which is so noble a
game' and 'hawking with gentle hounds and hawks for the heron
and the river be noble and commendable'.[20]

In his introduction to the late fifteenth-century manual *The Boke
of Saint Albans*, William Blades comments that the subjects of
hawking, hunting and heraldry were 'those with which, at this
period, every man claiming to be "gentle" was expected to be

familiar; while ignorance of their laws and language was to confess himself a "churl"'.[21] The alleged authoress of this popular manual, Dame Juliana Berners, stated in her introduction to the treatise on hawking that 'In so mach that gentill men and honest persones have greete delite in hauking . . . . Therefore thys book fowlowyng in a dew forme shewys veri knowlege of such plesure to gentill men and þ[er]sonys disposed to se itt.'[22] Similarly, her introduction to the treatise on hunting reads, 'to sych gentill personys the maner of huntyng for all maner of beestys'.[23] *The Boke of Saint Albans* was the first hunting treatise to be printed in England and was reprinted twenty-two times between 1486 and 1615.[24] Its influence upon the hunting fraternity must have been enormous. Of later date, 1575, but continuing this same tradition, George Turbervile says he wrote his book, *The Booke of Faulconrie or Hauking*, 'for the Onely Delight and pleasure of all Noblemen and Gentlemen',[25] and he mentions in his dedication, 'I know sundry Gentlemen (my great friends) deeply addicted to that commendable sport of hawking'.[26] Even the reader is addressed by the printer as 'Gentle Reader',[27] a convention probably originally based upon the gentle status of the reading audience.

John Cummins makes the point that medieval hunting manuals written in English tend to be 'pervaded by the procedural and linguistic snobbery' which excludes the rest of society.[28] This is certainly true. In her edition of the fifteenth-century *The Tretyse off Huntyng*, which concentrates more on esoteric matters and procedure than on the practical considerations of the chase, Anne Rooney comments on the non-pragmatic aspects of the English manuals: 'Hunting to support life does not need the details with which the hunting manuals concern themselves; these are instead the features of the medieval chase which made it courtly and non-utilitarian.'[29]

These two opinions from eminent scholars support the view that for people of high or gentle birth, hunting, with its specialised vocabulary, symbols, motifs and above all, its social significance was an integral part of their lives. It does seems likely that this 'procedural and linguistic snobbery' was an indication that the gentle authors, and hence their audiences, were making a strenuous attempt to make or preserve hunting and hawking as exclusive pursuits of élite groups who felt they were under some pressure from less prestigious, but socially mobile, groups. The 1390 Statute of the Realm in which Richard II decreed that hunting with hounds, ferrets and snares of various types was prohibited to those who lacked 'lands and tenements to the value of 40s a year, or any priest or clerk if he has not preferment worth £10'[30] reflects this pre-occupation of the ruling classes with maintaining the perceived status quo. The statute tells us in the clearest terms that other classes were hunting, possibly in aristocratic ways, certainly for aristocratic quarry including deer and hares, and that by so doing, the commons were challenging the ancient privilege of those whose status was based upon that most incontestable of measures, land ownership and occupation. Even the stated commonalty types of hunting, such as the use of ferrets and snares, were now to be restricted to those permitted to hunt. This was a positive and punitive attempt by the king to restrict all hunting to the ruling classes, a major misjudgement of the common Englishman's perception of his rights to hunt.

This notion of hunting as the exclusive preserve of the aristocracy persisted for several centuries, even in England, arguably one of the more 'democratic' European nations. *The Institucion of a Gentleman*, an anonymous tract published in 1568, makes this very point:

> There is a saying among hunters that he cannot be a gentlemen which loveth not hawking and hunting, which I have heard old woodmen [yeomen foresters] well allow as an approved sentence among them. The like saying is that he cannot be a gentleman which loveth not a dog.[31]

In 1653 Izaak Walton included a commendation of hunting in *The Complete Angler*: 'Hunting is a game for princes and noble persons; it hath been highly prized in all ages.' Interestingly, Walton then cites the medieval conventional justifications, or functions, of the chase, demonstrating the entrenched attitudes and continuity of aristocratic mores:

> Hunting trains up the younger nobility to the use of manly exercises in their riper age. What more manly exercise than hunting the Wild Boar, the Stag, the Buck, the Fox, or the Hare? How doth it preserve health, and increase strength and activity![32]

For the English gentry, hunting and hawking methodology remained largely unchanged well into the seventeenth century. This is evidenced by the remarkable, possibly unique, cycle of wall paintings in the Turret Room at Madingley Hall near Cambridge, dated to between 1605 and 1633. The murals probably depict current practices and consist of bear hunting, boar hunting and hawking, plus two panels of decorative work, almost certainly commissioned by Sir Edward Hynde, the owner between these dates and a known enthusiast for hawking and animal-baiting.[33] In both the bear and boar hunting scenes, gentleman-hunters on horseback and more plainly dressed servants on foot use spears to slay the beasts which are being attacked by mastiffs and greyhounds. Bear-baiting was a popular entertainment and this particular bear provided the quarry for an unusual day's hunting. By this date, wild boar were long extinct in England and park-bred animals were used for hunting. The hawking mural illustrates a classic scene: hounds put up a partridge for a mounted falconer (incomplete) while a gentleman on horseback flies his bird at a mallard on the river.

The aristocratic involvement in hunting is, of course, indisputable. The textual evidence is not only provided by the hunting manuals; the hunting theme also commonly occurs in romantic and imaginative European literature. Its symbolism, the imagery of hunting and the hunting motif, all appear frequently in late medieval romances, narratives and stories. The hunt is often used as a vehicle for a hero on a journey or quest, the flight of the animal leading him to the next stage of an adventure.[34] This usage of hunting, one of the main activities of the upper classes, is hardly surprising as authorship of romantic and imaginative literature was almost invariably aristocratic and the intended and actual audience courtly, noble or of gentle birth. The invariably aristocratic authors included the material of a pastime which was familiar to their predominantly élite audience, weaving the theme of the hunt, with its recognisable progression and procedures, in with the less tangible topics of love, magic and religion. The chase as a narrative agent in aristocratic romances was thus infinitely flexible to the subject matter and apposite to a courtly audience.

Even the patron saint of hunting was portrayed as a member of the nobility, emphasising the exclusive nature of hunting. The legend of the conversion of St Eustace, or Eustachius, to Christianity was well known and a subject illustrated by several medieval and Renaissance painters, including Pisanello and Dürer. The story of Eustace is told in the *Golden Legend* and, briefly, is as follows. Placidus was a member of a distinguished Roman family and an officer of the Emperor Trajan, well known for his charitable works. While out hunting, he was transfixed by the vision of a stag at bay, a fine hart, supporting a glowing cross and an image of Christ between its antlers. Through the hart, or the image, Christ then spoke to Placidus:

> O Placidus, why are you pursuing me? For your sake I have appeared to you in this animal. I am the Christ whom you worship without knowing it. Your alms have risen before me, and for this purpose I have come, that through this which you hunted, I myself might hunt you.

The religious symbolism of the vision is interesting as the hunted beast can be compared to Christ who, in a role-reversal of hunter and prey, is actually hunting the pagan Placidus in order to convert him.

Placidus was at once converted to Christianity and changed his name to Eustachius, afterwards modernised to Eustace.[35] Some time later, Eustace, his wife and two sons, were put to death as Christians under Hadrian in AD 118. His feast day in the Roman Catholic calendar is 20 September.[36] A similar visionary conversion story applies to the equivalent of St Eustace in Germany, St Hubert of Tongres. He too was an aristocrat, said to have been a nobleman of Aquitaine and employed at the Court of Pepin of Heristal. Bishop Hubert converted many heathens to Christianity and performed several miracles. He died in AD 727 and his relics were enshrined in the ninth century in St Hubert's Abbey in the Ardennes. The feast of St Hubert is 3 November.[37]

The Vision of Saint Eustace was painted by Pisanello between 1438 and 1442, not as an altarpiece or mere narrative of the religious event but to demonstrate to his patron his remarkable skill in depicting animals, particularly those associated with aristocratic hunting. It appears from the style and pose of some of the animals that Pisanello's painting was informed by personal knowledge of the illuminations in *Livre de chasse*, and other key hunting treatises.[38] For example, the bear at the upper right-hand side of the painting appears to have been derived directly from the animal being hunted by Gaston Fébus in MS fr. 616 and also closely resembles the bears which appear earlier in the same manuscript.[39] Significantly, *Le Livre du roy Modus et de la royne Ratio* describes the vision of St Eustace in detail and links the ten tines of the hart to the Ten Commandments. Copies of *Roy Modus* and *Livre de chasse* were in plentiful supply at this time and were known in Italy.[40] Pisanello was a meticulous observer and painter of animals so it appears inevitable that he used such canonical manuscript illustrations as a basis for his hunting studies.

The rank and high status of Eustace is firmly established and maintained by Pisanello in three ways. Firstly, by the quarry, a magnificent hart; other noble quarry also feature in the picture, another hart, a hind, a fallow buck, a doe, a hare (being coursed by a greyhound) and a brown bear. Secondly, by the aristocratic method of hunting: on horseback with hounds, several specific types of which are shown including two greyhounds or gazehounds, two scenting or running hounds which were particularly useful in hunting stags, two alaunts and two spaniels, usually used for flushing small game, partridge and quail.[41] Thirdly, by the dress of Placidus: a golden fur-trimmed jacket and a extravagant blue headdress, the height of fifteenth-century court fashion. He carries a decorated hunting horn with gilded mounts and wears long rowelled gilded spurs, the latter denoting his knightly rank. Pisanello has painted not a Roman centurion but a fifteenth-century Renaissance prince, out hunting alone with his hounds.[42] In reality, solitary hunting of this variety did not, and practically could not, occur, the rest of the hunt, comprising other noble hunters, professional hunters and hunt servants was irrelevant to the main subject of the painting. Pisanello may well have been depicting his patron as St Eustace, but the patron and exact date of this small panel painting remain unknown.[43]

The symbolism and icons of hunting and aristocratic love have long fascinated scholars of Middle English and European literature; much has been written on this very complex and esoteric subject. Romances and imaginative literature are brimful of imagery for the initiated. So, for example, the hart can represent a lover, his lady, desire, thoughts, longevity, and even, as has been shown, Christ himself.[44] The imagery of animals very much depended upon the situation or need. The coney or rabbit was associated with women and the hound with men, a clear and erotic connection which can be seen in a number of manuscripts.[45] However, it is the exclusive nature of aristocratic hunting and aristocratic love which is under discussion here, and Michael Camille's masterly interpretation of an illuminated page of a late thirteenth-century French songbook or *Chansonnier* illustrates this point superbly. The page of music, words and visual scenes is of a complex motet for three voices by Pierre de la Croix concerning love's sorrows and delays. The illustrations relate to each voice, the *triplum*, *duplum* and *tenor*. The hunting/love motifs are explicit and Camille comments, 'The lady fondles her own smirking rabbit and her lord's thigh while he strokes his puppy and places his white-gloved hand on the lady's shoulder'.[46] The *bas-de-page* illustration is of stag-hunting, featuring an archer, hound and mounted hunter, viewed by another grinning rabbit. Obviously, to read such a complicated picture with its multilayered and hidden messages successfully, the medieval audience would have been expected to be educated and well versed in such interpretations. This view is borne out by the comments of the medieval musical theorist Johanees de Grocheo, who claimed that such motets could not be appreciated by the common people, but were 'for the learned' and 'those seeking subtleties in the arts'.[47]

The exclusive nature of hunting in respect of rank and status which is the main message gained from the main primary sources has, understandably perhaps, been perpetuated by many secondary source writers. In 1963, Derek Brewer expressed this conventional view as follows:

> The amusements of most men in the court were active and outdoor. Of these hunting was the chief, and the sound of the dogs [sic], the bustle and excitement of gaily-clad riders, the thrills of the chase, the triumphant chanting of the horns, were amongst their highest joys.[48]

In 1970, A.C. Spearing commented:

> Hunting was felt to be the most characteristic activity of the medieval aristocracy, the appropriate means by which in peace-time the aggressive instincts of what was still a warrior class might be given a dignified outlet.

He, too, highlights the importance of procedure and ritual, continuing, 'There is a proper way of doing everything, even cutting up the dead beast, and knowledge of this way is a prerogative of the aristocracy and their skilled servants.'[49]

Spearing believes the Gawain-poet was a 'jantylman' (gentleman) writing for other 'jantylmen', learned in the lore and language of hunting;[50] there is no doubt this is correct as the anonymous author displays his own learned knowledge of hunting deer, wild boar and fox in all its procedural detail. There are 280 lines of the poem devoted to the hunting scenes compared with 370 to the conversations between Sir Gawain and the lady, an indication of the significance of hunting to the courtly narrative.[51] Interestingly, Rooney comments that *Sir Gawain and the Green Knight* provides us with the only complete description of a stag hunt available in Middle English literature.[52]

More recent historians of the medieval period continue in the same vein. Nicholas Orme, writing of the education of the medieval English kings and aristocracy, says that hunting came second only to fighting as the most prestigious physical activity and it was widely practised by male and female aristocrats.[53] He further remarks that throughout the later Middle Ages hunting was a favourite sport of royal princes, but the 'lust for hunting' was not confined only to royalty in the fourteenth and fifteenth centuries; it spread throughout the aristocracy, right down to the children of the gentry. Hawking was equally popular as an aristocratic pastime but less demanding and more leisurely without the same educational status, presumably because of its lack of personal danger or resemblance to warfare.[54] Marcelle Thiébaux writes 'that men in the Middle Ages were passionately fond of the hunt', and the Anglo-Saxon and Norman kings of England restricted vast areas of forest for their own sport, notably the New Forest in Hampshire. The noble hunters, who had inherited or purchased legitimate rights, hunted as a form of recreation and military exercise.[55]

The sport of falconry, or hawking as it is more often called in the hunting texts, was, like the mounted chase, a prerogative of the nobility and gentry. In Spain, for example, the aristocratic Chancellor of Castile, Pero Lopez de Ayala, saw falconry as a superior and appropriate pastime for the aristocracy.[56] The historian Abram, writing in the introduction to *The Art of Falconry*, believed that 'the sport pre-eminently associated in our minds with the Middle Ages is hawking'.[57] Although hawking was pursued by the same social groups as the chase, it was in some ways completely different from the fast, noisy and dangerous excitement of mounted hunting in which hounds pursued quarry that was often out of sight. It was, in contrast, a single combat, like that between knights, usually in full view of the participants.[58] It was also a rather more sedate and introspective pastime, better suited to older men and ladies. Intelligent and truly dedicated falconers, such as Holy Roman Emperor Frederick II, doubtless enjoyed the exacting nature of their sport. Falconry also lacked the ritualistic procedures of hunting, thus appealing to the individual and the aesthetic hunter, allowing the development of a more intimate relationship between man, falcon and quarry. However, hawking had a major drawback in that there was a frustrating period during the year when the birds were *mewing*, or moulting, in the dark of their quarters or mews, and therefore unfit to fly and hunt. Edward, Duke of York, comments adversely on this aspect in the Prologue to *The Master of Game* when he compares hawking and hunting:

> For though it be that hawking with gentle hounds and hawks for the heron and the river be noble and commendable, it lasteth seldom at the most more than half a year. For though men find from May unto Lammas [1 August] game enough to hawk at, no one will find hawks to hawk with.'[59]

Noble falconers valued their hawks more than any other of their possessions.[60] The expense of buying and equipping falcons naturally restricted this mounted sport to the aristocracy, as did the provision of proper accommodation, and the long hours required to train a hunting bird. The gift of hunting birds was much favoured by kings and nobles; it frequently occurred in practice and often features in medieval literature. Indeed, hawks and falcons were so highly regarded that they were sometimes used to pay ransoms.[61] The demand for good birds was constant in England and on the continent; prices were consequently high, and there was a profitable trade collecting and distributing falcons and hawks. Flanders, particularly the city of Bruges, was the main staging point.[62] *The Cely Letters* of 1478–79 show that George Cely, a Merchant of the Staple, was trading in hawks, and probably dogs and horses too, from Calais and Bruges. An abundant family correspondence gives us a rare and fascinating insight into the cross-Channel luxury trade in hunting birds during the later fifteenth century. In 1478, the Vicar of Watford wrote to George Cely: 'Ferthermore, I pray you to remember [me] in thys seson for a goshawke or a tarsel. . . . Also I pray you to send me a bylle of your wellfare, and the prys . . . .'

In October 1478, Richard Cely the elder at London wrote to Richard Cely the younger at Calais: 'Also youre gosehawke, the weche was delyuerd to my Lorde of Send Johnys, ys dede for defayte of good kepying, for the weche I wolde we hadde kepyt the hawke the weche Wyll Cely bravthe home and ys delyvered to the Vekery of Watforde.'

A later letter to George, or perhaps Richard, Cely, Merchants of the Staple at Calais, instructed the purchase of another goshawk at the considerable price of 8 or 9s for Lord St John: 'yeff ye covd bey any at Callas for viij or ixs., and he would pay for the sayd hauke hemselffe for the pleser of my Lord'.[63] On 12 October 1479, John Roosse at Calais wrote to George Cely at Bruges, 'that I scholde com to Breges to you for to helpe to conuey your haukys into England'. These birds would be conveyed via Calais. He mentions that 'I bowte a mewd hauke in Callys syn I cam; sche coste me x/s. and more, the wysche I have sent into Eyngland'. Later that year, Robert Radclyff at Calais wrote to George Cely at Bruges enquiring about buying a 'flecked spaniell' and a horse on his behalf;[64] it seems likely that both these animals were also purchased for hawking.

Throughout Europe, legislation protected and preserved hawks and restricted hawking to the privileged élite. Penalties for disturbing eyries could be savage, including blinding the culprit.[65] During Norman rule in England, the right to keep a hawk was restricted to the upper classes, but the Forest Charter of 1215 stated that every free man might have an eyrie (hawk's nest) in his own woods, from which he could lawfully take nestlings to train to hunt. A bird taken from the eyrie was termed an *eyass*, as opposed to a *haggard*, a hawk or falcon in mature plumage captured and reclaimed from the wild.[66] Stealing a hawk was regarded as a felony in England and any person who destroyed raptor eggs was liable to a year's imprisonment. The Church apparently approved and sometimes imposed these laws, the Bishop of Ely going to the lengths of excommunicating a thief who stole a hawk from the cloisters of Bermondsey.[67] Phillip Glasier must be referring to this incident in his classic *As the Falcon her Bells* when he recounts that:

'People took their hawks everywhere with them, even to church, and one bishop, hearing that his favourite falcon had been stolen from the cloisters while he was preaching his sermon, marched straight back into the pulpit and excommunicated the thief forthwith.'[68]

Like the quarry of hunters, birds of prey were classified by medieval writers. The basic division in the manuals is between *hawks of the tower* and *hawks of the fist*, which conveniently corresponds largely to the falcons (*Falconidae*) and the hawks (*Accipitridnae*).[69] The short-winged hawks were more popular with the French whereas the long-winged hawks, generically falcons, were more favoured in England. The latter birds include the peregrine, merlin and hobby, all of which were, and still are, used by falconers to fly at live quarry.[70] *Roy Modus*'s division differs somewhat from the basic classification. He places the peregrine falcon, lanner, saker and hobby as hawks of the tower, whereas the goshawk, sparrow hawk, gyrfalcon and merlin are classed as hawks of the fist.[71] The hawks of the tower were unhooded and allowed to climb on thermals before stooping on the prey which had been put up by spaniels or pointers, then come in to the lure, whereas the hawks of the fist were trained to come to the fist only, not to the lure. Only short-winged hawks were trained in this manner, never falcons.[72]

Strictly, the term *falcon* refers specifically to the female peregrine but it is sometimes used in medieval and other sources for the females of other species of the *Falconidae*. Usually the species is named, such as the gyrfalcon. The *tiercel, tercel, tassel* or *tarcel* denotes the male peregrine, from the French word *tierce*, meaning 'a third'. The male is a third less in size than the female. Again, this term is sometimes used incorrectly, referring to the males of other *Accipitridnae* and *Falconidae*, although not all male birds of prey are a third less in size than their female counterparts.[73]

By the fourteenth century, authors of hawking texts were linking social status to raptor species, and there are references to every rank of the ruling classes having its own associated falcons, the distinctions becoming more refined as time passes. A passage in MS Egerton 1995 in the British Library shows this increasing trend: 'The namys of hawkys, and to what maner of Personys that they longe vnto euery man afyr hys owne degre and ordyr'.[74] The *Boke of Saint Albans*, written in 1486, exemplifies the late medieval preoccupation with classification and division in the natural and human worlds, cataloguing and assigning particular birds of prey to persons of appropriate rank and status. The *Boke's* list reads:

Theys haukes belong to an Emproure
Theys be the names of all maner of hawkes . First an Egle .a Bawtere .a Melowne . The symplest of theis .iii. will flee an Hynde calfe .a Fawn .a Roo. a Kydde . an Elke . a Crane . a Bustarde a Storke. a Swan. a Fox in the playn grownde. And theis be not enlured . ne reclaymed . because that they be so ponderowse to the perch portatiff.. And theis .iii. by ther nature belong to an Emprowre .

Theis hawkes belong to a kyng .
Ther is a Gerfawken . A Tercell of a gerfauken . And theys belong to a Kyng .

ffor a prynce .
Ther is a Fawken gentill . and a Tercell gentill . and thys be for a prynce .

For a duke .
Ther is a Fawken of the rock . And that is for a duke

For an Erle .
Ther is a Fawken peregryne And that is for an Erle

ffor a Baron .
Also ther is a Bastarde and that hauke is for a Baron

Hawkes forr a knight
Ther is a Sacre and a Sacret . And theis be for a Knyght .

Hawkis for a Squyer .
Ther is a Lanare and a Lanrett . And theys belong to a Squyer .

For a lady
Ther is a Merlyon . And that hawke is for a lady

An hawke for a yongman
Ther is an Hoby . And that hauke is for a yong man And theys be *hawkes of the towre*: and ben both Ilurid to be calde and reclaymed

And yit ther be moo kyndis of hawkes
Ther is a Goshawke . and that hauke is for a yeman
Ther is a Tercell . And that is for a powere man .
Ther is a Spare hawke . and he is an hawke for a prest
Ther is a Muskyte . And he is for an holiwater clerke

And theis be of an oder maner kynde . for thay flie to Querre and to fer Jutty and to Jutty fferry.[75]

The last sentence of the list specifying 'moo kyndis of hawkes' refers to those birds known as *hawks of the fist*, mentioned in the classifications earlier, which were cast or flung (*jeter*) from the fist to strike (*férir*) the quarry. These birds of prey carried considerably less status than the *hawks of the tower*, as their terminal position in the list indicates.

It is significant that quarry species of animal were not classified in this hierarchical way and were never formally identified with corresponding human ranks in medieval society. The hawk or falcon is always identified with the human hunter, so an appropriate comparison between particular birds of prey and social ranks can be quite properly made. In contrast, wild beasts, whatever their individual 'noble' attributes, always remain the quarry and are therefore in a subservient role to the hunter.

Dame Juliana Berner's allocation of species has aroused much controversy over the years, some authorities accepting the list as a piece of social reality, others dismissing it as nonsense. It was described as 'interesting but fanciful' in the 1920s, and 'pretty fair nonsense' and 'partly a piece of fun' in the 1980s.[76] These twentieth-century observations contain much truth, no doubt, as particular occupations qualified for satirical comment. John Cummins points out that the physically fragile musket, the male sparrow hawk, 'would suit the holy-water clerk because it hardly eats anything and because its neurotic behaviour would drive a profane layman to perdition'.[77] This is also probably a jibe at the established Church as priests were supposedly forbidden to indulge in hunting or hawking.[78]

However, whether or not the catalogue reflected reality, part-reality or merely the barbed wit of its author is not really the point. What is important is that the list reveals an underlying social comment, which tells us that not only was late medieval society deeply divided into upper and lower strata (common knowledge and hardly new) but that medieval writers felt it was necessary to highlight the division between rich and poor. Whether their illustration is serious or satirical is less important than the underlying social point and this has been successfully communicated to us, the literate audience, for hundreds of years.

Of course, the list in the *Boke of Saint Albans* can provide a perfect vehicle for lampooning society, and to the medieval mind birds of prey were ideal subjects for this sort of social satire. There are many different species, each with its own distinct and well-known characteristics which could be compared to members of the ruling élite. Also, like humans, they come in all shapes and sizes, from the huge, imperious eagle to the tiny, delicate merlin. Add to these natural points that hawking was seen as a pastime of the upper classes, and one has all the ingredients necessary for successful hierarchical imagery which can be read on several levels.

What, then, of the two birds near the end of the list allocated to common men, the goshawk for a yeoman and the tiercel (here, the male of the species) for a poor man? Do these categories indicate that commoners were involved in hawking? The answer is both yes and no. The goshawk was cast off from the fist, and had a reputation for being very highly strung, difficult to man (tame) and keep healthy. However, it would take partridge, pheasant, bustard, hares and rabbits. The goshawk has been called the most dynamic

45

and successful of all hunting birds and John Cummins remarks that they were 'a great asset to the kitchen, but rather on the level of modern rough-shooting as compared to driven game'.[79] They were very effective hunters but did not possess the 'nobility' of the peregrine and gyrfalcon, so in the medieval mind may have been consigned to lesser ranks of men. In *The Goshawk*, T.H. White, who acknowledges the authority of the *Boke of Saint Albans*, remarks of his own newly acquired bird, 'a goshawk was the proper servant for a yeoman, and I was well content with that'.[80] However, it is unlikely that the 'yeman' of the *Boke* would be a landholder of intermediate social status, a man who had to work his land for a living, or an artisan living and working in a town. Rather the term refers to a man of intermediate status employed in an aristocratic household who had the time to hawk, perhaps as part of his employment as an officer of the establishment and companion to his lord. Alternatively, it is a yeoman falconer who is referred to in the *Boke* and flying a goshawk formed part of his training as a professional falconer in the mews of the lord.[81] This leaves the 'powere man' with his goshawk tiercel, a bird of less weight and power, of lesser status than the female and even more difficult to man. The author of the list is using the word 'poor' in an ambiguous way. An economically poor man, or a peasant, would not have the means to buy and equip, train and maintain a hunting bird. The phrase 'poor man' is therefore most probably one of sympathy for the poor gentleman who has not the means to acquire a decent hunting bird, or the unfortunate mews employee with the wearisome task of caring for and flying such a fractious and, at times, unrewarding bird.[82]

For practical purposes, the falconer, whatever his station, relied principally on a handful of hunting species: the peregrine usually referred to as the 'gentle' falcon, the gyrfalcon or gerfalcon, saker, lanner, alphanet, merlin, hobby, goshawk and sparrow hawk. However, it was the peregrine, the northern race of which was called the nebli, which was most favoured by gentle and professional falconers alike because of its devastating stoop and fierceness. This bird was also identified with, and a physiological extension of, the knight in armour.[83] *The Booke of Faulconrie or Hauking*, written in 1575, endorsed this notion, assigning various knightly character-istics and virtues to the peregrine:

> There are seauen kindes of falcons, and among them all for hir noblesse & hardy courage, & withal the francknesse of hir mettell, I may, & do meane to place the Falcon Gentle in chiefe. The falcon is called the Falcon Gentle, for his [*sic*] gentle and curteous conditions and factions. In hart and courage she is valiant, ventrous, strong.[84]

The emphasis is on the 'gentle' or 'noble' nature of the bird, linking falcon and falconer in mutually reflected rank and status.

Textual and illustrative sources clearly show that hawking was an enormously popular pastime in England and Europe during the later Middle Ages and the Renaissance. By the reign of Queen Elizabeth I there were no restrictions on the possession of hawks or falcons and it appears likely that the sport reached its zenith in England at this time, paralleling the emergence of the new Tudor gentry out of the upper yeomanry. Shakespeare was certainly aware and conversant with the vocabulary, care and methodology of hawking, as is indicated by a speech by Petruchio in *Taming of the Shrew*, IV. i. 191, written 1593/4:

> Thus have I politicly begun my reign, /And 'tis my hope to end successfully. /My falcon now is sharp, and passing empty; /and, till she stoop, she must not be full-gorged, /For then she never looks upon her lure. /Another way I have to man my haggard, /To make her come, and know her keeper's call, /That is, to watch her, as we watch these kites /That bate, and beat, and will not be obedient. /She eat no meat to-day, nor none shall eat; /Last night she slept not, nor to-night she shall not.[85]

Petruchio's speech is, of course, allegorical and he is using the imagery of falconry to describe his developing relationship and control over his wife Katharine, once a 'shrew' but now a 'falcon'.

In this context, Shakespeare's apposite use of specialised hawking language demonstrates his understanding of both falconry and the female psyche. Such words include: 'stoop', the dive of a falcon on to prey from a great height; 'lure', the imitation quarry, often a pair of wings with a piece of meat attached, swung around by the falconer to tempt back his falcon; 'haggard', an adult bird taken from the wild; and 'bate', the wing-thrashing tantrum of a bird hanging upside down on her jesses. He is also well aware of the complexities of feeding a falcon and keeping her 'sharp', on the edge of hunger, before using her to hunt live prey, and obedient to being called to the lure with its attendant reward. Bloated birds refused to hunt and, when released, would often fly off and perch in a tree until hunger drove them back to the lure.

Illustrative sources clearly show that royal and noble hunters tended to dress up, even extravagantly, when hunting and hawking. The noble hunters of the hart in *Livre de chasse* wear bright red, pink, blue or green robes and tunics, as do their counterparts in the 1465 version of *Roy Modus*.[86] Thus mode of dress can be used to differentiate between the upper and lower (or 'other') classes and, rather more obviously, between men and women. However, this can be a misleading generalisation as 'correct dress' varies according to the authority consulted and upon the attitude of the individual hunter. For example, Emperor Frederick II, writing in 1248, includes advice on hunting garments in his chapter entitled 'On the Equipment suitable for a Falconer Hunting Cranes (with a gerfalcon)'. He is very specific:

> The skirts of his garments must be short (habeat pannos vestimentorum suorum curtos), so that they do not hamper his movements, and of a single colour, preferably beige or an earthen tint, and of such material as peasants wear; for such cloth may be exposed freely to the inclemency of the weather and to use in rough places. If when he goes out to hunt he wears fine clothes of various colours (that are easily distinguished), the birds he hopes to capture with the falcon will at once see him and will not tarry but will easily escape. He should wear a wide hat to make his face

less visible to the cranes, who will, in consequence, be less frightened by his appearance.[87]

He also recommends that heavy leggings be worn.[88]

What a contrast this functional but drab gear makes with the gorgeously apparelled nobles riding out to hawk in the Calendar picture for August in the early fifteenth-century manuscript, the *Très Riches Heures du Duc de Berri*. In this, the second lady rider is particularly sumptuously dressed in a blue houppelande with gold decoration, and a white headdress, her horse caparisoned with a scarlet and gold saddle-cloth.[89] Here, appearance is obviously much more important than trying to ensure success by blending in with the landscape. In contrast, the Morgan codex of *Livre de chasse*, made around 1410, possibly for John the Good of Brittany (1399–1442), has more sensible advice for noble hunters. The text prescribes dress of green cloth for the hunter in summer, with leather leggings to protect him from branches. His equipment includes a sword, a knife and a horn. Folio 59 of the manuscript shows two riders and four hunt servants, all of whom are dressed in green robes or tunics with brilliantly coloured leggings.[90] The advice on summer wear from Fébus implies that hunting dress varied with the seasons. Probably in practice it had to, especially on the continent with its more extreme winters. The two snow scenes of the Calendar of MS Egerton 1146 demonstrate this practicality of keeping warm when out hunting. In both the illustrations for November, the boar hunt on foot, and December, the boar hunt on horseback with hounds, the hunter is shown warmly clad and muffled-up against the cold, as also is his lymerer in the latter miniature.[91] In the picture for December, both men's faces and headgear are covered in frost, an unusual detail of realism in illustrations of this type. In *The Hunters in the Snow*, painted in 1565, Pieter Bruegel the Elder skilfully emphasises the bitter cold of the Flemish winter by his rendering of the unsuccessful peasant hunters, dejectedly huddled into their inadequate rustic clothing.[92]

By the mid-sixteenth century, hunting and hawking dress for royalty and the nobility had become even more elaborate and less practical. The twelve months of hunting scenes of *Les Chasses de*

Maximilien, woven in Brussels by the 1530s,[93] well illustrate the emphasis on making an opulent impression in the Renaissance hunting field, particularly for gentleman-hunters. The month of December shows Maximilian's grandson Ferdinand on horseback, spearing a huge wild boar. He is wearing a short, frocked hunting-jacket in deep red with gold decoration and a fur collar. Even the hunt servants, who are on foot, are gorgeously apparelled.[94] This was probably not always so, particularly for the less well off and lower gentry, and in his edition of William Twiti's *The Art of Hunting: 1327,* Bror Danielsson writes that 'As yet (*c.* 1300) there did not exist any special hunting dress. Everybody moved about in their everyday dresses, varied according to social status, even though the colour might be adapted to the environment.'[95]

Danielsson's assertion is rather misleading, because in spite of the opening statement, it clearly intimates that there *was* a special hunting dress and that it was green or some other natural colour. Hunting dress in the fourteenth century may well have been undifferentiated for many aristocratic hunters but this seems unlikely as a general rule. Hunting all day on horseback over every sort of terrain, but particularly in woodland, required some sort of appropriate wear which was protective, comfortable and denoted status. The pen drawings of hunting scenes in *Queen Mary's Psalter* show the gentry and nobility wearing wide, pleated ankle-length dresses with wide sleeves, round, open rolled necks and hoods. The king wears a white Spanish cloak on top of this, whereas the nobility wear a pelerine or overcoat. Gloves with long cuffs are worn, indicating gentility. Male headgear includes crowns, an assistant's hat and a felt hat, peaked out in front belonging to 'probably a distinguished gentleman'. The ladies wear long smooth dresses, covering the whole of their feet when on horseback. These are simple garments with long sleeves, often supplemented by a smooth or pleated overcoat slit up to the hip. A scarf tied round the head, chin and neck secured the hood. A cleric in hooded, half-sleeved dress accompanies the king and his retinue out hunting.[96]

However, we must be careful here on the representation of hunting dress in art, whether it is found in an illuminated *bas de page* in the Calendar of a Book of Hours, a psalter or a royal tapestry. The great problem is assessing how close to reality the visual evidence is. Usually we have no way of knowing what the patron of illustrative material ordered in detail or the relative inputs of artist and patron. Did he or she require the artist to show the hunters in their 'best' outfits? Were the hunt servants well dressed to enhance the overall richness of the illustrative scene and the status of the patron and the dominant figures? The answer to these two questions is probably 'yes', given human nature and the desire to achieve several points with one work of art. Perfection in illustration is understandable and can be compared to a posed photograph. Whether these pictures represent the total reality of dress in the hunting field is another question, to which the most sensible answer is 'probably partly'. No doubt there were royal and major aristocratic hunting days and events for which everybody, including the professional staff, was required to dress up accordingly and in the height of current hunting fashion, but for most hunting and hawking forays the mode of dress was probably less elaborate, more practical and certainly less expensive.

The upper classes hunted on horseback and two small but important items of dress or equipment which indicate high status are connected with the horse. The first can clearly be seen in *Queen Mary's Psalter*. The noble or gentle hunters wear small spurs of the strap-on 'prick' variety. Danielsson's text, however, states that none of the huntsmen carried spurs, which is puzzling.[97] The dismounted professional huntsmen certainly do not (and why should they?), and it would be strange if the huntsmen of rank were not wearing spurs. Spurs were an essential aid to horsemanship and control of the war and hunting horse in the Middle Ages, and for centuries to come. If the illustrations in *Livre de chasse* are examined, the nobles are invariably portrayed equipped with the large rowelled spurs of the early fourteenth century; in contrast, the hunt servants do not wear any, as was apparently the norm. The plate for Chapter 28 shows the mounted huntsman, wearing rowelled spurs, instructing an apprentice in the recognition of a warrantable hart. His high social status is indicated by the authoritative directing stick he is carrying while his spurs are another mark of his knightly rank. He is not just a huntsman or even a gentleman-huntsman, he is the Master.[98] Another illustration from *Livre de chasse* is of the Master instructing his apprentice hunters on the correct method of blowing the hunting horn.[99] Only one young hunter is wearing spurs, and these are of gold with rowels. Presumably, he is of gentle birth while the others are commoners training to be professional huntsmen. The plate for Chapter 55, hunting and killing the wolf, shows a blue-robed noble with a tapered hunting sword, and an unarmed, more plainly dressed mounted man.[100] The noble wears golden spurs whereas the other man's are of silver, plainly indicating the lesser rank of the latter, who is perhaps the noble's esquire or private gentleman. Steel, silver and gold spurs were items of equestrian equipment which denoted ascending social rank.[101]

The second item of dress is mentioned in the text analysing the hunting illustrations in *Queen Mary's Psalter*. Bror Danielsson writes, 'Some ladies of rank . . . carry trappings showing their family arms'.[102] The public display of arms was one of several hallmarks of rank and gentility,[103] so this was to be expected in the hunting field where one was surrounded by neighbours, peers and servants. It was important to be known and recognised as a member of the ruling élite, and a coat of arms specifically identified the bearer's family as well as indicating ancient gentle ancestry.

Arms and weapons of the chase are also important indicators of social rank and status. Those illustrated in the most lavish, beautiful and detailed illuminated manuscript copy of *Livre de chasse*, MS fr. 616, are listed by W.A. Baillie-Grohman in the Appendix of the 1904 edition of *The Master of Game*. Included are the longbow, used with barbed arrows for large and hairy game, and blunted arrows for small game and birds; the crossbow, firing short bolts (quarrels) of barbed and blunted varieties; the javelin, particularly used for hunting wildcat; the three-pronged otter spear; the ordinary spear for use against all quarry; the hunting sword, a specialist weapon used by the aristocratic hunter for large game, with a very broad base tapering to a point; the *Couteau de chasse*, the hunting knife carried by varlets and underlings for 'unmaking' of deer and 'undoing' of wild boar.[104] Gaston Fébus also used the *Espieu*, a javelin with a narrow and short head easily withdrawn from the quarry and which could be thrown or held as a lance.[105] An interesting variation on the standard hunting sword is being used by Ferdinand, Maximilian's grandson, to despatch a wild boar, depicted in 'December' of *Les Chasses de Maximilien* tapestries in the Louvre. His boar sword has a thin shaft, broad leaf-like point with twin tines or toggles, essentially 'stops' to prevent over-penetration and, very usefully, the boar running up the shaft and reaching the hunter and his horse.[106] This archaic safety measure is similar to that of the hog-spears used in British India for pig-sticking until Partition in 1947. Indeed, the German manufacturing firm of Pumas based at Solingen, still advertises such a hog-spear (*saufeder*) in its 2002 catalogue.[107]

In *Livre de chasse*, Fébus provides us with a typically exact and detailed description of a hunting weapon, the so-called English or Turkish bow, which he includes in his instructions for bow and stable hunting.[108]

William Twiti's treatise hardly mentions edged weapons, referring only briefly to the hunting knife: 'and he þat ouzt þe knyf with wiche he is vndo schall haue þe chyne.'[109] The hunting illustrations in *Queen Mary's Psalter* are more informative on weaponry and include the longbow, with arrows carried in the belt rather than in a quiver, and assistants bearing a hunting-axe, useful for breaking up large carcasses.[110]

Personal hunting weapons of royalty and the nobility, particularly crossbows, swords and hunting-knives, often became family heirlooms, and some examples from historical figures survive in European collections. Schloss Ambras, near Innsbruck in the Austrian Tyrol, has a particularly fine and extensive collection of late medieval and Renaissance hunting weaponry, including examples that belonged to Charles the Bold of Burgundy, King Louis XII of France and Emperor Maximilian I. The Hunting Gallery of the Royal Armouries at Leeds also has a small but interesting collection of aristocratic hunting weapons from this period, including hunting swords, boar-spears, crossbows, quivers and bolts, and two hunting-trousses. The *trousse*, or *garniture*, was a practical but often finely crafted and richly decorated set of cutlery carried for the special purpose of unmaking the hart or other large quarry. It typically consisted of two broad-bladed knives for severing bone, two narrow-bladed knives for cutting out the finer muscles and a two-tined fork for the handling of delicacies, all carried in a purpose-made scabbard or sheath.[111] The German garnitures in the Leeds Royal Armouries Hunting Gallery collection are excellent examples of such equipment, well made but meant for practical use in the field.

The horse was a vital element in the equipment of the gentle veneur and falconer. Maurice Keen remarks that to live nobly, 'Knights and Esquires should be well mounted' and even the lesser nobleman was expected 'to keep hawks and hounds, and to talk knowledgeably of them'.[112] The gentleman 'type' should have, among his many accomplishments, skill in horsemanship and on the hunting field.[113] While not synonymous with being a nobleman, enjoying the right to ride a horse was of considerable importance and related to the idea of the 'chevalier'. The horse gave the rider rank and status, whether in the field of war or the chase. In the higher levels of the hunting profession, the huntsman was mounted,[114] as were the senior foresters in the forest hierarchy. The gentle amateur veneurs were invariably mounted, unless the hunt was specifically on foot. The chase at speed provided 'the personal elements of exercise, prowess and emulation of the individual distinguishing himself'. The knight was expected to show himself off to his best advantage and this apparently applied particularly to the English upper classes in the hunting field.[115] An old Welsh proverb states: 'A gentleman might be known by his hawk, his horse and his greyhound.'[116] These personal living and expensive items were the icons of social identification which differentiated the gentleman from the ungentleman. A man could not be publicly acknowledged as a gentleman without them.

By the eleventh century, the art of horse breeding was long established in Byzantium and especially in the Arab countries where there was a wealth of established breeds suitable as warhorses.[117] The

Byzantines had long used hunting to keep their warhorses and cavalrymen fit.[118] However, at this time in Europe selective breeding appears to have been only just beginning, with few references in the available literature to breed provenance, the exception being some Spanish sources. Many good horses both from Byzantine and Moorish origins were entering Europe and these must have provided material and inspiration to horse breeders. Ann Hyland comments that the Bayeux Tapestry provides a rough guide to the European type of Norman warhorse, the size confirmed by her own researches into Norman horseshoes held at the Museum of London: 'a medium-sized animal of approximately 14.2–15 hh, with no particular distinguishing features, other than hinting it was fairly stocky'.

A Persian work, the *Qabus Nama* of Kai Ka'us ibn Iskander, written in 1082 by the Prince of Gurgan for his son, outlines his princely education. This syllabus appears similar to that of a European noble's son and includes riding, javelin-throwing, archery, wielding the spear, throwing a lasso, polo, hunting, hawking and falconry. It also contains prudent fatherly advice on buying a horse which could be applied to a purchase in any age. Ann Hyland has put together the following generic description:

A suitable horse should have a good head, attention being paid to the dentition, special reference being made to avoidance of parrot mouth. The facial plane should be straight, the forehead broad, ears long, fine and erect. The neck should be long with an open gullet, and it should be set well into the shoulder without coarseness. The barrel should also be fine with a long underline. The chest should be broad, the loins short-coupled. Limbs should be substantial. Hooves should be black and long, the sole round. The tail should be long with a short dock, and there should be absence of hair on the lower limbs.[119]

This demonstrates not only the high level of knowledge among royal and noble buyers but also the quality of horses available in the Near Eastern horse markets of the eleventh century for the purposes of war, hawking and hunting.

Hawking took place from horseback, and in 1248 Holy Roman Emperor Frederick II of Hohenstaufen provided sound advice to the falconer regarding the character of his mount:

> the horse should be gentle and stand quietly, must not gallop without permission, not increase gait when the falconer drops his reins, must be quick to obey, agile to left or right, swift, not frightened by unforeseen or unusual objects, must not whinny on duty, not difficult to handle or hard-mouthed ('dure boce'), lest when he hurries to bring assistance he may trample on the falcon.[120]

Such an animal must have been highly trained and thus an expensive item. It is significant that Emperor Frederick does not mention either the breeding or conformation of his ideal mount; presumably these were not regarded as important, whereas the patient training of a potentially suitable animal was the paramount factor.

The horses of the huntsman and falconer depicted in *The Luttrell Psalter* are medium-sized nondescript animals with broad backs and powerful quarters, displaying little of the 'quality' or weight of modern hunters. In contrast, the mounts of the Magi show the great weight and muscle conformation associated with purpose-bred late medieval warhorses.[121] Line drawings in *Queen Mary's Psalter* from the early fourteenth-century show the horses of the huntsmen of rank to be rather low in height, of medium weight with a small head, strong hind quarters and a long tail. Horses of people of high rank had their manes neatly tied up or plaited. The long curb-chains (joining the long extended ports of the bit), suggest a swift but easily turned riding-horse.[122] In modern terms, the nearest equivalent is a 'handy' horse with polo-pony qualities of instant response and man-oeuvrability, essential for negotiating the rough and varied terrain of late medieval England and Europe. Henry Savage, writing in 1933 of medieval hunting, concurs with this generalisation: 'The animal in use was, of course, not the war-horse or destrier but a lighter (and probably faster) beast.' Savage further observes that the hunting manuals place less emphasis on the horse than on the breed and conformation of the hound,[123] and this lack of preciseness regarding the hunting mount is borne out in *The Boke of Saint Albans*. Dame Juliana Berners gives her opinion on 'The propretees of a goode hors' as follows:

A good hors shulde have XV ppretees and conditions./yt. is to wit iii. of a man. iii. of a woman'/iii. of a fox/iii. of a haare and iii. of an asse./Off a man boolde prowde and hardy./Off a woman fayre brestid faire of here. e esy to lip uppon,/Off a fox a faire tayle short eris with a good trot./Off an hare a grete eygh a diy hede, and well rennyng/Off an asse a bigge chyne a flatte lege, and goode houe.[124]

These medieval notions of a horse suitable for hunting appear vague and confusing, particularly when compared with the exacting points of conformation and type detailed by the Prince of Gurgan four centuries earlier. It is interesting to compare both descriptions with a modern definition of an English hunter used for fox hunting, the Prince's horse conforming surprisingly closely to the English counterpart:

Hunter. Not a breed but a type, which is largely influenced by the nature of the country over which it is to be used. The Show Hunter, however, which is the ideal, is Thoroughbred, or nearly so; it has power and scope, giving a good length of rein, and a strong back and loins, hocks of great propelling power, with the best of galloping actions. It must ride with balance and courage, carry its head in the right position, and be responsive to its rider.[125]

This type of animal appears larger and more powerful, but less handy, than its medieval counterpart, with the added vital ability to jump fences, ditches and walls. The idea of selective breeding, to establish and reproduce specific breeds with certain physical and behavioural characteristics, was largely unknown in Europe and the Thoroughbred was centuries in the future. However, Pisanello's superbly painted stallion in *The Vision of Saint Eustace* (*c.* 1438–42), exhibits many of the features of a modern medium-weight hunter including a deep chest, strong neck and shoulders, a short back and powerful quarters.[126]

As with horses, so hounds (rather than dogs) conveyed notions of status and Baillie-Grohman comments that no hound seems to belong so peculiarly to the age of chivalry as the greyhound, 'and one cannot picture a knight without one'. He also quotes a supposedly old law of King Canute which decreed that a greyhound may not be kept by any person inferior (in rank) to a gentleman.[127] However, this use of the term 'gentleman' seems rather suspect within the context of the period, it being a rank which was not precisely defined until the early fifteenth century. Nigel Saul writes that after 1415 the vernacular use of 'gentleman' is employed quite precisely 'for the limited purpose of denoting the lowest order of the gentleborn'.[128]

Dame Juliana believes a gentleman should also learn the conformation of a good greyhound as part of his education. As with her description of a good horse, she draws upon the physical characteristics of other animals, hence 'The properties of a goode Grehound' in *The Boke of Saint Albans*: 'A Grehounde shulde be heded like a Snake. And /necked like a Drake. Foted like a kat. / Tayled like a Rat. Sydd lyke a Teme. /Chyned like a Beme.'[129] Greyhounds quite commonly appear in the illustrations of Gothic manuscripts, often in pursuit of a stag or hare. It is significant that a greyhound chasing a hart is traditionally used as a marginal motif on the opening page of Books of Hours. The location of such a cameo scene is revealing and it may be that the greyhound represents every Christian who should follow Christ, himself symbolised as a wounded hart and shedding blood to make the pursuit easier.[130] MS Egerton 1146, a German Book of Hours, from about 1500, begins with a beautiful example of such a scene, the hart's left side spotted with blood.[131] *The Hours of Philip the Bold, Duke of Burgundy*, completed around 1370, has a marginal picture of two greyhounds coursing a hare.[132] MS Douce 62, a French Book of Hours dated from about 1400, has a much more unusual scene, a *bas-de-page* illustration of a greyhound chasing an antelope.[133] The antelope is identified by its jagged horns, the standard device used by illuminators of bestiaries and manuscripts to depict this particular cloven-footed ungulate.

Greyhounds are by far the commonest hunting dog to appear in late medieval illustrations, particularly manuscripts, the reasons perhaps being twofold. Firstly, although there was no single breed of these swift hounds which hunted by sight, giving rise to the old term of 'gazehounds', they all tended towards a lithe and elongated 'type'. Secondly, illustrations show them in all manner of domestic situations, in living- and bedrooms, at the board when their owners are at meals, sitting by the fireside and even at mass. Of all dogs, they appear to have been the most constant of companions of their masters during journeys, in war and at home.[134] It is therefore no surprise that the type appears so often in illustrated sources, particularly those which portray scenes of everyday life. Artists produced images of what they and their audiences knew about.

It is interesting that possession of a greyhound today is not an indication of high social status – usually the very opposite in fact, greyhounds being associated in the public mind with the stereotypical images of the cloth caps and racing pigeons of working men in the industrial north of England. This is undoubtedly due to the change of role of greyhounds by the eighteenth century, from that of hunting deer, hare, wolf, boar and fox to that of coursing hares in organised matches. Coursing involves the use of two greyhounds, termed a 'couple', which are 'slipped' as the hare, which has been driven up by beaters, passes them. Greyhound racing evolved from coursing[135] and it is probably this sport, with its associated betting, which gives the modern greyhound, and its owner, relatively low status compared to the past.

Another breed of hound, the possession of which conveyed the notion of gentlemanly status, was the spaniel. Both *Livre de chasse* and *The Master of Game* devote short chapters decorated with illustrative miniatures to these small hounds and their nature. Fébus refers to them as *chiens doysel*, meaning bird-dogs, or *espaignolz*, meaning spaniels.[136] The present-day Brittany, incorrectly called a spaniel by the uninitiated, is said to be descended from these medieval *chiens d'oiseaux*. They are still, like their ancestors, excellent at hunting-up and flushing game birds and starting small game. They are good in water and useful for retrieving duck and other waterfowl. In the Middle Ages these hounds were particularly liked by falconers owing to their great ability at finding and flushing partridge and quail.[137] They were thus associated with the gentle country pastime of hawking, *The Master of Game* commenting: 'It is a good thing to a man that hath a noble goshawk or a tiercel or a sparrow hawk for partridge, to have such hounds.'[138] However, both Fébus and Edward agree that spaniels can be quarrelsome, undisciplined and bark too much, the Duke of York adding to Fébus's comments that he would not have any, 'especially there where I would hunt.'[139]

Aristocratic hunting was defined, above all, by two factors, the quarry species and methodology. Although common hunters took the beasts reserved for gentle hunters, they did it illegally and would suffer punishment if caught, usually in the form of a fine suited to their status. It is significant that taking 'noble' quarry did not confer gentility on common hunters while poaching of other people's game by aristocrats did not diminish their own status. It was not what was hunted and caught, but how the hunter did it which defined him as a gentleman or ungentleman.

THREE

'Bestis' and 'Crafte'

The medieval classification of quarry species is complex and confusing, much depending upon which source is consulted. Broadly, the quarry species which are illustrated in most pictorial sources and figure in almost all textual sources are the red deer stag or hart, the red deer hind, the hare, the wild boar, the wolf and the bear. These beasts were traditionally categorised as 'noble' and their lawful pursuit identified the hunter as a 'gentle hunter'. Some French and English hunting books divide game into two distinct categories, the 'beasts of venery' and the 'beasts of the chase'.[1] Additional categories of 'folly' or 'rascal' and 'vermin' are sometimes mentioned.[2] In general, gentle hunters pursued the first two categories of quarry, at least publicly, the first group being regarded as the most prestigious. William Twiti, huntsman to Edward II and author of *The Art of Venerie*, gives the basic classification:

To venery y caste me fyrst to go/ Of wheche iiii bestis be, that is to say,/ The hare, the hert, þe wulfe, the wylde boor also;/ Of venery for sothe þer be no moe . . .

And then ben othyr bestis v of chase:/ The buck the first, the do the secunde,/ The fox the thryde, which ofte haþ hard grace,/ The ferthe the martyn & þe last the Roo,/ And sothe to say ther be no mo of tho . . .'[3]

Juliana Berners' *Book of Huntyng* declares: 'Fowre maner beestys of venery there are,/ The first of theym is the hert, the secunde is the hare,/ The boore is oon of tho,/ The wolff, and not oon moo.'[4] Later, the *Boke* continues with the beasts of chase but also introduces the category of 'rascal' or, in other words, everything else:

61

I shall yow tell which be beestys of enchace./ Oon of theym is the bucke, a nother is the doo,/ The fox and the martron and the wilde roo./ And ye shall, my dere chylde, other beestys all,/Where so ye hem fynde, rascall ye shall hem call/ In fryth or in fell/ Or in forest, I yow tell.[5]

Notice that Dame Juliana does not mention the red deer hind, but David Dalby comments as an aside to German stag-hunting practice that 'Hinds were sometimes hunted with hounds, and were usually driven into nets rather than pursued across country'.[6] Hinds gave inferior sport to harts as they did not run so strongly and in consequence were regarded as mere suppliers of venison. There was thus no shame in driving them, sometimes in groups, into fixed nets.

The bear does not feature in *The Art of Venerie* or the *Boke of Huntyng*, the logical reason for its exclusion being its complete extinction in England centuries earlier.[7] However, it was still common on mainland Europe in the late medieval period and was hunted both on horseback and on foot, particularly in southern and mountainous regions. Bears were hunted on horseback with hounds by the princes and nobles of the north Italian city states in the Renaissance.[8] Both Gaston Fébus and Emperor Maximilian I regarded bears as worthy and dangerous quarry.[9]

Pictorial and textual sources clearly indicate that it was the red deer which was the favourite quarry species of medieval aristocratic hunters. For example, while the cycle of twelve hunting illustrations in the Calendar of MS Egerton 1146 includes the five major quarry species, there is a heavy emphasis on red deer. The frequency is as follows: red deer appear seven times, wild boar twice, and the hare, bear and wolf only once each. Overall, it is the stag, or more correctly the hart, with its great rack of antlers, that dominates both textual and pictorial sources as the icon of nobility hunting. Referring specifically to Germany, but equally applicable to the rest of Europe, David Dalby states: 'During the German Middle Ages, the stag was the most important quarry for noble huntsmen . . . and other deer are mentioned less frequently.'[10] He later remarks 'the stag chase became the favourite hunting sport during the "courtly centuries"' meaning after the twelfth century. Stag hunting required a high degree of skill and technical know-how, and importantly involved much élitist ritual, making it suitable as a courtly pastime.[11] One German manual illustrates the importance of the stag to German noble hunters by its very specialisation. *Die Lehre von den Zeichen des Hirsches* is an instructive examination of the tracks and signs of the stag, all indications of whether the beast was chaseable.[12] A sixteenth-century German hunting manual, *Die Hohenloheschen Handschrift*, contains a series of detailed diagrams showing the different slot-marks (tracks) of deer for the instruction of hunters assessing age, size and condition of quarry.[13] In the appendix to his edition of *The Master of Game*, William Baillie-Grohman emphasises the expertise required of both the professional and aristocratic stag hunter and notes that

> One of the first essentials for a huntsman in the Middle Ages was to learn to know the different *signs* of a stag (according to German Venery there were seventy-two signs), so as to be able to 'judge well'. These signs were those of the *slot*, the *gait*, the *fraying-post*, the *rack or entry* (i.e. the place where the stag entered covert), and the *fumes*.[14]

It was the 'great hart', however, which held the premier position as noble quarry. These beasts, at least six years old with ten points or tines to their rack of antlers, were often described as 'warrantable' in the hunting treatises.[15] *The Master of Game* specifies the male red deer as correctly being termed as in 'the fifth [year] a stag; the sixth year a hart of ten and first is he chaseable, for always before shall he be called rascal or folly'.[16] The hart was regarded as royal game, and so belonged to the king or ruler of the country. Hunting the wild hart was thus a royal prerogative and a courtly activity, although special licences to take red deer and other game were granted on occasion by the sovereign to specially favoured courtiers.[17] The social primacy of the hart is indicated by two early hunting texts. The surviving version of *De arte bersandi*, written by Guicenna(n)s in Germany in the early thirteenth century, is the beginning of a comprehensive instruction on the hart hunt. It is also the earliest medieval hunting text which survives and the only known hunting treatise written in Latin. The earliest vernacular hunting treatise is *La Chase dou cerf*, written in Picardy in about 1250. This poem treats of all aspects of the hart hunt, from the chase to breaking-up the carcass.[18]

Edward of York's observations make it clear why the hart was regarded with such esteem throughout Europe: 'The harts be the lightest beasts and strongest, and of marvellous great cunning.'[19] They were also fierce and dangerous quarry and therefore worthy of the respect of noble hunter-warriors. As Edward graphically decribes:

> And then they are bold, and run upon men as a wild boar would do if he were hunted. And they be wonderfully perilous beasts, for with great pain shall a man recover that is hurt by a hart, and therefore men say in old saws, 'after the boar the leech and after the hart the bier.' For he smiteth as the stroke of the springole, for he has great strength in the head and the body.[20]

The risks of injury or death while out hunting are seldom mentioned by the authors of the hunting books, so this rare grim reminder is interesting as well as thought-provoking. Understatement of the dangers of hunting and other noble pastimes was characteristic of medieval aristocratic culture and to some extent has endured as part of English 'stiff upper-lip' attitudes.

Because of its admirable warrior-like natural characteristics, the hart was thus elevated in medieval minds to a special position of 'nobility', making its pursuit a 'noble sport' and in turn bestowing high status and glory on its hunter. However, unfortunately for aristocratic hunters, numbers of the red, or 'high', deer in England fell dramatically during the later Middle Ages. This decline was largely the result of a decrease in suitable habitat, much former wilderness and waste being brought under cultivation, particularly as grazing for sheep, the mainstay of England's premier industry. Felling timber for charcoal burning, iron, copper and lead smelting also reduced wild red deer habitat. In addition, much of the land used for game reserves and parks was also used to provide grazing and timber, and in order for this dual function to work careful woodland and pasture management was necessary. Woodlands which were excessively exploited became degraded, the classic case being Thorpe Wood which lay across the River Wensum near Norwich. In 1100 it was covered in oak woodland, but owing to overgrazing and excessive timber extraction it had degraded to heathland and been renamed Mousehold Heath by the early sixteenth century.[21] Roger Manning estimates that by 1539 the numbers of red deer in the royal game reserves in the north of England had dwindled to around two thousand. In southern England it was necessary to boost low numbers by breeding programmes in parks. Stags are notoriously aggressive during the rutting season so imparked red and fallow deer had to be kept apart. Herds of red deer were still to be found in Windsor Forest, Ashdown Forest and at least three other parks in Sussex in the reign of James I.[22] So, although the great hart survived in the English hunting manuals as the premier large quarry of the nobility, in reality its place was increasingly taken by the imparked fallow buck, an animal which was far more available and still gave good sport. Stocks in forests and private parks were partly maintained by buckstalls and deer-leaps. The buckstall was a woodland enclosure, surrounded by a fence of wattle hurdles within which was a broad and deep ditch called the deer-leap. The low fence allowed driven deer to leap into the enclosure but the deep ditch on the other side prevented them from escaping. The captive deer would be fed ivy, holly, oak twigs and other browsings within the fenced enclosure until they were required for stocking or meat.[23] Another function of these one-way structures was to allow tenants to drive deer from the unenclosed forest into their own fenced preserves. In addition, it allowed access by hunters in the surrounding Forest who were following up wounded deer which had taken refuge in the park. This was an arrangement of benefit to both parties: the owner of the game rights and his tenant.[24]

Although fierce and brave, the wild boar comes a poor second in the nobility stakes. Its relative position is commented upon by Dalby: 'Of lesser importance than the stag in the medieval hunt was the wild boar. The boar hunt is mentioned or described in MHG [Middle High German] sources much less frequently than the stag chase.' He continues that the boar was more dangerous to hunt than the stag and required great skill with a weapon to despatch. Hunting boar was a less refined sport than stag hunting and was the dominant form of the chase in German lands until the eleventh or twelfth centuries. The boar is often compared to a fierce warrior in the German sources, reflecting an earlier and more heroic age.[25] This imagery is similar to that awarded to the hart and in the same way made the boar a worthy and noble adversary. Gaston Fébus approved of hunting the boar and in *Livre de chasse* devotes eleven chapters and illustrations to its nature, hunting and trapping.[26] He considered the wild boar the most dangerous quarry, admiring and respecting the fierceness of the beast.[27]

The Master of Game translates only one of the chapters on the wild boar from Fébus, but Baillie-Grohman comments that the reason for this omission was probably because Edward of York considered the stag and hare to be 'the royal sport *par excellence*, and not because there were none to hunt in England in his day'.[28] It is quite probable that wild boar were extinct in the wild in England by the mid-thirteenth century, but what is interesting is that they were still regarded as a 'noble beast' by aristocratic families and lived on, not only in semi-captivity in parks but also in the public mind, in heraldry and romance.[29] A boar appears in *The Luttrell Psalter* (1320/40), but as he lacks hair and has distinct dark skin patches, he is probably a domestic rather than a wild pig.[30] In comparison, Pisanello's *Wild Boar* (*c.* 1430–35), appears to be the authentic hairy forest monster.[31] The late fifteenth-century *Boke of Huntyng* contains specific information on the aging and procedures of undoing the wild boar,[32] so in aristocratic minds it must still have been an existing beast of venery in England. It continued to thrive on mainland Europe, extensive forests being essential to its survival, and was hunted with varying degrees of enthusiasm and dedication by royalty and the nobility. However, to judge by the surviving manuals and by its appearances and role in imaginative literature, the boar was most valued as a quarry species in the Iberian Peninsula and Germany.[33]

The third beast of venery is the hare and both late medieval English and French hunters regarded this animal with great esteem. William Twiti begins his treatise with the hare, a sign of its quarry status, as he deems it 'þe most merveylous beste þat is in þis lond', the reasons being, 'For as miche as he beriþe grese and crotyth and rongith'.[34] By this he meant that the hare produced grease, voided excrement and was a ruminant, thus having the ability to chew the cud. This latter point is not in fact correct as the hare does not have a compound stomach; she can, however, regurgitate food and give it a second mastication.[35] Edward, Duke of York, repeats this sentiment almost word for word,[36] a good example of the plagiarism which is a feature of the late medieval hunting books. He places the hare first in chapter order in *The Master of Game*, reversing the order of *Livre de chasse*, thus emphasising the hare's importance to English aristocratic hunters. Gaston Fébus also regards the hare highly and gives it much space in his text, but places it second to the deer in chapter order, reflecting the priorities of French *veneurs*. John Cummins comments that hunting the hare, '*par force . . .* was a microcosm of the most complex and subtle aspects of the medieval chase'.[37] The widespread appeal of hare coursing with greyhounds lay in the long chase and also, very importantly for keen hunters, that it could be practised at any time of day or year. Nor did coursing require the elaborate preparation of the stag hunt; hence it was more suitable as an informal pastime.[38] While this may seem at odds with the importance of ritual and procedure in the stag hunt, in spite of the informality of coursing it was clearly regarded as an aristocratic sport in England and France. Coursing was also cheaper than stag or boar hunting and the danger and excitement were provided by the extended chase, not by the quarry, again unlike the pursuit of the hart or wild boar. Surprisingly, this lack of the 'warrior' aspect of the hare does not appear to have detracted from its value as a noble quarry. It is significant that German sources of the period show that stag hunting and hare coursing were the pre-eminent forms of the chase, as practised by the German nobility during the Middle Ages'.[39]

The high status and popularity of the hare as a quarry species in England are reflected in its widespread appearance in pictorial sources. The hare often appears in the margins of illuminated manuscripts as a hunter of men, exemplifying the 'world upside-down' of medieval moralists and satirists in which role reversal and topsy-turvy situations upset the divine rational order of things. A well-known *bas de page* from a manuscript in the Bodleian Library, Oxford, shows two hunter-hares, one with a crossbow, the other carrying the quarry, a man with bound hands, from a game-pole, while a smirking leveret looks on in admiration.[40] However, it was not only illuminators who used the hare in such imagery. Painters and wood-carvers did too. The Brabantine painter Hieronymus Bosch (*c.* 1450–1516) provides an excellent example in his triptych *Garden of Earthly Delights*. The right wing illustrates *Hell* and in the foreground a large hare, readily identifiable by his long ears with dark tips, blows a hunting horn and carries his slain quarry, a shapely woman bleeding profusely from a huge gash in her belly, slung from the type of pole commonly used for carrying hares and rabbits on hunting forays.[41] In the right wing of another triptych, *Haywain*, Bosch has used world upside-down imagery in a slightly different way. In the foreground of the hell scene, a devil-hunter blows his horn and carries his human quarry on a game-pole, a man paunched from throat to genitals like a hare or rabbit.[42] Wood-carvers also utilised such humorous world upside-down imagery, and hunter-hares appear on some misericords in ecclesiastical settings. Thus this situation of hunter turned hunted is found on a misericord in Manchester Cathedral where hares roast a hunter on a spit over a fire while his hounds boil and are seasoned in cauldrons. This scene, inaccurately called *The Rabbits' Revenge* as the animals are hares, was copied by the Manchester wood-carver from an elaborate engraving by Israhel van Meckenem (d. 1503).[43]

Although long extinct in Britain, bears were abundant in Europe and outlasted wolves in the Alps.[44] In continental hunting treatises, the bear was included as 'noble' quarry for aristocratic hunters. In his Foreword to the first edition of *The Master of Game*, President Theodore Roosevelt, an acknowledged historian and sportsman, comments: 'The kings and nobles, and the freemen generally, of the regions which now make up France and Germany, followed not only wolf, boar, and stag . . . but [also] the bear.'[45] Gaston Fébus devotes several chapters to the nature and hunting of the bear. It must have been a familiar quarry in the Pyrenees as Fébus begins by saying, 'Ours est assez comune beste, si ne me covient ja dire de sa faisson, quar pou de gens sont qui bienn'en aient veu.' He respected the beast for its great strength but not for its low intellect, 'il sont tous estourdiz, et, si fort y sont feruz'.[46] Rather ironically, Fébus died in 1391 after returning from a bear hunt in the forest of Sauveterre.[47] In Iberia the bear had high quarry status, both Alfonso XI of Castile and John I of Portugal regarding it as royal game.[48] The Holy Roman Emperor Maximilian I was also an ardent bear-hunter. In his book *Thuerdank*, there are three sections on bear hunting and in his *Hunting Notebook* Maximilian advises, ' You must go hunting with a spear, and always have one – go after him with the spear . . .'.[49] His favourite method was to tackle the beast in its lair, on foot and single-handed, armed only with a short hunting spear or hunting sword.[50] This almost suicidally brave technique reflects Maximilian's regard for the fighting qualities and courage of the bear, making it a worthy foe to take on face-to-face. The bear thus emerges as a personal challenge to the fanatical hunter, rather than as a quarry beast providing a prolonged and exciting chase. In spite of dedicated enthusiasts such as Fébus, Alfonso XI and Maximilian, opinions on the big beast varied and *The Lexicon of the Mediaeval German Hunt* says of the bear, 'Amongst other heavy game . . . even the brown bear is of little importance'.[51] German sources do mention the bear but its value as a quarry species is generally regarded as being considerably inferior to that of the stag, boar and hare. However, bears sometimes feature in manuscripts and MS Egerton 1146, a Germanic manuscript, has two illuminated illustrations of these beasts. In the *bas de page* of October in the Calendar, the mounted hunter thrusts a cross-hilted spear into a huge black bear which is being harried by hounds, whereas in a marginal illustration the hunter is on foot, using a long spear to despatch the bear.[52]

The wolf was widespread in mainland Europe, and to a lesser extent in Britain, during the later Middle Ages.[53] Fébus confirms this in the beginning of his chapter on the nature of the wolf, saying, 'Lou est assez commune beste, si ne me convient ja dire de sa faisson, quar pou de genz sont qui bien n'en aient veu'.[54] Medieval man had an ambivalent attitude towards the wolf; peasants feared and hated the beast as it was a public danger to stock and human life whereas hunters appreciated its natural abilities. The wolf's strength, speed, strong scent and self-confidence made it an interesting and challenging quarry.[55] The wolf was also a dangerous and cunning beast to hunt. Wolf hunting was complex, required thought and proper preparation, and according to John Cummins, it also presented 'an economic insouciance beyond the possibilities of the average yeoman'.[56] Thus the considerable outlay necessary for successful wolf hunting in itself made the sport an aristocratic preserve. Included in *The Boke of Huntyng* as a beast of venery,[57] the wolf must have qualified on its sporting potential alone as its flesh is totally inedible.

Gaston Fébus rated the wolf highly, giving it far more folio space in his book than the hare, but then he admired the strength and fighting qualities of quarry in preference to their social values. *The Master of Game* places the wolf between the wild boar and fox in chapter order, as does Fébus, but Edward omits the later chapters on hunting and trapping the wolf, probably for reasons of snobbery. The large amount of space allocated to the wolf in both *Les livres du roy Modus et de la royne Ratio* and *Livre de chasse* indicates its high status as a quarry species hunted by the nobility in France.[58]

In Germany the attitude towards wolves appears more practical than sporting. Wolves were regarded as vermin with no legal restrictions on their hunting and trapping. This was probably a response to the threat posed by their large numbers in rural Germany. They are briefly mentioned in some German sources, but as Dalby comments, 'these animals were not normally chased by noble sportsmen, in Mediaeval Germany'.[59] Wolves appear

70

occasionally in manuscript illustrations, such as in the February *bas de page* of the Calendar of MS Egerton 1146, in which a wolf is being pulled down by hounds, the hunter galloping up to despatch the beast with his drawn sword.[60]

In England, the Norman kings enjoyed wolf hunting on horseback with hounds and wolf hunting tenures were common, probably surviving for some time beyond the wolf. For example, in 1370 Thomas Engaine held lands in Pitchley on condition that he provide dogs (wolfhounds) to be used in the hunting and destruction of wolves and foxes; in 1427 Robert Plumpton held wolf-hunt land in Nottingham 'for the winding of a horn' and wolf chasing in Sherwood Forest.[61] Edward I organised a largely successful campaign to exterminate wolves, employing a certain Peter Corbet to take and destroy all the wolves in Gloucestershire, Worcestershire, Herefordshire, Shropshire and Staffordshire.[62] Records confirm the presence of wolves at Marske, west of Richmond in the North Riding of Yorkshire, until 1369. John of Gaunt, Duke of Lancaster, was for a time Lord of the Swale Marches in Yorkshire, and he hunted a vast chase stretching from Wensleydale to Stanemoor (*sic*) which abounded with wolves and great herds of red deer. Traditionally, John of Gaunt is credited with personally slaying the last wild wolf in England, near Leeds.[63] The final documentary evidence in England mentioning wolves dates from 1394 to 1396, and records that the monks of Whitby were paid 10*s* 9*d* 'for tawing 14 wolfskins', indicating the survival of wolf packs on the North Yorkshire Moors. It is likely that wolves were hunted to near extinction in England by the end of the fourteenth century with odd pockets of breeding pairs holding out in the remoter areas of the northern hills and forests. In Scotland they survived until the early seventeenth century; the last positive record is of an enormous bounty of £6 13*s* 4*d* paid for a wolf slain in Sutherland in 1621. In Ireland there were wolves until the early eighteenth century, the last ones being killed in County Cork between 1709 and 1710.[64] In the seventeenth century they must still have posed a considerable threat to stock and humans, as the Irish Council offered cash bounties on wolves: £6 for a bitch, £5 for a dog and 40*s* for a cub.[65]

Overall, hunting this fierce and cunning beast *par force* not only tested the hunter's own abilities and courage to the full, important aspects for the true venator, but was also a public indication of superior economic and social standing. Undoubtedly, wolf hunting, like bear hunting, was a more restricted aristocratic sport than stag, boar or hare hunting, only appealing to fanatical aficionados of venery.

Although it is perhaps obvious that for the single reason of food procurement alone, hunting must have been a universal necessity and pastime for medieval man, both the English and continental sources unequivocally testify that certain forms of venery were reserved for, and restricted to, the ruling élites. The hunting manuals and treatises specify not only quarry species but also methodology, vocabulary, ritual and procedure. However, this information is not restricted to the hunting books; it is also commonly encountered in the romantic and imaginative literature of the period. The hunting passages in *Sir Gawain and the Green Knight* and *The Parlement of the Thre Ages* are cases in point. Both these late fourteenth-century Middle English poems contain detailed descriptions of how animals were hunted and properly broken-up, set within a rural or romantic context.[66] As has been indicated already, this type of literature was written for a courtly audience and an understanding of hunting language and methods was integral to its production and presentation. A.C. Spearing comments on this élitism of procedure and vocabulary: 'There is a proper way of doing everything, even cutting up the dead beast, and knowledge of this way is a prerogative of the aristocracy and their skilled servants.'[67]

Nobles were 'lerned' in the language and techniques of hunting as a result of their education and Spearing likens this upper-class learnedness to the most sacred rites of Catholicism, referring to the élitist vocabulary as the 'liturgy' of the aristocratic 'sacrament',[68] so highlighting its quasi-sacred importance within court society. To be conversant with hunting jargon was not only a social necessity, it also defined a person as belonging to the ruling classes.

In addition, pictorial images were almost invariably of animals and birds being hunted in particular ways, the accepted aristocratic ways. The great majority of illustrations contain two of the vital elements of aristocratic hunting, horses and hounds. Dalby remarks on this definitive European practice: 'The classic form of the mediaeval hunt was the open stag chase, i.e. the pursuit of a stag with horses and hounds'.[69] There are numerous references in English, French and German sources to this traditional method of hunting the stag, and to a lesser degree, the hare. The fallow deer, roebuck, boar, wolf, bear and fox, were also hunted by nobles in this manner. So, as with literature, members of the audience were presented with upper-class imagery with which they could identify, reinforcing the idea of exclusiveness which appears increasingly necessary to the ruling élites in the later Middle Ages.

The classic method of hunting on horseback with a pack of hounds was known as *par force de chiens*, or 'by strength of hounds'. Gaston Fébus describes 'a force' hunting in great detail, devoting two of his lengthier chapters to this method of stag and hare hunting: 'Si devise comment le bon veneur doit chassier et prendre le cerf a foursse', and 'Ci devise comment le bon veneur doit chassier et prendre le lievre a *foursse*'.[70] Roy Modus uses the term 'a forche' in the same manner.[71] Two fourteenth-century German allegorical works, Hadamar's *Jagd* and the anonymous *Die Jagd der Minne* provide details of this method of the chase and its terminology.[72]

At this point it is necessary to provide a short description of a day's *par force* hunting in order to understand the context and significance of literary and illustrative sources, and some of the vocabulary of aristocratic hunting. The rare full and many partial descriptions of the chase which survive from the Middle Ages have enabled modern scholars to present a comprehensive and detailed reconstruction of this method of hunting. Similar sequences, using slightly differing terminology owing to distinct linguistic sources, can be found in two recent works, *The Stag of Love* and *The Lexicon of the Mediaeval German Hunt*.[73]

Hunters rose early to quest, probably having gone out the evening before to locate and move a warrantable stag, preferably a hart of ten or more tines. Hunt officials called lymerers, each accompanied by his scenting hound, the lymer, on a leash, looked for signs which revealed the quarry's size, age and value. Along the way, each huntsman placed branches to help him locate the path back to the quarry on the hunt's return and also to indicate that a defined area had been reconnoitred. The hunt officials then joined the *assemblée*, a formal gathering at a pre-arranged point, where the lord or Master of Game assessed the huntsmen's reports and examined samples of droppings, termed 'fewmets',[74] which indicated the quality and age of the beasts to be hunted. After feasting and good fellowship at the hunt breakfast, a horn was blown, signalling that the hunt was about to begin. The pack of hounds moved off, encouraged by cries from the hunters, and was put on to the scent of the selected beast. Once he was moved out of covert, the hart could be expected to double back, or 'ruse', and then take a wide leap off in a new direction to confuse the hounds. This was awkward and it was therefore important to drive the hart out of its familiar thickets and hiding places into open country over which it could move at speed, providing a quality chase. If in its flight the beast left part of the pack behind, the 'perfect' chase became termed 'forloyne', meaning the quarry or hounds, or both, had out-distanced the hunters. This was signalled to the field by a horn note.[75]

After a long chase, the beast would become hard-pressed and exhausted, sweat heavily and emit a stronger scent, exciting and encouraging the hounds. The stag would often plunge into water, both to cool itself and to try and lose its scent. This act, known as 'soiling', was regarded as a sign that the beast was ready to be taken by the hounds in the water, on the bank, or after a short chase. Finally, at the end of its strength, the hart would turn 'at bay' to the hounds. The Master, one of the huntsmen or a noble, would move in behind the beast and disable it by severing the hough-sinew in a hind leg. The stag was then despatched by piercing the spinal cord between the antlers and neck with a sword or hunting knife.[76] Alternatively, a sword was thrust through the heart from behind the shoulder. Either move was very dangerous to a dismounted hunter and required great skill and much practice. Less commonly a bow or crossbow was used to finish off the beast held at bay. A highly skilled and courageous hunter could despatch the quarry from horseback, using a sword or crossbow. The sources make it clear that the death was as quick as was practicable, given the dangerous character and strength of the larger beasts hunted. Was there 'blood lust', a common accusation aimed at modern hunters and shooters? For some participants no doubt there was, but this was probably satisfied at the kill, the climax of vigorous and exciting action. From this point events slowed down, and ancient ritual and procedure took over the gentle hunter's consideration.

Once the beast was despatched, the hounds were given brief leave to leap upon the carcass, bite the flesh and lap the blood, urged on by the hunters. This was part of the hounds' training, particularly the younger intake, encouraging them to recognise the quarry, be keen and to work hard the next time.

Two important formalised ceremonies now followed. Firstly, the ritual of breaking-up the beast took place, this procedure following a well-established sequence detailed in the hunting books and other literary sources such as *Tristan, Sir Gawain and the Green Knight* and *The Parlement of the Thre Ages*. In *Tristan*, a version of the legendary romance of Tristram and Yseult written by Gottfried von Strassburg in about 1210, the elaborate French method of unmaking the hart is introduced to the naive Cornish gentry by the young but courtly and sophisticated foreign hero. Von Strassburg relates how after the hart is killed, Tristan is shocked when the Huntsman-in-Chief lays out the beast on the grass 'on all fours like a boar' and proposes 'to split it clean down from the head and then into four, so that none of the quarters is much bigger than another. That is the custom of this country'.[77]

Tristan explains that in his own country the hart is 'excoriated', and he is asked to demonstrate this unknown manner of breaking-up. With help, he turns the hart on its back. He makes an incision under the muzzle and from here slits it down the belly. Then he returns to the fore-quarters, flaying (skinning) first the right then the left. Next, he flays the two hind-quarters. Then he peels the hide from the flanks and everywhere from 'the holds', working his way down from the head. Then he spreads the hide on the ground.

He detaches the two fore-quarters from the breast, leaving it entire or whole. These he lays to one side. Then he severs the breast from the chine (the backbone) and from the flanks, making sure to leave three ribs on either side. The two hind-quarters are removed as one piece. He leaves the two steaks at the top of the loins as belonging to the haunch. Then he severs the ribs on both sides and removes them from the chine and the paunch as far as the great gut. Finally, he lays the breast, sides, fore- and hind-quarters, in a neat pile, completing the break-up. This was all done 'according to the rules of the chase'.

This is not the end of the lesson, however. The next stage is the *fourchie*, again unknown to the Cornish nobles. Tristan cuts a forked stick, a *fourche*, and then cuts out the liver, the numbles and pizzle. The three pieces are bound firmly to the fork and tied up with green bast (flax). The *fourchie* is then given to a groom to hold. Tristan then demonstrates the third stage, the preparation of the quarry, the ritual feeding and rewarding of the hounds.[78]

This, and related texts, established Tristan as the original master of hunting lore and language[79] and, not surprisingly, later medieval authors took their cue from him. In *Tristan*, Gottfried von Strassburg sets down procedural practice with which he, as a knight of the early thirteenth century, is familiar. It is clear that these practices were already well established as part of French court culture and thus an important part of a noble's education. The antecedents for these procedures are not known, the earliest extant medieval hunting text being the early thirteenth-century *De arte bersandi*, written in Germany and the only hunting treatise in Latin.[80] The term 'excoriate', used by Tristan to mean skinning the hart, is one I have not found repeated elsewhere in hunting texts. It derives from the Middle English word *excoriaten*, from the Latin *excoriare*, meaning 'to strip of its skin'.[81] The terms 'breaking-up' and 'Break-up' in the sense used by Tristan,[82] clearly include both the skinning and butchering of the hart, and occur frequently in later hunting texts. Interestingly, the ritual butchering of the carcass is referred to as *dightande* by Robin Hood when he performs the task for the abbot/king in *The Gest of Robin Hood*, the fifteenth-century ballad.[83]

The hunting texts instruct that there were three stages in the chore of dressing the deer, this total process being variously called 'breaking', 'unmaking' or 'undoing' the carcass: the deer was *undone* (cut open), *'fleaned'* (skinned) and then 'brittled' (cut up). In *Livre de chasse*, Gaston Fébus is shown instructing the hunters in these procedures.[84] Certain pieces of the carcass were presented to the guests and chief personages of the hunt. The haunches and head were removed and portions of the carcass reserved for various people and purposes. *The Tretyse off Huntyng* details that the hunter who slew the hart with a bow would have the skin, the person who broke up the carcass had the chyne, or chine, the parson had the right shoulder, poor men were given a quarter and the parker had the left shoulder.[85] Gottfried von Strassburg's instruction differs; having removed the head and horns from the neck and placed them with the breast, Tristan exclaims to the servants: 'Here, quick! Take this chine away! If any poor person should have a mind to it, make him a present of it or deal with it according to your own custom.'[86] The chine basically comprised vertebrae with some flesh still attached and was definitely not a succulent piece of venison, so was an acceptable gift to the professional hunter or a deserving poor man.

A piece of gristle called the 'corbyn bone' was always removed and flung to the crows or ravens as an offering. *The Boke of Saint Albans* is specific on this latter point of procedure: 'The baly to the side from the corbyn bone/ That is corbyns fee: at the deeth he will be.'[87]

The Tretyse off Huntyng gives two sets of precise instructions on the correct procedure for breaking-up the hart. These directions form a considerable part of a treatise of only 254 lines, demonstrating the importance placed on proper practice.

The first refers to the procedure after hunting the hart without the help of a scenting hound or lymer:

And quen he is dede þan oweth he to blowe also many reans as mony motez. & þen be we aboute to opyn hym & fley hym, & now behoueth þat we taken owte his bowellez & ber hym to þe water & washe hem. Now we be aboute to quarter þe beest;

when his bowellez bene wasshen þan shall þe quyletez be cutted in þe hyde, & þan shall we take þe hede & ley hyt on þe quylettez. þan shall we blawene & take vp þe hede – also mony reans as mony motez. And þan shall a man know off what age the hert was. And for þe houndez ben fedde on þe huyde, so is yt clepyt 'aquyrry'.'[88]

The second description is more graphic and detailed, and in the manuscript is entitled, 'To breke þe hert':

Atte þe fyrst begynnyng he reuerseth hym & slytteth hym from þe herber to þe tuell, and crosseth from þe ryght leg to þe lyfte. He turneth off þe huyde & þan makez þe herber & arereth þe shulders, & from þe splent bone rytteth hym downe to corbyns bone, and þan gederez þe suet. & þan vnpaunchet hym & takez owte þe ratte & þe mawe, & dyyght hytte who so wyll, & kyt þe slent bone & clene þe brest. Shape his aunters & arere þe noumblez, a crosse & disseuer þe haunch fro þe sydez togedyr, & cutte þe quylettez & ley on þe skyn, & ley þe hede aboue, & blow a forloyn & geder þe houndez to þe halowe.[89]

The final two lines of this quotation from *The Tretyse* signal the second great ritual, the *curée*, thus called as the reward fed to the hounds originally took place on the hide or *cuir* of the beast.[90] The paunch and small intestines were emptied, washed and chopped up, mixed with blood and bread and fed to the hounds. Sometimes the heart, lungs and liver were included.[91] This was fed on or under the hide, to the accompaniment of hunting cries and notes on the horn by the noble and professional huntsmen. The head of the hart was placed with the mess on the hide, as described by Gaston Fébus, or under it with the antlers still attached in order to hold the hide up, as described by Edward of York.[92] According to *The Master of Game*, the lymers were rewarded after the other hounds, never being allowed to take their share with the rest of the pack.[93] Both *Livre de chasse* and MS Egerton 1146 contain graphic illustrations of this ceremony.[94] The *curée* was performed as a ritual but its underlying purposes were practical. As Gottfried von Strassburg has Tristan say: 'And believe me, it was devised for the good of the hounds. It is a beneficial practice, since the bits one lays on the hide serve to flesh the hounds, being sweet to their taste from the blood.'[95]

Precise directions in the late medieval hunting treatises as to the sequence of events, including horn blowing, signal both the practical and ceremonial importance of the *curée*. It fed and trained the hounds by the association of reward after a successful hunt, and it provided a pause and symbolic end after the physical excitement of the mounted chase. The noble huntsman was also paying his last respects to his quarry, as well as rewarding his faithful hounds. According to French hunting tradition, if the hart was worthy sport for a noble, then it was fitting that it should receive not only an honourable death, usually at the hands of a nobleman, a 'social equal', but also the proper post-death rituals. These procedures of formally breaking-up the carcass and *curée* were regarded in France as the personal responsibility of a noble. However, these ceremonies of French aristocratic hunting did not become fully established in Germany until the sixteenth or even seventeenth centuries. By then, many French-derived stag hunting terms, including *curée*, were part of the language of German hunters.[96] Clearly, however, Gottfried von Strassburg, a German knight and probable member of the Strassburg urban patriciate,[97] was perfectly conversant with such practices in the early thirteenth century and it is significant that his hero Tristan is a French gentle hunter.

It is interesting that in spite of the insistence placed by French hunting practice on a noble undoing the hart, this procedure was not regarded as particularly important in England. *The Master of Game* provides the English alternative:

But on the other hand if the lord will have the deer undone, he that he biddeth as before is said, should undo him most woodmanly and cleanly that he can and wonder ye not that I say woodmanly, for it is a point that belongeth to woodmanscraft, though it be well suiting to an hunter to be able to do it. Nevertheless it belongeth more to woodmanscraft than to hunters, and therefore as of the manner he should be undone I pass over lightly, for there is no woodman nor good hunter in England that cannot do it well enough, and better than I can tell them.[98]

The good hunter, in this context a gentleman-hunter, needed to know how to undo the hart, and he would be conversant because of his aristocratic education, but the professional woodman, meaning here a yeoman forester and hunter who was trained in the practical procedure of undoing, would actually perform the task. Usefully, this gave him the right to the chine, as stated in *The Tretyse off Huntyng*. Why was there this ambiguity? Did the English gentleman consider that breaking-up a beast was below his dignity? Was it perhaps that he disliked getting his hands dirty, or worse, covered in blood? There is probably some truth in both these notions, but I think that there is another very English reason, for which I have no evidence whatsoever from the hunting books. Englishmen have never placed much worth on unnecessary ceremony, especially that imported from the continent, and a gentleman-hunter perhaps considered that once the hart was hunted and slain, then his part of the job was completed. The messy chores of breaking-up and *curée* were the necessary jobs of underlings who were paid to do such things and 'tidy up'.

Only when these rituals were completed was the remainder of the carcass trussed up and carried to the lord's gate where the hunters blew the prise to inform everyone of the successful capture and slaying of the hart.[99] This marked the end of a perfect day's hunting in pursuit of a single and carefully selected beast.

Aristocratic texts, both instructional hunting books and romantic literature, place great emphasis on these two rituals at the end of the formal chase of a single hart, as do many images from the time. To medieval society, they were powerful representations of noble hunting, marking it as different from any other type of hunting, which it was, but also attempting to present it as the only legitimate form of hunting. This is nonsensical, of course, and may be regarded as the presumed prerogative of the medieval ruling élites. In addition, these ritualistic bases for class division are not particularly special when examined in relation to their practicality. The two-fold value of the *curée*, fleshing and training the hounds, has already been discussed and, in that context, appears eminently sensible. What about breaking-up the carcass? The idea of chopping a deer's carcass into four equal portions, as advanced by the Huntsman-in-Chief in *Tristan*, is totally impractical, and physically almost impossible. No hunter in his right mind could have ever seriously considered such a possibility, even a peasant desperate to dismember a poached deer and cart off or hide the pieces. The procedural way of breaking a carcass is simply the best way of tackling a not too difficult problem, the requirements being a good sharp, strong knife, patience and a minimum of training. In fact, confronted with such a task, by the nature of the anatomy of the animal, an intelligent person would almost inevitably follow the main logical steps as detailed in the hunting manuals.

Obviously, gentle authors introduced the particular obligatory sequence, like dealing first with the fore-quarters and then the hind-quarters and so on, plus the odd item of superstition such as the 'ravens' portion', in order to add mystery and exclusive veracity to the whole ritual. Regarding the origins of such procedures, there are no clues in the Classical Greek or Latin texts, which tend to deal with hounds, horses, nets, trapping and recognising important features of the prey,[100] but this is hardly surprising. There is one good way to break-up a deer and it is certain that this had been known to hunters, and probably those who sold and cooked venison, for thousands of years. The need to write it down as a component of rank and status would not arise until the development of French court culture from the eleventh century.

However, the chase of a selected beast provided special sport and, perhaps as a gesture of respect to the quarry, the carcass deserved special treatment. When many deer were slain in sport, as in bow and stable hunting, the carcasses could not be given such time-consuming treatment. In this event such tasks were traditionally apportioned to various individuals, both hunters and non-participants. Edward, Duke of York, tells us in his own words:

And than shud þe kyng telle þe maister of þe game what dere he wold were þen and to whom [and a list follows, including] . . . and delyuere it to þe procatours of þe chirch þat owen to haue it [and] . . . some to gentilmen of þe contre bi enfarmacion of þe forster or parker, as þei han be frendly to be balv and . . . þe sergeant of þe larder [and finally] þe remenaunt to officers and to hunters as hym good liketh.[101]

Hunting large quarry *par force*, particularly the hart or boar, was undoubtedly the most challenging, and also the most dangerous, form of aristocratic hunting technique. On the other hand, 'bow and stable', in which herds of deer (red and fallow), hinds and does as well as younger males, were driven towards standing huntsmen, was also frequently practised in late medieval Europe. In this method, also aristocratic, numbers of deer were 'unharboured' or 'put up' by lymer hounds, kept on the move and driven by beaters, shot as they came upon the hunters at their stations, and pulled down by pursuing greyhounds if wounded. This must have often been the case as even modern archers wound, rather than kill, large game and have to follow it up. The technique was not new in England. Large-scale driving of red and fallow deer, called 'drifting', now a term applied to the rounding up of ponies, had been practised by hunters in the New Forest since the late eleventh century.[102] William Twiti explains setting up *Archers and Greyhounds and Stably* in a strange combination of vocabulary drawn from English, French and Latin:

An oþer chace ther is whan a man hath/ set vp archerys and greyhoundes e de/ establie, and the best passe out the/ boundys and myne houndes after. Than/ shall Y blowe on this maner: a mote/ and aftirward rechace . . .[103]

This is done:

De aver les genz que sunt entour la/ chace a moy e rechater vpon my houndys/ that be past the boundys. Whech be the boundes? þer as the [h]oundes/ ben, þei that we assigned, as Y haue sayd to-fore.[104]

Horn motes end the hunt, informing his men to assemble and recall the hounds.[105]

The *Master of Game* is more informative than Twiti on this type of hunting, perhaps because it was becoming an increasingly fashionable event, culminating in the *grandes battues* of the Renaissance. Edward comments that it was the duty of certain tenants to attend the king's hunts and to act as part of the stable. It was part of the Master's duty to provide guaranteed sport and when arranging a day's hunting, the Duke of York, as the royal Master of Game, placed his stations to keep the game within certain boundaries so as to force it to pass the stand of the king.[106] The *Master of Game* also is specific that the king takes up his stand accompanied by his yeoman of the bows (or bowbearer) and the fewterers with their hounds ready to let slip.[107] According to the *Black Book* of Edward IV, the monarch retained his own yeoman of the bows and a yeoman for his hounds.[108] Arranging such an event must have been complex and have necessitated the liaison and close cooperation of royal huntsmen and servants with the officials of the local hunt establishment. In a large, especially royal, hunt, courtiers and any gentle companions were directed to their own stands, each with their own bowbearers and fewterers. Other hunters, who included the professional hunt staff and foresters, were stationed around the boundaries of the Forest section, in order to drive any 'great deer' (harts) back towards the royal party and to take lesser game themselves.[109]

The place, or station, where the noble archer stood with his bowbearer and fewterer to receive the game was also known as the 'tryst'. The game might be driven to him, or, if he had not been directed to a particular station, he might have placed himself in a likely position from which to shoot at passing game. In French this was called shooting *a l'affut*, from the Latin *ad fustem*, meaning near the wood, as the hunter leant his back against, or hid behind, a large tree, thereby concealing himself from the game.[110]

Not surprisingly, the lexis of bow and stable hunting is an important element of imaginative and romantic literature. In the deer hunt in the third fit of *Sir Gawain and the Green Knight*, the dreamer poet tells us how early in the morning

There were a hundred choice huntsmen there, whose fame/ Resounds. / To their stations keepers strode; / Huntsmen unleashed hounds: / The forest overflowed/ With the strident bugle sounds.[111]

So skilful are they at the tryst, and so strong the hounds, that the game is brought down as fast as one can look. It is significant that respecting the fence month (close season), the castellan and his hunters take only hinds and does, the harts and bucks being allowed their freedom.[112] This highlights the importance of the legality of aristocratic hunting, even in imaginative literature. Did courtly audiences perhaps need to be reminded of this aspect of their favourite sport and pastime?

In Chaucer's *Book of the Duchess*, the poet dreams of participating in a great hunt given in honour of the Emperor Octavian. Chaucer's vivid description demonstrates his own intimate knowledge of aristocratic hunting, the result of his gentlemanly education. He includes elements of both *par force* and bow and stable hunting, for at one stage the narrator tells his audience, 'How they would slee the hart with strength' and use 'many relaies and limers', yet at another point describes how 'I was go walked fro my tree', obviously his tryst or stand, by a whelp (young hound) into a magic Greenwood of huge trees, full of all three species and ages of deer.[113] So led by the theme of the chase, the audience enters an area of magic and forest fantasy, paralleled by the May forest of *The Parlement of the Thre Ages*.

By the middle of the sixteenth century, bow and stable hunting had developed into a complex and hugely expensive demonstration of wealth and power, much favoured by great nobles and European royalty. The original idea of a sporting occasion was prostituted into one of slaughter and self-indulgence, the idea being to guarantee sport for royalty. Two paintings of the time illustrate the beginnings of this departure from true sport. *The Stag Hunt of the Elector Frederick the Wise*, completed by Lucas Cranach in about 1529, shows dozens of deer, having been driven into a lake, being shot by hunters from their stands or trysts. The

Elector Frederick and Holy Roman Emperor Maximilian I are easily recognised. *The Stag Hunt for the Emperor Charles V at the Castle of Torgau*, painted by Lucas Cranach the Younger in about 1544, is a similar scene of slaughter but on a grander scale, taking place in front of the impressive castle at Torgau.[114] This sort of guaranteed hunting could degenerate and become even more symbolically ritualised. To celebrate the marriage of Leonello d'Este to Maria of Aragon in 1444, there was a St George play, followed by a joust and a 'hunt'. The latter event involved the slaughter of animals released into the piazza in the middle of Ferrara.[115] *Bullfighting and other Games in the Piazza del Campo, Siena*, painted in about 1600 by Vicenzo Rustici, is a further development of this notion of guaranteed sport, again making use of the great central square of a Renaissance city.[116]

There are two other related ways in which aristocratic hunting differs markedly from commonalty hunting and these are the 'fence month', the season of non-hunting or disturbance of red deer, and approved seasons for hunting quarry. It could be rightly argued that the imposition of a close season is not a technique of hunting, but it is certainly part of aristocratic methodology in its wider sense, as is the season when it was best to hunt specific beasts.

The concept of a close season, imposed on hunters for whatever reason, is intimately bound up with the whole aristocratic attitude towards quarry and methodology. The fence month is specifically mentioned by Edward, Duke of York, and at the end of the fifteenth century, *The Boke of Saint Albans* is also exacting about the times when certain beasts may be hunted or allowed relief. Only the hart and the hare are given the privilege of a close season. Of the hart, Dame Juliana Berners comments: 'From the Annunciacion of owre lady day/ The hert then releues the sooth for to say/ Till saynt Petris day and paule.'[117] This made sense as early summer is the time when red deer calves are born and a regime of protection and lack of disturbance was essential to the well-being of both youngsters and nursing mothers. Prohibiting hart hunting thus also guaranteed the protection of hinds and calves, ensuring stock for the following year. William Baillie-

Grohman uses the 1598 edition of Manwood's manual to illustrate this point. Manwood's fence month was

> fifteen days before and ended fifteen days after midsummer. During this time great care was taken that no men or stray dogs should be allowed to wander in the forest, and no swine or cattle were allowed to feed within the precincts, so that the deer should be absolutely undisturbed during three or four weeks after the fawning season.

The deer had complete precedence; it was clearly imperative and doubtless enforced, that no commoner or his animals entered the forest. He continues to explain the origin of the term:

> in this month there must be watch and ward kept with men and weapons for the fence and defence of wild beasts, for that reason the same is called fence or defence month.[118]

The use of the term 'fawning', rather than 'calving', may indicate that Manwood was generally referring to fallow rather than red deer, the latter's numbers being in decline by the end of the Tudor period. This tradition of imposing the fence month continued for centuries in England, C.J. Cornish commenting in 1895:

> 'Defense de chasser' is probably the origin of the ancient term of venery which heads the notices, posted during May and June at the gates of the royal deer parks, requesting that during the 'fence-months' visitors will prevent their dogs from disturbing the deer.[119]

In spite of this special privilege accorded red deer, in general the advised hunting seasons were related to when animals were fit and in prime fat condition, not to the modern considerations of mating, pregnancy and nursing young. The concept of a season as a period which included the time when it was best to hunt deer and other animals because they were fat, or *in grece*, was pragmatic and economically based, very different from a period of relief imposed on hunters out of consideration for the quarry. Baillie-Grohman compiled a useful list of seasons from various medieval sources in his Appendix to *The Master of Game*. Inevitably, some of these sources were contradictory and the following is a simplified version:

Red deer stag: June 14th. to September 14th., but probably from May onwards.

Red deer hind: September 14th. to January 6th. or February 2nd.

Fallow deer buck: June 24th. to September 14th.

Fallow deer doe: September 14th. to February 2nd.

Roe deer buck: Easter to September 29th.

Roe doe: September 29th. to February 2nd.

Hare: September 29th. to February 2nd. or June 24th., but Twiti, Gaston Fébus and Edward, Duke of York, like hare hunting as it 'lasteth all the year'.

Wild boar: September 14th., 29th. or Christmas Day to February 2nd.

Wolf: Christmas to March 25th. but probably all year.

Fox: September 8th. or Christmas Day to March 25th.

Otter: February 22nd. to June 24th.

Martin, badger and rabbit were hunted at all seasons.[120]

Hunting seasons and non-hunting seasons were not legislated under statute law at this time, although the Forest Laws did specify hunting seasons for most animals. This sort of control by the ruling élites over their own pastime must also have been the result of two factors which were very different to the practical aspect of 'grease time': respect for their quarry and conservation of the species.

This 'respect' for the 'dignity' of the hunted beast, which is eventually to be killed, is one of the continuing ambiguities of hunting throughout the ages. The medieval hunter perceived and classified certain animals as 'noble', and so applied human rules of chivalry to those favoured beasts. This sportsmanlike regard was essentially one of honour and 'fairness' by one gentleman to another of equal status, somewhat akin to the Plains Indians' respect for the American bison, but also, in our case, involving notions of rank and status. The aristocratic hunter was very definitely identifying himself and other sportsmen of his class with the accepted 'beasts of venery', an aristocratic form of anthropomorphism, more profound than simple humane respect for the quarry. In the English language, we are familiar with the term 'sportsman', which is used in a complimentary way. The equivalent term in the medieval Middle German manuals is '*Weidmann*',[121] indicating an attitude of decent consideration for the quarry and other hunters, and of general good behaviour in the hunting field.

The preservation of stocks and the continuity of species for future hunting must also have played a significant part in assigning a fence month to high status species. The medieval aristocratic hunter was an educated and well-versed man and he undoubtedly realised that the supply of large game was not endless. Imparking of unenclosed land and the rearing of deer and wild boar to stock such parks were understandable reactions to the decline in numbers of large quarry species. The idea of conservation in the later Middle Ages was thus complex and to a large extent based upon completely different philosophies from the fundamentally humane ideas of modern hunters and legislators.

Remarkably, the fence month is actually illustrated in one high-quality German manuscript, the Calendar pictures of which form a cycle dedicated to aristocratic hunting. The *bas de page* miniature for May of MS Egerton 1146 shows a peaceful pastoral scene of

1 Gaston Fébus educating young hunters: practising blowing horns and holloaing. (*Bibliothèque nationale, Paris, Livre de chasse, MS fr. 616, Ch. 26, fol. 54*)

2 The conversion to Christianity of the Italian patron saint of hunting. *The Vision of St Eustace*, by Pisanello, *c.* 1438–42 (*National Gallery, London*)

3 High status dress for falconry. (*Musée de Condé, Chantilly*, Très Riches Heures du Duc de Berri, *MS 65*, Calendar for August, *fol. 8v*)

4 The boar hunt on foot. The hunter, in winter clothes, despatches his quarry caught in a rope snare set in a gap in wattle fencing. (*British Library, London, MS Egerton 1146, Calendar for November, fol. 12v*)

5 The boar hunt on horseback with hounds. Both men's faces and headgear are rimed in frost, an unusual touch of realism. (*British Library, London, MS Egerton 1146, Calendar for December, fol. 13v*)

6 Maximilian's grandson, Ferdinand, in extravagant hunting dress, spearing a wild boar from horseback. (*Musée du Louvre, Paris*, Les Chasses de Maximilien, *tapestry for December*)

7 (above) and 8 (overleaf) Early fourteenth-century English horses for hunting and hawking. (*British Library, London,* The Luttrell Psalter, *Additional MS 42130, fols 43v and 159*)

8

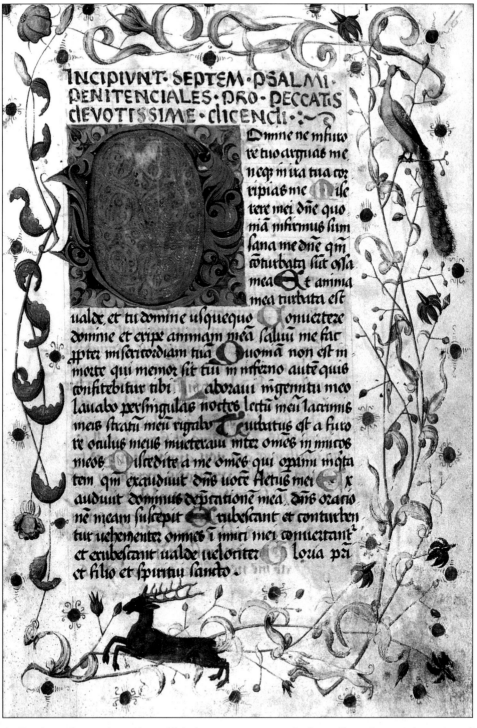

9 Greyhound pursuing a hart. This is a common marginal motif on the opening page of Gothic manuscripts. (*British Library, London, MS Egerton 1146, fol. 16r*)

10 Spaniels or *chienz doysel*, useful small hounds for wild duck, partridge and quail. (*Bibliothèque nationale, Paris, Livre de chasse, MS fr. 616, Ch. 20, fol. 50*)

11 The 'world upside-down'. *Garden of Earthly Delights*, right wing of the triptych *Hell* (lower detail), by Hieronymus Bosch, *c.* 1500. A giant hare with his bag, triumphantly blowing a hunting horn, carries a naked young woman on a stick. (*Bridgeman/Museo del Prado, Madrid*)

cos meos. Et preces omnes qui tribulat
animam meam quoniaz ego servus tuus si.
SEQVITVR · LETANIA · MAIOR ·
· IN MEDIATE · POST · SEPTEM ·
PSALMOS · DEVOTE · DICENDA
yrieleyson. Cristeley
son. Criste audi nos.
Saluator mundi ad
iuua nos.
Sancta maria, ora,
Sancte Michabel.
Sancte Gabriel ora
Sancte Raphael.
Omnes sancti ange
li et archangeli. orate p
Sancte Johannes baptista. ora pro nob'
Omnes sancti patriarche et prophete orate
Sancte Petre. Ora p
Sancte Paule. Ora p
Sancte Andrea. Ora p
Sancte Jacobe. Ora p
Sancte Johannes. Ora p
Sancte philippe. Ora p
Sancte Thoma. Ora p
Sancte Bartholomee. Ora p
Sancte Mathee. Ora p
Sancte Jacobe. Ora p
Sancte Symon. Ora p

12 A dangerous game. Bear hunting on foot, the hunter using a cross-hilted bear-spear. (*British Library, London, MS Egerton 1146, fol. 20r*)

13 A wolf is pulled down by hounds, while the mounted hunter wields his sword. (*British Library, London, MS Egerton 1146*, Calendar for February, *fol. 3v*)

14 A good start to the day: the assemblée, or hunt breakfast. (*Bridgeman/Bibliothèque nationale, Paris. Livre de chasse, MS fr. 616, Ch. 38, fol. 67*)

15 Classic aristocratic *par force* hunting: on horseback with a pack of hounds. (*Bibliothèque nationale, Paris, Livre de chasse, MS fr. 616, Ch. 39, fol. 68*)

16 The hunter poised to despatch the hart in water, while a lymerer struggles to restrain his scenting-hound. (*British Library, London, MS Egerton 1146*, Calendar for July, *fol. 8v*)

stags, hinds and calves grazing in a wood beside a stream.[122] Significantly, this is the only miniature of the Calendar in which hunters are absent. The occurrence of such an illustration in this manuscript surely reflects not only the occupational accuracy of the whole hunting cycle but also the forbearance and sportsmanship of the patron, two essentially chivalric ideals of aristocratic medieval hunters which separate them from their peasant counterparts. Of course, gentle hunters could afford to indulge themselves in these idealistic and generous ways whereas peasants could not, particularly if they were poaching venison. The snares, traps and other 'engines' used by peasant deer poachers in royal forests demonstrate skilful efficiency but also unspeakable cruelty, the object being to incapacitate the deer, not grant an honourable and quick death after a long chase.[123]

In conclusion, although quarry type was a vital element in defining the aristocratic medieval chase, methodology, seasons, lexis, ritual and procedure were perhaps more important indicators of an élitist pastime, a 'sport apart'. After all, anybody could poach a deer or hare, but this did not make a man a gentle hunter or indicate social status, in fact very often the exact opposite, although many poachers were aristocratic or ecclesiastic in origin. It was only a minority of the population who could afford to hunt on horseback and equip themselves adequately and also be members of that properly educated élite, regarded as 'lerned' by both peer and socially inferior groups. Their premier pastime and sport had to be, and be clearly seen to be, remote from the commonalty and unattainable by any but those of noble, or at least gentle, birth. This was an important part of the public face of the European ruling classes.

FOUR

Everyman

As the previous chapters have demonstrated, there is a wealth of evidence in hunting manuals, treatises and imaginative and romantic literature on the European upper classes hunting and hawking. All of this contemporary literature was written by gentle authors for a gentle, or courtly, educated audience. Inevitably, the immediate impression given by this great and varied mass of material is of the almost total exclusion of the rest of medieval society, who did not possess the privilege of leisure. The Third Estate, or commons, had to work for a living. The great majority of people of this rank dirtied their hands pursuing an occupation. Whatever their status or wealth within this feudal category, they could not claim the title of 'gentleman'. However, in spite of the humble status of common hunters, a few textual sources, notably some canonical French manuscripts, indicate that hunting was a widespread activity throughout the community. The *Livre de chasse* and *Roy Modus* include descriptions and instructions catering for the needs of the general rural population, in addition to those for the courtier and aristocratic landowner.[1] *Roy Modus* is indeed invaluable on peasant methods of taking birds. His manual of instruction is presented in the well-established form of a dialogue made up of question and answer, and includes chapters in which King Modus responds to a poor man's questions on methods of taking birds. The text is clarified with illustrations. *Livre de chasse* is also a precious source of commonalty methods but is confined to hunting mammals, lacking any instruction on taking birds, or on hawking. The MS fr. 616 and MS M.1044 manuscripts of *Livre de chasse* contain particularly good quality and useful illustrations of commonalty methods.

Movable type, first successfully used by Johann Gutenberg at Mainz from around 1454/5, expanded and accelerated the production of aristocratic hunting and hawking books. However, it is significant that there were no specific texts for the instruction of common hunters for nearly two centuries. Probably the first such text was German, Johann Conrad Aitinger's *Brief and simple report on bird-catching with snares*, written in 1631. Snaring birds was the most popular form of hunting for the mass of society. The fact that a book on commonalty methods was in print and available to a more literate public reflects changes in attitudes and the general unrest in Germanic society at this time.[2]

Texts other than hunting books can prove useful for providing additional pieces of information on commonalty hunting. *The Luttrell Psalter*, a beautiful illuminated manuscript created as a status symbol for Sir Geoffrey Luttrell somewhere between 1320 and 1340,[3] shows some few pictures of peasant methodology as well as the expected aristocratic hunting and hawking illustrations. Janet Backhouse comments, 'It is however abundantly clear from the flavour of the original work that the craftsmen engaged to produce this splendid and expensive manuscript had been given very specific guidance about at least some of its desired contents.'[4] This manuscript is a unique record of everyday life on the Luttrell estate at Irnham in Lincolnshire in the early fourteenth century. As such, it is interesting that the patron, Sir Geoffrey Luttrell, very probably instructed the artists that illustrations of peasant hunting as well as gentle hunting were to be included, thus giving a rounded picture of estate life.

The humble hunter and villager, as far as is known, neither wrote nor read hunting treatises, so presumably relied upon oral tradition for instruction from family and friends on hunting methodology and techniques, as well as for advice on poaching. Using Forest court evidence on peasant deer poaching, Jean Birrell comments, 'Fathers passed on their skills to their sons, and . . . fathers, sons and brothers often hunted together'. In peasant communities, those who were related would not only know each other well but would also feel able to trust each other on illegal hunting forays.[5] Thus both lone hunting and small-group hunting were widely practised by English and European peasant hunters. According to Nicholas Orme, 'Ordinary children were unlikely to take part in hunting itself, but it is hard to believe that some did not follow to hold open gates or simply to watch what went on.'[6] Orme is clearly referring to aristocratic hunting and the mounted chase. However, the sons of commoners undoubtedly did hunt, not only in their own traditional ways, including poaching, but also in a formal manner if they became employed in the king's or a great lord's hunt establishment.

What little information we possess on the practices of the commonalty from hunting manuals and treatises is often socially biased, even if presented accurately in the texts. Hunting books are peppered with remarks indicating distaste and disapproval. Thus, the Duke of York, writing on snaring hares with cords, comments disparagingly, 'Trewly I trowe that a good hunter wold sle hem so for no good.'[7] Gaston Fébus remarks with repulsion on French peasants using a spring-trap, loaded with a hunting spear, against bears and other beasts, 'Plus n'en vueill parler de ce, quar c'est vilaine chasce.'[8] It is undoubtedly significant that Fébus purposely uses the word 'vilaine' at this point in his text. His adverse comments on the method of driving deer into fixed nets, a practice commonly used by rich and professional hunters (legitimately) and poor hunters (illegally) to obtain supplies of venison, also show his contempt for unsporting 'villainous' techniques.[9]

However, one of the fascinations for historians studying *Livre de chasse* is the considerable inclusion of commonalty methods of taking game. Why did this Prince of the Pyrenees include such lower-class material in a how-to-do-it book for nobles? The answer may be that Fébus, a wise and intelligent man, included these non-sporting techniques for the instruction of 'all men who hunt in all ways', which is legitimate enough in a comprehensive book on how to hunt. There is, in addition, a probable subtext to the inclusion of such material; it is so that a gentleman might be conversant with all the techniques of taking birds and animals, including those covert methods of the commons. This knowledge could prove invaluable not only in his dealings with his tenants and the rural peasantry but usefully in outwitting poachers, whatever their background.

This possibility, that gentle readers could benefit from knowing what the lower orders might do in this respect, raises the interesting question of the role of hunting manuals and whether 'instruction' encompassed a wider remit than simply quarry, method and correct lexis. Perhaps feudal 'man-management' was a recognised part of their purpose. This seems an eminently sensible concept and in line with the philosophy of the times; there were instruction books on many subjects including hunting, hawking, heraldry, fishing, and how to bring up boys and girls from birth to puberty.[10] In a society that was largely rural, instruction on the proper management of labour, in all its many aspects, appears *de rigueur*. A vital point is that Fébus, and some other nobles, recognised that men of few or no means, with no apparent rights of warren, were hunting by their own methods in order to obtain food and raw materials, and to protect their lives and property. No doubt, the pleasure of hunting was an additional factor and motive also, with John Cummins commenting on 'the less fortunate men finding valid fulfilment creeping along hedges with a bundle of rabbit-nets, sitting inside a bush luring small birds, and making traps'.[11]

The right to hunt and to do so freely was one of the demands made by the peasants in the 1381 revolt. Wat Tyler demanded of the youthful Richard II: 'All warrens, as well in fisheries as in parks and woods, should be commen to all; so that throughout the realm, in the waters, ponds, fisheries, woods and forests, poor as well as rich might take the venison and hunt the hare in the fields.'[12] To symbolise their claim to take game in the abbot's chases, the rebels at St Albans carried a rabbit tied to a lance.[13] These demands for commonalty rights to hunt and fish freely were echoed in later European revolts and were among the first to be made by German peasants during the Peasants' War of 1524/5.[14]

That hunting by the English commons was widespread, posing a threat to the established privileges of their social superiors and also to law, order and stability is evident in a petition to Parliament in 1390, which was added to by Richard II and passed as a Statute of the Realm. This is the first of the Game Laws whose justice was administered by Common Law courts and not by the eyres of the Forest courts. It is thus a landmark in the laws concerning taking game and reflects changing attitudes in society.

> Also pray the Commons that whereas artificers and labourers, this is to say, butchers, shoemakers, tailors, and other low persons, keep greyhounds and other dogs, and at times when good Christians on holy days are at church, hearing divine services, go hunting in parks, rabbit-runs, and warrens of lords and others, and destroy them entirely; and so they assemble at such times to hold discussions, and make plots and conspiracies, to make insurrections and disobedience to your majesty and laws, under colour of such manner of hunting.
>
> May it please you to ordain in this present parliament, that any kind of artificer or labourer or any other who lacks lands and tenements to the value of 40s a year, or any priest or clerk if he has not preferment worth £10, shall not keep any greyhound, or any other dogs, if they are not fastened up or leashed, or have had their claws cut, on pain of imprisonment for a year. And that every justice of the peace shall have power to enquire and punish every contravention.[15]

Richard II, having been instructed in venery from an early age like all royal princes,[16] may himself have had sufficient knowledge of lower-class hunting methods to add, 'hounds, ferrets, hays, nets, hair-pipes, cords and all other devices to take or destroy beasts of the forest, hares or rabbits or other sport of gentlefolk'.[17]

The king certainly meant to cover all eventualities of commonalty practice and restrict hunting of any description to those with some property, presumably those more likely to be supporters of the monarchy and the status quo. However, the basic property qualification of 40s a year indicates the lowest level of lesser gentry, perhaps even the upper yeomanry, so the law was to some extent inclusive and certainly was not an effective attempt to restrict hunting to the rich and noble members of society. The preamble to this statute expresses an important concern on the part of the authorities that commoners were holding meetings, ostensibly to hunt but in reality to plot and conspire insurrection against the king and the laws of the land. As Professor A.J. Pollard dryly remarks, 'as probably they were, since the rights to game were a highly contentious issue'.[18] Significantly, this new game law applied to the whole kingdom but not to the royal or seigneurial forests where Forest Law still applied. It was thus very definitely a restrictive piece of legislation, designed to legally exclude the great mass of the English population from hunting. The 1390 Game Law abolished the ancient right of all to take game from the common fields and woods of England, thus paving the way for hunting to cease being the contended monopoly of the Crown and become the privilege of the upper classes.[19]

Setting aside Marxist notions of class persecution and of Ricardian political motivations, the significance of the statute to historians is obvious – it indicates that an increasing number of commoners were participating in hunting to a considerable extent and, moreover, using their own effective methods to take quarry which was regarded as 'noble', particularly the hare. These common folk were apparently getting above their station and had to be firmly reminded of their proper place in society. The sumptuary laws of Edward III, enacted in 1363, and of Edward IV, enacted in 1463,[20] were another expression of the governing classes' unease at an increasingly socially mobile commonalty. It is significant that these laws regulating dress and public status largely affected, and were principally aimed at, the emergent 'up-start' middling sort or *mediocres*, that is, the yeomen of the countryside and the merchants, artisans and shopkeepers in the expanding towns. These yeomen were less than gentlemen: they worked.[21] On the other hand, the sumptuary laws can be interpreted quite differently; as a pragmatic move on the part of the rulers of late medieval society to accommodate the new middle classes. Maurice Keen describes this as 'a more determined and careful effort to bring merchants, substantial artificers and townsmen into equation with landed people, in terms of dress and degree'. This attempt to create a parity made up of different social groups indicates the increasing importance of commerce and the esteem in which it was held by those in power.[22]

From the meagre evidence available it is difficult to assess whether hunting by the commons was largely restricted to the rural population or whether and to what extent townspeople were also involved. There are great problems in defining what was a town or urban, and what was rural. Where did towns begin and end? Most were small and did not possess walls to separate town from country. In any case, an enclosing wall was not a particularly valid physical division between the two areas as commercial premises and housing developed beyond most town walls, medieval York being a good example. Another problem is which residents could be classified as townsmen. Most residents probably lived and worked within their town but some people lived in a town but worked in the nearby countryside. However, common sense dictates that a good number of town residents must have regularly forayed into the countryside, and indeed the 1390 statute specifies five occupations (butchers, shoemakers, tailors, priests and clerk) which could indicate urban origins for at least some of these troublesome hunters. To people living in most towns, the potential hunting grounds in field, woodland and the king's Forest were near at hand and easily accessible. A statute of Henry V enacted in 1421, relating to university discipline, makes it clear that some residents of Oxford were hunting, although illegally:

> VIII. Item, Because that many Clerks and Scholars of the University of Oxford unknown . . . have hunted with Dogs and Greyhounds in divers Warrens, Parks and Forests . . . and taken Deer, Hares and Conies . . . .[23]

These student-poachers kept the right kinds of dog for successful forays into other men's preserves and were obviously prepared to take game of any variety. The quantities which they were taking must have been considerable to warrant a specific inclusion in the statute. For many, educated as nobles or gentlemen before going up to the university, hunting was part of their way of life and it is hardly surprising that they wished to continue actively to participate as students, whether legally or illegally. Doubtless, this also applied to Cambridge students.

In his researches into the local codes of law in Iberia, John Cummins has found that the medieval townsman, as well as the villager, had rights of hunting which varied regionally and from town to town.[24] This is, of course, legitimate hunting by the commons, but it surely indicates that townsmen in the Iberian Peninsula were not divorced from the countryside and still wanted or needed to hunt wild quarry. There is no reason to suppose that this need or desire should not have applied to any person in England or the continent at this time, or indeed for centuries to come.

Dress for the medieval common man out hunting was, of necessity, strictly practical and utilitarian. Peasants and other poor folk had few, if any, changes of clothes and almost certainly they performed their labours and went hunting in the same set of garments. A recent analysis of the February miniature from the *Très Riches Heures du Duc de Berri*, painted in about 1416 by the Limburg brothers, points out that the inhabitants of the factor's house were not poor as several pieces of spare clothing hang on the walls. In contrast, 'the poor possessed only one set of clothes'.[25] The Sumptuary Statute of 1363 specifies the dress of persons with goods and chattels below the value of 40*s* (£2) to be blanket cloth and russet stuff which could be bought at 12*d* (1*s*) per yard. This applied to most rural folk including 'carters, ploughmen, cowherds, oxherds, dairymen, shepherds, other keepers of beasts and threshers of grain'.[26] However, this plain rustic clothing had distinct advantages over the bright, flamboyant dress usually worn by the nobility out hunting, exemplified by the figures in the Maximilian tapestries. Simple, drab or russet clothing blended better into the landscape and probably a little dirt assisted this process. It is significant that both freedom of movement and muted, natural colours were considered important factors when dedicated noble hunters decided what to wear out hunting, and some of them wisely took their cue from the local rural peasantry. In the mid-thirteenth century, Emperor Frederick II realised the wisdom of rustic wear when out hawking and advised, 'Garments must be short . . . preferably beige or an earthen tint, and of such material as peasants wear'.[27] John I of Portugal said that colour was of no importance, but that practicality mattered to some extent. He advised narrow sleeves, or leg-of-mutton sleeves which were narrow from the elbow to the wrist, that the tunic should not come below knee level, even for the mounted huntsman, and that boots were essential.[28] The hunting drawings in *Queen Mary's Psalter* show the lowest class of professional hunter, the hunting assistants, all wearing a plain knee-length dress, with a circular hole for the neck, and long sleeves. This simple garment is girdled round the waist and tucked up at the front for more freedom of movement.[29] The peasant netting partridges is dressed in similar fashion with the addition of a small, unattached half-hood.[30] Nearly two centuries later, plain natural colours for hunting clothes are recommended by Emperor Maximilian in his *Private Hunting Book*; he advises, 'You shall wear gray and green clothing, partly gray, partly green'.[31] Maximilian loved to hunt alone, dressed as a 'real' hunter, but there were more formal occasions, such as when he was the honoured guest of the Elector Frederic the Wise. Naturally, Maximilian dressed in the height of courtly fashion for such politically important events, as is shown in the stag hunting painting by Lucas Cranach the Elder.

For the lone hunter, out to fill the pot and have some rare sport, concealment and camouflage were vitally important to success. The European forest was a vast store of potential food, to be harvested using every possible advantage. Wearing green in the Greenwood, like the legendary outlaws and heroes of the peasants, Robin Hood, Little John and Gamelyn, made practical sense.[32] The illustration of undoing and breaking-up the hart in the Manuscrit français 616 version of *Livre de chasse* shows ten hunters, but of different rank. The three nobles are dressed in bright red or pink whereas the seven hunt servants are in green hunting dress, including three with green knee-stockings.[33] In fact, green was the livery colour not only of professional hunt servants but also of the employed forestry officials, the so-called Yeomen of the Forest. In the fifteenth-century

Robin Hood rhymes, Robin and his Merry Men are portrayed as such yeomen who fled to live in the Greenwood wearing their occupational uniforms.[34] What else did they have to wear? It is natural that they were described by the Robin Hood poets as being in green; the audience, whether gentle or common, would immediately understand, and indeed probably expect, such a point of reference in the description of yeomen foresters.

In *The Parlement of the Thre Ages*, Youth is portrayed as a gentle hunter, but 'He was gerede alle in grene'.[35] and is referred to as 'the gome alle in grene'.[36] The dreamer-poet represents himself as a lawless hunter, a literate game-thief and dreamer without status.[37] He carefully camouflages himself with foliage before stalking the deer, 'Both my body and my bowe I buskede with leues',[38] and then hides beside a tree (his tryst?) and waits for a hart to appear. The use of natural foliage as camouflage is vividly represented in a miniature in *Livre de chasse*; the hunter is stalking deer using a 'charnette' or stalking-cart. Hunter, horse, cart and attendant groom are all camouflaged with leaves and branches.[39] The point here is not the status of the hunter, but rather that Fébus was showing that camouflage was a recognised technique of concealment which enabled hunters to approach game closely in order to maximise the success of a shot. Fébus also writes of approaching game (deer) using a stalking-cow, described as 'une toile qui semble a un buef'. However, the miniature in the Manuscrit français 616 version of *Livre de chasse* shows a stalking-horse in which two assistants are concealed,[40] akin to the traditional English pantomime horse! Manning remarks that stalking-horses were often used by hunters of all classes to approach deer which only feared two-footed predators.[41] The references in *The Parlement of the Thre Ages* to gentle but lawless hunters wearing green and using leaves to aid concealment indicate that these techniques were probably well known, if not universal, and employed in the field by hunters of different status but for the same reason. The use of natural materials in the art of concealment and camouflage must go back thousands of years to the earliest hunters, as must the use of dummies in approaching wild quarry. The ultimate aim of any hunter was to be as effective as possible, particularly if fresh meat was the main objective. For the rural lower orders brought up in the countryside, concealment and camouflage would have been second nature, valuable skills taught by their elders and passed on by word of mouth and practical example.

Undoubtedly, at the appropriate time, such as when out stalking deer, nobles wore green clothing and perhaps natural camouflage; commonalty hunters did so because green was their occupational livery or because they possessed nothing else. Thus what constituted 'correct' dress out hunting depended upon who was hunting and for what purpose. The basic problem for the upper classes was whether to dress for status or practicality and, of course, aristocratic *veneurs* had this pleasant choice whereas common hunters did not. Thus, we cannot judge status purely on dress code, although it can be a significant indicator, depending upon the context of hunting which is described or illustrated. The one factor which is clear is that the aristocratic authors of the most informative late medieval hunting texts agree that green was the correct colour to wear for 'true' hunters. However, as John Cummins comments, there appears little consistency in the colouring of hunting garments in medieval illustrations, although there can be some consistency within one manuscript, such as between mounted hunters and assistants on foot.[42] The unknown factor is that illustrations may not always have reflected practice in the hunting field, the reason being that illuminated pictures in manuscripts had decorative and status purposes as well as a purely instructive function.

Quarry hunted by the commonalty included virtually every living bird and animal but it all had the same factor in common – edibility. Wolves and foxes, to be killed without mercy and indiscriminately, were the exceptions.[43] Vulpicide was considered as a favour to the community, not as a sin.[44] Here, gentle and humble hunters' interests collided. Nobles hunted wolves and foxes on horseback *par force* but these beasts were also hunted on foot by common men as they were predators and yielded a valuable pelt. A marginal picture in *The Luttrell Psalter* shows such a huntsman about to let slip his brace of greyhounds at Reynard.[45] Bears (hunted in the wild on the continent but in England the product of bear-baiting), badgers and squirrels made good eating. Red deer, being royal game, were rigorously protected as were fallow deer and, perhaps to a lesser extent, roe deer. Hares, although the favourite quarry of English gentle *veneurs*, were also hunted by humble persons using different methods to the upper classes. A chapter in *Roy Modus* explains how to hunt the hare with running hounds, a common enough method today, while a later chapter tells of the poor man who has only a *reseul*, a pocket or bag net, and how he is to capture hares in the fields and vineyards.[46] *The Master of Game* comments that 'any poor gentleman with a couple of greyhounds or a few *raches* [small hounds running by scent] could have a good run with the hare, even though he might not possess a horse'.[47]

Note that this hunter although presented as 'poor', was still a 'gentleman' so his real social status remains ambiguous; or does it? Perhaps Edward is conceding that there were poor hunters who pursued noble game but, naturally, they were still gentlemen. William Baillie-Grohman comments in *The Master of Game* that the writings of the French *veneurs* illustrate how rich and poor pursued the hare, if not always by the fairest methods.[48] He also relates that Gace de la Buigne tells how small farmers would assemble with their hounds, some forty of different breeds and sizes, and hunt hares with great enjoyment and success.[49] These French farmers were using whatever resources they had between them, to hunt the hare in a manner which was a humbler version of hare hunting by a trencher-fed pack from an aristocratic hunt establishment. Their methodology was loosely based on gentle hunting but they lacked the wherewithal and education to pursue it 'correctly'. However, their enjoyment was probably just as intense as that of their aristocratic neighbours. François Villon in writing his will, *The Testament*, comments satirically on two friends, down-at-heel gentlemen, who are also difficult to classify socially:

As for Merbeuf and Louviers,/ I leave them neither bull nor cow/ for they're no stockmen. More truly they/ are men to carry hawks (now, now,/ don't think this is a joke!) to bow/ and stoop on partridges and plover,/ without a failure anyhow-/ at Madam Machecoue's and under cover.[50]

Gaston Fébus gives instructions for pot-hunting but at the same time makes it clear he does not approve of such methods for the sportsman: 'Also one can take hares in divers methods with cords, for which I would that they who take hares thus should have them [the cords] round their own necks.'[51]

However, as a social indicator, the evidence for the practice of netting game is mixed. Two pictures in *Livre de chasse* show two commonalty methods of taking hares. 'Hare driving with bells' is a cunning technique in which a long-net is stretched between a wood and the field where the hares are feeding. The hunters hold a rope which has bells attached to it and as they walk towards the wood across the field, the bells ring, driving the hares into the long-net. In netting 'hares in their muses', the nets are stretched across runs habitually taken by hares at the crossing of rural roads. Hunters with spears are hiding nearby to despatch the hares when they become entangled in the nets.[52] This method of taking hares also appears in *Roy Modus*.[53] Both these methods are simple and effective, as well as requiring a minimum of equipment, making them ideal for rustic hunters.

Nets of various types and snares were commonly used by practical hunters to take most forms of game, birds and animals. Gaston Fébus was familiar with nets and netting both large and small game. An illustration in *Livre de chasse* shows the manufacture of snares, running nooses and nets from rope, together with an explanation of method entitled, 'Si devise comment on doit fere et lassier toutes manieres de las'. Other illustrations demonstrate the methods of netting deer, wild boar and wolves with large nets and rabbits with small nets.[54] The lively *base de page* miniature for April in the Calendar of MS Egerton 1146 is of a mounted hunter with hounds chasing a stag and hind into a large net stretched between two trees.[55] These illustrations show the blurring of upper- and lower-class methodology. Who netted what and when? As regards deer and other large game, the answer seems to be 'everybody' when the occasion demanded fresh meat, a continuing problem for all classes in the Middle Ages. As in France and England, some German manuals exhibit élitist bias on methodology. For example, the *Jagd der Minne* includes a contrast between the sportsmanlike hunting methods of the '*Minnejäger*', a member of the lower nobility, and those of the '*Becken-jeger*', the bad huntsman, who employs nets and snares during the chase.[56] This latter practice was presumably used to purposely bring the hunt to an abrupt but more predictable conclusion than the open chase. However, not all contemporary evidence inclines to this view and the use of nets and snares in the German medieval chase was not always considered unsporting. Indeed, some literary passages describe both stags and hinds being netted and trapped during the chase.[57]

As with wearing green, it is clear that the practice of using nets is not indicative of commonalty hunting as netting was socially widespread. This very effective method of taking all types of game from deer to rabbits was a well-established practice which continued for centuries. Roger Manning comments, 'Hunting with toils or nets was a very common practice in the Tudor period among all classes from kings to peasants.' Even Queen Elizabeth hunted in this manner at Theobalds in the 1590s.[58] Certainly, as we have seen, the nobility used large fixed nets to ensnare big game, particularly deer and wild boar, yet there is persuasive evidence that commoners probably used netting as an everyday method more than nobles. It appears scale of net was important; smaller nets were cheaper to buy or manufacture and were easily concealed and dismantled on clandestine outings. This is not to say that small-scale netting by commonalty hunters was easier, less ingenious or lacking in skill, probably the contrary. An illustration in *Roy Modus* shows a clever rigid-framed trap for catching squirrels. One animal is already inside the trap, greedily eating the bait, while a second descends from a nearby tree to claim his share. A worried peasant waits some distance away to pull the cord which will close the trap entrance.[59] A line drawing in *Queen Mary's Psalter* shows a peasant netting a small covey of partridge using a net several feet long stretched across a tapering wooden frame. Two ropes are attached to the wider end, suggesting the structure may have been thrown or, more likely, is being pulled by the hunter.[60] *Roy Modus* shows two peasants each holding a large framed net over sitting larks while a third rings a bell to put the birds up into the nets.[61] Another type of net was the *cokeshote* or *cockshut*, a large net suspended between two long poles and employed to catch, or shut in, flying woodcock.[62] The device was held upright and clapped shut by the hunter when the bird flew into the netting. The woodcock's habit of 'roding', or coming in to roost at the same time along an identical flight path each evening, made the bird an easy prey to stealthy, observant hunters skilled in woodcraft. The *Percy Bailiff's Rolls* of the fifteenth century record a reference to purchasing five 'cokshotes' for this purpose: 'Et de 1s. receptis de redditu V cokshotes sic dimissorum diuersis tenentibus per forestarium ididem.'[63] In this case, the cockshotes were purchased for the local Forest establishment, but these simple aerial trapping structures were easily made by any skilled countryman. This ancient practice of taking woodcock is commemorated in the place-name Cockshut Wood, a small wood situated on the east shore of Derwent Water, near Keswick, in the Lake District.

The alternative to using a cockshote can be seen in a charming, though patently ludicrous, illustration in *Roy Modus*. The method is jokingly described by Modus as *a la folletoere* (a bit of nonsense) and involves the hunter dressing up as a woodcock, including a long nosepiece like a beak, approaching the bemused bird on his knees, then snaring the quarry around the neck with a horsehair noose tied to a rod.[64] This was surely the ultimate in optimistic camouflage techniques!

Such a simple but effective device as a cockshote could clearly be used for taking other medium- to small-sized birds. A variation on the cockshote is shown in a margin of *The Luttrell Psalter*. Here, a peasant is netting a small bird using a simple but ingenious contrivance, consisting of a long pole with a triangular net at the top attached to a moveable cross-piece. The mouth of the net can be closed by means of a draw-cord held by the hunter when a bird is caught.[65] Peasant hunters also used clap-sticks to catch small birds which were lured in to mob a live owl decoy. This method is also illustrated in *Roy Modus*.[66] The practice of using live or artificial decoys to attract prey is an ancient one, the decoy being either of the same species as the quarry or a predator type, such as an owl or hawk, likely to be attacked by the quarry. A favourite trick was to cover twigs and small branches with a thick layer of glue made from lime, and then attract small birds in to perch on the prepared twigs. *Roy Modus* shows a peasant hidden in a bush with a songbird attached to his wrist, the bird's song attracting others of the same species on to the limed twigs of nearby bushes.[67] John of Salisbury, writing in the third quarter of the twelfth century, mentions various peasant practices of taking wild birds, including snares, nooses and of luring them 'by tunes or whistle'.[68] Again, this latter well-known technique is illustrated in *Roy Modus*. The concealed peasant hunter plays his whistle to attract songbirds which fly in and mob an owl decoy attached to a nearby perch; the songbirds land then become stuck to limed branches.[69] A *bas de page* to a picture of the 'Mouth of Hell' in the *Hours of Catherine of Cleves* shows a man using caged songbirds to catch birds. Attracted by the live decoys' song, wild birds fly in to perch on a limed string stretched between a tree and a stake.[70]

John of Salisbury indicates that such methods were used by common folk who believed 'that birds of the sky and fishes of the deep are common property', a notion which perhaps understandably annoyed the local gentry who apparently punished offenders severely.[71] This punitive approach by landlords may appear harsh, and it probably was rather an exceptional action at the time, given the legal standing of the Forest Laws. It was likely a reaction to the truculent and socialistic attitudes of the local peasantry, not a serious attempt to stop them taking small birds which would have been legally untenable, and practically impossible to enforce. The Forest Laws, of course, were concerned with protecting the verte and venison and not with prosecuting peasants for trapping small birds. It was a convenient but popular belief that wild beasts were the property of no man, but the legal doctrine of *ferae naturae* was only first advanced in the mid-thirteenth century by Henry de

Bracton (d. 1268).[72] As Peter Coss reminds us, the ideal world
envisaged by the peasants at Mile End and Smithfield in 1381 was a
secular commonwealth which included free access to the beasts of
the forest and fowls of the river.[73] This radical belief was not
restricted to England or to the late fourteenth century. In the 1520s,
peasants from Stuhlingen in Wurttemberg demanded the right,
according to 'the divine law of God', to 'hunt and shoot' all kinds of
game 'and to satisfy our hunger'.[74] Even temporary legal restrictions
challenged not only the debateable right of all men to hunt, but
more importantly, denied common men a vital food resource.

Large game birds were a tempting target for the common hunter,
but their successful capture required some careful preparation. A
simple method illustrated in *Roy Modus* of securing a cock pheasant
is to lay a trail of grain to the trap, a wicker basket whose edge is
held up by a figure-of-four support. The pheasant follows the grain
and stands on a bar or trigger which releases the basket, capturing
the bird alive.[75] An added refinement is a small mirror propped up
under the basket which is supposed to anger the cock bird who,
perceiving a rival, rushes in and trips the trigger.[76] A useful marginal
sketch shows the reader how to make and set the ingenious trigger.[77]
Game birds are not commonly depicted in illuminated manuscripts,
and this bird in *Roy Modus* appears to be the common, or dark-
necked pheasant, a variety regarded as the strain that originated in
Central Asia and south-east Russia and was introduced into
continental Europe sometime before the eleventh century.[78] A very
good illustration of the same variety of cock pheasant appears in the
margin of Egerton 1146.[79] However, the outstanding game bird
picture in this German manuscript is that of a cock red-legged or
'French' partridge, possibly the only example of a single clearly
identifiable bird of this species in a late medieval manuscript.[80]

The wild boar was a particular and dangerous nuisance to farmers
in the Middle Ages and indeed still is so in Bearn, south-west
France, where it remains a favourite quarry of hunters. An ingenious
rustic method of trapping this marauding beast, which has been
raiding a farmer's apple orchard, is described in detail by Gaston
Fébus. He advises that if it has been noticed that for several nights

animal raiders have been feeding on apples in an orchard or on sheaves in a cornfield, a feeding place with corn or apples should be prepared, surrounded with hurdles or stones to a height of about one ell (about a metre or yard). To get at the feed the beast has to jump over these obstacles. After the game has taken the bait for three or four nights, you should then dig a pitfall in the middle of the feeding place, near the spot where the animal lands after it has jumped over the hurdle or stone wall.[81] The beast falls through the covering into the pit where it can be despatched by the farmer.

Other large animals could be trapped using this peasant method. The wolf was hated and feared by country people and every effort was used to exterminate it. Aristocratic wolf hunting was not sufficient to control the packs which pillaged stock and threatened human lives. Baiting meat with poison was a much favoured method and one used in Spain until very recently. Fébus describes various ways in which wolves were taken including 'Si devise comment on puet prendre les lous aus aguilles'.[82] In this method needles or hooks were inserted into chunks of meat which were left at the end of a blood-trail. The wolf found the bait by scent then greedily gulped it with agonising and eventually fatal results. A large hook concealed in a chunk of meat suspended on a rope tied to a bough was a variation. In this case, the wolf leaped up to grab the bait and impaled itself on the hook.[83] Wattle fencing, universal in rural areas during the Middle Ages and for centuries to come, was often used to direct the quarry to bait, a pit, snare or net. An illustration in *Livre de chasse* shows a wolf hanging from a wooden beam. The precursor to this would be as follows: having been guided by portable wattle fencing to the bait, which was laid within a rope noose tied to a pivoting beam, the wolf has taken the bait, sprung the snare and been hoisted into the air.[84] Another miniature shows temporary fencing set up in an X shape, used by hunters to guide a wild boar to a pit, the bait being laid on straw over the pit mouth.[85] Spring-traps set in fence gaps were a favoured way to protect vineyards and orchards against animal poachers. A trip-device in the gap released a spear or bolt fixed to a bent bough. Peasants used this device against bears and other large beasts.[86] The Calendar

107

miniature for November in MS Egerton 1146 shows a large boar, snared by a rope noose set in a gap in wattle fencing, about to be despatched by a hunter on foot using a boar spear.[87] This effectively illustrates peasant methodology successfully utilised by a German noble, who quite possibly had read Gaston Fébus's book of instruction, *Livre de chasse*, as part of his hunting education.

As small ground-game, rabbits were naturally one of the main targets of commonalty hunters and a number of appropriate and effective netting techniques had evolved since the Norman Conquest for catching them. The line drawing in *Queen Mary's Psalter* of women ferreting and netting rabbits illustrates the most common method of taking conies.[88] Mark Bailey, in his study of the East Anglian Breckland, maintains that occasionally polecats, which are larger and fiercer than ferrets, were also used. Most warreners and trappers presumably reared their own ferrets, although there are records of medieval ferret-breeders in East Anglia. As the nets or 'hayes' into which ferrets drove their prey were expensive items. Bailey quotes 30s. for a long net of perhaps 180 feet in length, trappers probably wove their own from locally grown hemp. He marshals evidence which clearly points to local peasants having a wide knowledge of trapping techniques regarding rabbits and predators.[89] Although his research is mainly on the husbandry of rabbits in warrens in East Anglia, it seems reasonable to surmise that peasant expertise and methodology would be similar in other parts of England and Europe where rabbits were found. This is supported by information included in *The Master of Game*, which mentions conies as a quarry of the bisshunters and says, 'þei hunte hem with ferrettis and wiþ long smale haies'.[90] In this context 'smale' could mean 'low' or possibly refer to the small mesh of the long-nets. The use of ferrets and nets was undoubtedly the commonest and most effective method of bolting rabbits from preserved man-made warrens, also known as garrenas or conigers, or natural warrens.[91] A *bas de page* in *The Luttrell Psalter* shows a rabbit warren with conies entering and leaving their bolt-holes, and sitting in the sun. However, a ferret or polecat is just about to enter the central burrow and spoil their fun. There are no nets visible in this miniature.[92] Long-nets were not the only type of net to be used with ferrets. A delightful fifteenth-century Burgundian tapestry shows a group of peasants using ferrets and purse-nets to take rabbits in a warren. The men are setting nets over bolt-holes and extracting netted rabbits while their womenfolk assist by handing them equipment and pointing to newly caught conies.[93]

Although a great magnate, Gaston Fébus did not ignore the humble rabbit as he knew its value. The MS fr. 616 version of *Livre de chasse* includes a chapter on the nature of rabbits, accompanied by a delightful illustration of rabbits and their warren. Fébus advises that if one wants good sport, rabbits should be kept near their warrens by hunting them two or three times a week with spaniels and that the area should be fenced in.[94] In a later chapter, he gives more precise instructions on rabbit hunting, including working 'flushers', such as spaniels, through hedges and thickets in order to drive them into their holes. One should then block or cover all the bolt-holes with purse-nets, except one, into which the muzzled ferret is dropped. The ferret is muzzled to prevent it killing a rabbit, feasting upon it then falling asleep. The ferret flushes the rabbits which try to bolt out of the holes and become enmeshed in the purse-nets. Fébus further explains that in open country the burrow can be surrounded with long nets and that purse-nets and snares can be set at holes in hedges along runs. If there is no ferret available, one can bolt the rabbits by smoking them out. Small bags containing orpiment (yellow arsenic), sulphur and myrrh are lighted and dropped into the holes. The accompanying miniature shows all the methods described necessary in taking rabbits: bolt-holes blocked with sticks; lighting a big fire at an entrance; putting the orpiment into a hole; dropping the muzzled ferret into a hole; a spaniel chasing two rabbits while another kills a rabbit; a rabbit caught in a purse-net; a hunt servant carrying away a couple of rabbits suspended from a stick over his shoulder.[95] This thorough instruction contains no rituals or procedures and is totally practical in its nature. The techniques described by Fébus have remained unchanged to this day, except for the ingredients of the smoking-out mixture. It is quite possible that he was setting down ancient peasant methodology, tried, tested and perfected over many centuries in south-western France.

The carved and hinged seats of choir-stalls found in many English monastic and collegiate churches and cathedrals provide an unusual visual source of hunting motifs. Christa Grössinger remarks that hunting is one of the most popular occupations shown on misericords and she continues, 'A great number of misericords reflect the interest in hunting as an everyday occurrence'.[96] Intended as antidotes to the strict and celibate regime of monkish life, misericords portray humorous, bawdy, religious, chivalric and world upside-down themes. Many misericords are of everyday life and no doubt poignantly reminded monks and clerics of their previous existence outside monastic orders. Both aristocratic and commonalty methods of hunting are depicted, stag hunting predictably being the most common theme.[97] However, some misericords show scenes of rabbit hunting by common hunters. An example in Ely Cathedral reveals three aspects of the walked-up hunt; that is, the pursuit of quarry by a lone hunter with the aid of a hound. In the left supporter, the hunter, with a stick over one shoulder and blowing his horn, walks through an oak wood, followed by his hound, while a rabbit flees through an oak thicket in the right supporter. The quarry is clearly a rabbit, with its characteristic short ears, and not a hare. In the centre, the successful hunter walks homeward, his brace of leashed hounds by his side and the slain rabbit slung over his shoulder.[98] One cannot help wondering if this was a legal hunt or a poaching expedition. The horn and brace of hounds indicate legitimate hunting as silence and a single dog were the customary prerequisites for successful poaching. In Worcester Cathedral is an unusual misericord called *The Rabbit Hunt*, the central feature of which is a nun writing at a lectern. The right supporter is of a hunter, with a dead rabbit on a pole over his shoulder, who is using a ferret or possibly a polecat, to flush rabbits from a warren.[99] This is an excellent example of a misericord illustrating an episode in the everyday life of an ordinary villager. The lone pot-hunter, with his ferret and a handful of small purse-nets to peg over individual bolt-holes, has taken rabbits in this way for centuries, and still does so. Two further misericords are particularly interesting as they illustrate both noble and commonalty hunting. The first is in King's Lynn Museum and depicts a stag pursued by two hounds as the main theme, with a rabbit peeping from its burrow as a marginal figure. The gentle hunter's presence is cleverly indicated by a horn and arrow incorporated into initials either side of the main carving. The second is in Holy Trinity, Coventry, showing a stag at bay with a hound holding its muzzle while a rabbit looks on. The tiny figure of a hunter stands behind.[100]

The evidence, although scattered and sometimes of an indirect or ambiguous nature, indicates that the commonalty were hunting to a considerable extent. The methods they employed were usually markedly different from those of gentle hunters, although there were areas which overlapped, such as netting and trapping larger game. Quarry type differed too; the emphasis in commonalty hunting had to be on smaller game, particularly small birds; in other words, animals and birds which were not regarded by the ruling élites as worthy of hunting, or 'chaseable'. Again, there was some overlap, particularly in the cases of predators and vermin. Clearly, commonalty hunting methods lacked the ceremonial and ritualistic aspects associated with aristocratic hunting. This is largely because obtaining fresh meat and protecting crops were the main objectives, rather than impressing one's peers and superiors and deliberately creating an event which highlighted the social exclusiveness of the ruling classes. In addition, unlike *par force* or bow and stabley hunting, commonalty hunting usually only involved a handful of people out to acquire extra food. Procedures were thus irrelevant, unnecessary and time-consuming. However, it is worth noting that there were certain basic procedures in dealing with a carcass which were ritualistically performed by gentle hunters but to common hunters were simply the best ways of slitting, skinning, cleaning and butchering. Common hunting also differed in regard to numbers of participants from the large numbers involved in the aristocratic chase. Lone hunting was possibly the most widely followed commonalty method as it required little preparation, caused the least amount of disturbance and could be very effective. The same factors apply to hunting in small groups, with the added advantage of cooperation between individuals perhaps producing a bigger bag. These latter remarks apply equally to illegal hunting, discussed in the second half of the next chapter.

One of the very few paintings specifically featuring peasant hunting is *The Hunters in the Snow*, signed and dated 1565, by Pieter Bruegel the Elder.[101] This is one of five remaining paintings from a sequence of probably twelve (perhaps six, one for every two months) large-format pictures, the idea based upon the labours of the months found in the Calendars of Books of Hours but actually illustrating the seasons. *The Hunters in the Snow* represents January and incidentally illustrates one of the severest winters of the Middle Ages. The dejected hunters, accompanied by a variety of equally downcast hounds, are returning to their village from a hunt which was not for sport but for necessity. Their meagre bag, slung on the back of a hunter, is a scrawny fox. A detail at the left margin of the picture is the inn sign, which in Old Dutch reads, 'Dit is In den Hert', meaning, 'This is in the heart'.[102] The painted figures of the sign are of a saint with a golden halo kneeling in front of a red deer stag. Bruegel intended the whole sign to be read as a pun. The saint is undoubtedly St Hubert, the Germanic patron saint of hunting, who had a vision of Christ on the cross, which miraculously appeared between the antlers of a stag he had hunted and forced to stand at bay. He had offended Christ by hunting on Good Friday, the day of the Crucifixion. (The same story applies to St Eustace, but in Italy; this was discussed in a previous chapter.) Hubert was immediately converted to Christianity, thus becoming pure 'in his heart'. The chaseable stag is also correctly termed a 'hart' or 'hert', and represents Christ. The inn sign can also be read as an icon of irony, the stag highlighting the legal inaccessibility of the hart and its venison, and the inedibility of the only quarry killed by the hunters, a fox. In addition, the inn sign hangs by only one hook, a symbol which can be read in two ways. Perhaps, as Penelope Le Fanu Hughes points out, it may be a comment on humanity's lack of spirituality.[103] Karel Van Mander comments that Bruegel and his merchant friend Hans Franckert liked to disguise themselves as peasants and attend rustic feasts in order better to observe country people.[104] It is possible that Bruegel has developed an empathy for these rural people and their hard way of life. The inn sign may reflect this empathy and be a pointed social comment by Bruegel, that St Hubert was the patron saint of aristocratic hunters who cared little for peasant hunters and their success. Finally, the picture is one of great contrasts: the dejection of the hunters returning from the hunt, a complex occupation which is especially problematic in the winter, with the simple pleasures of the skaters on the ice in the village below, enjoying a rare opportunity for leisure provided by the harsh winter.

Gaston Fébus makes it perfectly clear that the lower orders in the village communities of south-west France were actively engaged in hunting when he remarks, 'Assez en ay dit, quar c'est chasce de vileins et de communs et de paysanz'.[105] Febus's writings in *Livre de chasse* often demonstrate an essential human quality, perhaps rare in a late medieval aristocrat. His empathic style gives us the distinct impression that he realised the necessities and enjoyment of hunting to common men, and probably would have viewed with regret any curtailment of their traditional pleasures.[106] Emperor Maximilian I also appreciated the hardy peasants' pleasure and expertise in hunting, and one of his own joys, when hunting in the mountains of the Tyrol, was that he could be approached by the humblest of his subjects.[107] No doubt many a hunting anecdote, and more, was exchanged during these meetings. It seems that hunters, whether peasant or prince, have always been able to communicate on some level as they have so much in common to talk about. This is not idle chitchat or mere gossip. In hunter-gatherer societies today, like that of the Inuit, discourse involves the oral passing on of up-to-date hunting news, such as recent sightings of game, game movements, other hunters, poaching and so forth. It often includes useful reports on the hunting environment, such as flooding, freezing and weather predictions. These unplanned meetings and conversations helped provide a useful basis for hunting trips then, and still do, particularly where remoteness and the environment make normal communications difficult. Also it cannot be denied, hunters love talking about hunting! There is no peasant equivalent of the aristocratic medieval literary texts praising the varied joys of hunting, so talking, tale-telling and singing of hunting provided the peasant equivalent of a literary tradition. Human nature being what it is, it is fairly safe to assume that peasants, and other humble hunters too, took pride in their skills and pleasure in their outings. Written or pictorial material is not needed to demonstrate these natural human emotions; their unrecorded pleasure can safely remain as taken for granted.

FIVE

Crossing the Barriers

The three previous chapters have been concerned largely with comparisons, stressing the differences between upper- and lower-class hunting, emphasising in particular quarry type, methods and techniques. These differences highlight the barriers of class division, a continually reiterated subject which is dear to the hearts of many historians. However, it is apparent, perhaps surprising, that the uniting factor between all classes was a love of hunting. This common ground provided the base for organised hunting on a large scale and was vital to the successful running of a royal or noble hunt establishment.

This organisation resembled a pyramid in its hierarchical structure and it recruited men and youths from a wide social background. The sons of yeomen, and lesser men, shared a common culture with aristocrats and gentlemen when they joined such an establishment. It was a way for the non-gentleman, and his son, to rise up the social scale. Distinctions of class increasingly became blurred and there was confusion over the meaning and validity of gentility.[1] By Tudor times, their dress, weaponry (which included swords), speech and manners gave them the appearance of gentlemen.[2] Some of this could be said to be a necessary part of their training as hunt servants within the noble household, but some was also the result of concern with their own image in the hunting field, a direct reflection of their master's wealth and prestige. Of course, their masters were also responsible as they held the purse strings which financed such finery. However, some commentators were critical of yeomen imitating their social betters, exemplified by the comment in *Polychronicon Ranulphi Higden* of a 'yeman arraieth hym as a squyer'.[3] Certainly, in pictorial sources of Renaissance hunting, such as *Les Chasses de*

115

Maximilien, it is often difficult to differentiate between gentle and professional hunters. This is not the case in earlier illustrations, such as those of *Roy Modus* and *Livre de chasse*, in which the hunt staff are much easier to identify. Compared to the gentle hunters, the servants are purposely painted smaller, even those in the foreground; more simply dressed and often in green; carry hunting knives and horns slung on baldrics but not swords; and as most are on foot, lack spurs. Not only are the gentle hunters larger, they are also depicted as more elegant and stylish than the staff on whom the artist has skilfully bestowed a humble demeanour. There are few hunt servants portrayed in the Calendar cycle of MS Egerton 1146; they are only present in April (Netting Red Deer), July (Despatching the Hart), August (The Ceremony of the Curée) and December (The Boar-hunt on Horseback with Hounds).[4] However, their inferior rank is evident from their dress which is not only plain but ragged. The fewterer in April sports grey leggings lacking knees. The weary lymerer in July is shown wearing boots which have split from their soles, revealing his bare feet. The August lymerer wears a ragged blue tunic and he, too, has holey boots. The servants wear hunting knives but lack swords and spurs. In addition, their facial expressions are, to a man, glum and gloomy, a complete contrast to their master who is clearly having a tremendously enjoyable time. It appears likely that in this particular German manuscript, the artist is under strict instruction from his patron to portray the hunt servants as clearly identifiable and inferior beings. Why else depict them in rags? An alternative answer is that this *was* the reality, and the neatly dressed hunt servants in *Livre de chasse* and other illustrated hunting treatises was the conventional though sanitised version, more in keeping with the dignity of the proud owner of an expensive illuminated manuscript. Perhaps the patron of the Egerton manuscript was unusual in that he was determined to record every actuality of hunting in his lands.

The royal Forests in England, the large areas of varied habitat preserved for the pleasure of deer hunting by the king and his guests, were similarly staffed and organised in a strict hierarchical manner. Some such structure was obviously necessary in order to produce some guarantee of sport. It has already been remarked that there must have been close links between the hunt and Forest establishments, particularly leading up to, and on, royal hunting days, although we have little direct evidence of this liaison. It is evident that the hunt and Forest establishments were unusual late medieval organisations in that they both possessed a defined 'career structure' up which it was possible, with merit and ability, to ascend and achieve high rank. That this was possible, and in two areas of considerable employment, points to a significant flexibility within the feudal system now widely taken for granted by historians. Social mobility, it seems, was perhaps easier in rural England than was previously imagined, particularly after the Pestilence of 1348. These were employment areas into which the higher classes of rural people, described in the fifteenth-century documents as the *mediocres*, were moving increasingly in order to 'better' themselves. It appears that the opportunities were there and that the sons of husbandmen entered such employment for social and economic reasons.

Certainly, many of the professional hunt officials, the 'hunt servants' as they would be called today, stemmed from humble origins, yet they appeared to mix with their employers and social superiors at particular carefully delineated moments because of their specialised training, knowledge and skills. A.C. Spearing remarks that the knowledge of doing everything correctly, 'is a prerogative of the aristocracy and their skilled servants', and that the aristocracy were assisted by 'lerned servants'. These servants thus spoke and understood the élitist but technical vocabulary of venery which formed the 'liturgy' of the aristocratic 'sacrament', although they were 'lerned' not by birth but by training,[5] a fine point of social distinction. However, all had to be taught the correct language and procedures, 'whatever you be grete or litel'.[6] This training included the proper undoing of the carcass which, although within the practical knowledge of a noble hunter, was often performed in the English hunting field by a professional hunter or forester. *The Master of Game* makes this clear when instructing his audience, 'it is a point that belongeth to woodmanscraft, though it be well suiting to an hunter to be able to do it'.[7] Upon the thorough training of the hunt officials and their assistants depended the success or otherwise of hunting days and, ultimately, of the hunt establishment of each royal Forest and great lord.

The responsibility of the more senior hunt officials was sizeable and the bond of respect between a keen hunting monarch and his older huntsmen could be considerable. Similarly, the falconer who directly supervised the daily running of a noble or royal mews probably had a special relationship with his employer.[8] Frederick II of Hohenstaufen valued his falconers highly because of their qualities and skills, and, perhaps significantly, he does not refer to their lineage and birth.[9] He regarded the office of falconer as important, 'because its duties are manifold and exacting and call for rare qualities of body and mind'.[10] A surviving fragment of a register covering a few months of the years 1239 to 1340 mentions by name fifty of Frederick's falconers, including Master Walter Anglicus and his famous son, William[11] (the surname indicates that these falconers were probably of English origin), showing that these officials were regarded as of some importance by the Emperor. The post of Lord Falconer was a high office in many royal households, and even the royal falconers of lower status were sometimes from the landed gentry.[12] Those gentle hunters, or employees of lords' mews, who trained and flew birds of prey were divided into two distinct types, based upon the category of bird which they used to take quarry. The *austringer*, from the French *autour*, trained and flew goshawks, or short-winged hawks, in wooded and close country where his bird pursued the prey. In contrast, the *falconer* flew long-winged hawks (falcons), usually the peregrine falcon, in open terrain where his bird could gain great height before 'stooping' on to the quarry.[13] The trainer of a sparrow hawk, an unpredictable bird often carried by aristocratic ladies, was correctly called a *sparviter*.[14]

Surviving late medieval documents, such as the Hunting Ordinances of King Alfonso V of Portugal, provide us with information on the ranks of hunt officials, their duties, privileges and rights.[15] *The Master of Game* is also a valuable English source regarding the ranks and salaries of hunt officials, although John

Cummins comments that some of the gradations given in *Livre de chasse* are omitted.[16] It seems likely that salary was directly linked to both job-title and its attendant status. The hunt officials most often mentioned in documents before the end of the fifteenth century are as follows (all salaries are *per diem*):

Master of hounds or keepers of the King's dogs and chief huntsmen	12*d*
Master of Herthounds	12*d*
Master of Buckhounds	12*d*
Master of Harriers	12*d*
Keeper of King's dogs	12*d*
Huntsmen	4*d*, 7½ to 9½*d*
Yeoman at horse	4*d*
Otter-hunters	2*d*
Foxhunters	2*d*
Yeomen berners on foot	1½*d*, 2*d*
Fewterers, veutrers (attendants on greyhounds)	1½*d*, 2*d*
Limerer	2*d*
Bercelettar (yeoman of the bow or archer)	2*d*
Chacechiens (garcons, inferior attendants on hounds)	1½*d*
Grooms and pages	1½*d*
Foresters and Parkers	1*d*, 3*d* 17

Employment as a professional huntsman or falconer could be not only prestigious but also include valuable financial perquisites. The many falconers of the Visconti ruling family of Milan received tax exemptions and the 108 huntsmen of King Alfonso of Aragon in 1445 were all exempted from municipal taxation and jurisdiction. Alfonso also sent his senior Spanish huntsmen abroad on diplomatic missions, indicating his trust in their judgement and skills in statecraft. In 1443, Leonello d'Este, the elder brother of Borso, commissioned a votive portrait of a favourite falconer from the sculptor Nicolo Baroncelli.[18] There could hardly be a higher tribute to a professional servant. The falconers employed at the Scottish court were fortunate enough to be clothed by the king, and the 1491 treasurer's accounts clearly show a hierarchical structure in place, the higher placed professional receiving not only more cloth than his subordinates, but also cloth of varied kinds and some red-coloured.[19]

The Duke of York, as Master of Game to Henry IV, was an aristocrat by birth, but it was possible in the higher grades of royal huntsman to achieve nobility. John Cummins remarks, 'it appears that a huntsman not born into the nobility could aspire to become a squire and presumably, therefore a knight'. He then provides two examples of this type of ennoblement. Late fourteenth-century French hunting accounts name Messire Philippe de Courguilleroy, a *Maistre Veneur*, and describe him as a 'chevalier', or knight; one of the other *veneurs* named is Jehan de Courguilleroy, and he is described as an 'escuier', or squire. This same family appears many times in the hunting accounts and is a good example of the achievement of nobility through promotion within the hierarchy of the hunting establishment. The Franconvilles, another French family in which the profession of huntsman was a strong tradition, became squires.[20] Borso d'Este, who succeeded to the marquisate of Ferrara in 1450, was so passionately keen on hunting that he ennobled his falconer and the keeper of his hounds.[21]

In England, William Twiti, a man of uncertain but not noble origin, became (Chief) Huntsman to Edward II, presumably through promotion within the royal hunting establishment. The 1326 Exchequer accounts name William de Twyty, the King's Huntsman, as being in receipt of a wage of 9*d* per day. This salary of a commoner compares very favourably to the accounts of 1401 which give the 2nd Duke of York 12*d* per day as Master of the King's Harthounds. Old royal huntsmen were often provided for by grateful monarchs. Edward II's respect for Twiti resulted in his honourable retirement around 1327 to residence at Reading Abbey as a pensioner of the king.[22] The Abbot of Reading gave a later royal huntsman, Alan de Leek, the same honourable retirement as Twiti.[23] The Hunting Ordinances of Alfonso V of Portugal lay down that if a retired royal huntsman attained the age of seventy, he was to be lodged by the Master Huntsman and receive the same protection and privileges as an employed huntsman.[24]

17 The hunter uses a cross-bow to despatch the hart, held at bay by hounds, while the hind escapes. (*British Library, London, MS Egerton 1146*, Calendar for September, *fol. 10v*)

18 Gaston Fébus superintends the strict procedures of breaking-up the hart. The carcass is 'undone' (cut open), 'fleaned' (skinned), and 'brittled' (butchered). (*Bibliothèque nationale, Paris, Livre de chasse, MS fr. 616, Ch. 40, fol. 70*)

19 The ceremony of the curée. After the procedure of breaking-up the hart, the ritual of feeding the hounds takes place while horns are blown. *(British Library, London, MS Egerton 1146, Calendar for August, fol. 9v)*

20 A painting for political reconciliation. *The Stag Hunt for the Emperor Charles V at the Castle of Torgau*, by Lucas Cranach the Younger, c. 1544. This event never took place. (*Kunsthistorisches Museum, Vienna*)

21 The fence month; the close season when red deer were not hunted and had to remain undisturbed. The two stags are in velvet. (*British Library, London, MS Egerton 1146, Calendar for May, fol. 6v*)

22 How to shoot game using a 'charnette' or stalking cart. The hunter, horse, cart and assistant are all carefully camouflaged with leaves and branches. (*Bibliothèque nationale, Paris, Livre de chasse, MS fr. 616, Ch. 71, fol. 114*)

23 Vulpicide about to be committed by a commonalty hunter using greyhounds. (*British Library, London*, The Luttrell Psalter, *fol. 64v*)

24 'Hare driving with bells', an effective commonalty technique for netting hares before dawn. (*Bibliothèque nationale, Paris, Livre de chasse, MS fr. 616, Ch. 82, fol. 119*)

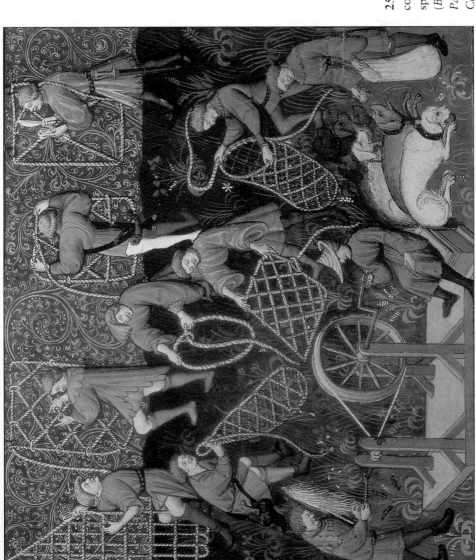

25 Making nets and snares from cord with the aid of a ropemaker's spinning wheel. (*Bridgeman/Bibliothèque nationale, Paris, Livre de chasse, MS fr. 616, Ch. 25, fol. 53v*)

26 Methods of hunting *par maistrise* (by cunning and skill) and catching deer, wild boar and wolves with cord nets. (*Bibliothèque nationale, Paris, Livre de chasse, MS fr. 616, Ch. 60, fol. 103*)

27 Netting red deer. The galloping hunter, assisted by swifthounds just released by his slipper, drives a stag and hind into vertical netting stretched between trees. (*British Library, London, MS Egerton 1146*, Calendar for April, *fol. 5v*)

28 Catching rabbits with small nets at a warren. (*Bibliothèque nationale, Paris, Livre de chasse, MS fr. 616, Ch. 51, fol. 92*)

29 Peasants trapping squirrels. *(Bibliothèque nationale, Paris, Les Livres du Roy Modus et de la Royne Ratio, MS fr. 12399, fol. 53)*

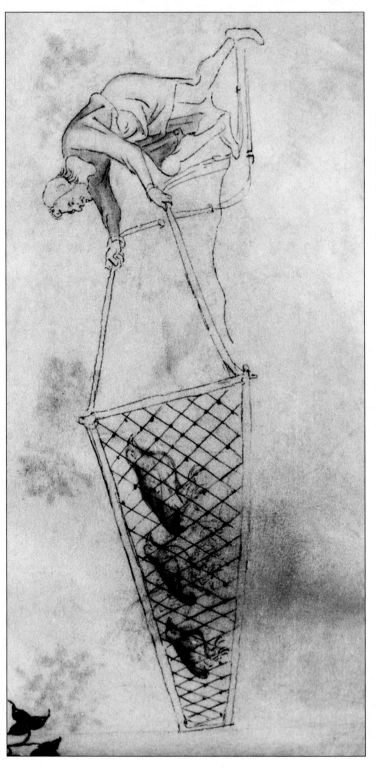

30 A peasant netting a small covey of partridge. (*British Library, London*, Queen Mary's Psalter, *MS Royal 2B VII, fol. 112*)

31 Peasants catching larks with a bell and nets. (*Bibliothèque nationale, Paris, Les Livres du Roy Modus et de la Royne Ratio, MS. fr. 12399, fol. 97*)

32 The ultimate in camouflage? Catching woodcock *a la folletoere*. (*Bibliothèque nationale, Paris*, Les Livres du Roy Modus et de la Royne Ratio, *MS fr. 12399, fol. 93*)

It was not only the officials of the upper echelons of the hunt who benefited from involvement in the hunt organisation. There were also particular occasions when the lesser employees enjoyed their privileges. Of course, there was a public formal relationship between professionals and the nobility, and this is apparent in the *assemblée* and *curée* ceremonies, sumptuously illustrated in *Livre de chasse* and other illuminated manuscripts. There is a distinct separation of figures based upon rank. Often this division is clear as the professionals are apparelled in green livery. Sometimes, particularly in the field, these differences are not clear. For example, a yeoman at horse appears very similar to a gentleman-hunter on horseback. However, at the same time, it is clear that the formalised events, important elements of the ritualistic procedures of a hunting day, must have dictated the public relationship between noble and professional hunter. These formal events were thus exclusive in that they catered for a restricted social membership, the nobility. However, in private, when hunters were not in the public gaze and could be more relaxed with each other, it was undoubtedly different and was inclusive. Social mixing and camaraderie occurred particularly at the special suppers given for all the huntsmen celebrating the successful taking of the first and last harts of the season.[25] *The Master of Game* relates, in the Duke of York's own words (so not included in its precursor *Livre de chasse*, from which much had been plagiarised):

And if it be þe frist hert slayn wiþ/ strength in þe seson or þe last þ shergeaunts/ or þe ȝemen shul goo on þeire offices bihalfe/ and axe þeire fees, þe which I reporte mo to/ þe old statutis and custumes of þe kyngges/ hous, and þis do þe maister of þe game ouȝt to/ spekis to þe officers þat alle þe hunters/ soper be well ordeyned and þat þei drynk non/ ale, for no þing but alle wyne þat nyght for þe/ good and grete labour þat þei haue had for þe/ lordes game and disport and for þe exploit and/ makyng of þe houndes, and also þat þei be more/ merily and gladly telle what ech of hem haþ don/ of alle þe day and which houndes haue best ronne and boldiest.[26]

It is clear that these suppers were important events in the hunting calendar, great occasions for drinking deeply of wine and not common ale, and recalling with gusto the day's events and which hounds performed best. There would be toasts to the slain harts and pledges by both gentle and professional hunters to each other, to times past and to future hunting. Such suppers were integral not only in breaking down class barriers but also to bonding together hunters who came from a wide range of social backgrounds. Such feasts can thus be termed inclusive events as they included all men who hunted in the hunt establishment. These twice-yearly occasions of good fellowship may be seen as the equivalent of the annual fraternity feasts,[27] partaken of by a group of men united not by trade or occupation but by hunting, the 'fraternity of the hunt', similar to the 'fraternity of the forest' to which the outlaw band of Robin Hood has been recently likened by Professor A.J. Pollard.[28] Tudor and Jacobean 'hunting fraternities' are discussed by Roger Manning, but these groups of men were poaching bands or gangs, not legitimate fraternities within the hunt or Forest establishments. Manning's fraternities were local vigilante groups who took it upon themselves to dispense popular justice to unpopular landlords including: 'those who failed to display neighbourliness and hospitality, to landlords who encroached upon common wastes and woods or who neglected to prevent their deer and rabbits from damaging the crops of tenants and neighbours'.[29] Manning suggests that the social gulf between gentry of all ranks and yeomanry was narrowed owing to mixed participation in these 'hunting fraternities'.[30] This would seem inevitable, just as the inclusive suppers of the hunt establishments promoted social mixing and equality.

It is significant that although ladies hunted on days organised by royal and noble hunting establishments, and were specifically catered for at these events, there is no mention of women hunters at the twice-seasonal socially democratic suppers. This is also a common feature of most medieval town guild feasts. 'Inclusive' did not apparently embrace the fair sex at fraternal hunting 'jollies', a profoundly puzzling view to modern fox-hunters whose social life for both sexes is centred around the local hunt calendar.

It must have been realised that enthusiastic cooperation and complete understanding between gentle and professional hunters in the hunting field were essential to success, and social events such as drinking and feasting were natural ways of encouraging them. Of course, the manuals of instruction present a perfect world and, in practice, it is likely that rank and position were rarely forgotten, merely set aside as necessity dictated. However, in a society where to be alone was probably an infrequent occurrence, men were inevitably closer to each other physically and spiritually than they are today. Differences in rank and station may or may not have been accepted with grace but they were part of what appeared to be an unchanging world which had endured since time out of mind. Camaraderie, respect and even friendship between persons of disparate status were possible in such an enclosed world, particularly one where there was the strong unifying factor of hunting.

It is interesting that extravagant feasts also took place after falconry expeditions, as well as after hunting days. *Picnic at the Court of Burgundy*, a copy of a lost Flemish original by the School of Jan van Eyck, captures such an event outside the Château of Versailles. This feast took place on the eve of Philip the Good's marriage to Duchess Isabella of Portugal in 1430.[31] However, unlike the inclusive suppers which relaxed social mores and brought together gentle and professional hunters for good fellowship, this is evidently an exclusive celebration feast for royal and noble guests. There appears no equivalent social event or supper for gentle and professional falconers, so was the democratic 'good fellowship' of the hunting fraternity absent in hawking? It appears so; another factor supporting the widely held belief that this sport was more socially exclusive than hunting.

However, as well as the élitist nature of hawking, there is another factor to consider here. A large hunt establishment required considerable numbers of employees to function properly, ranging from kennel varlets to master huntsmen. The large number of hunt servants necessary is not only indicated in the surviving records, such as the Royal Hunt Wages Account of Henry IV of 1470; servants also outnumber the gentle hunters in many illustrations of royal and noble hunting. In contrast, with the exception of some royal mews on the continent such as those of Emperor Frederick II and some Iberian monarchs, many aristocrats 'made do' with a single-handed falconer,[32] a professional with the skills to care for the needs of a few hunting birds and run a small mews establishment. Pictures of hawking rarely show more than two assistants accompanying nobles, often only one, such as the lone falconer on foot accompanying the mounted lords and ladies in the August miniature of the *Très Riches Heures*.[33] However, such illustrations may not reflect reality; with such a high-status pastime why should numbers of servants detract from the splendidly attired nobles and their ladies? The grooms and kennel men were not specialist mews employees, unlike the falconers or austringers, so cannot be included among those specifically employed in the mews. Thus there was not the social mix of people from different backgrounds in hawking, and it therefore follows that there could not be the same jolly good fellowship and inclusive feasting that were associated with hunting establishments.

The hierarchical structure of a large hunt establishment enabled those with ambition and ability to progress up through the various stages of page, varlet, assistant huntsman and huntsman, perhaps eventually reaching the ultimate post of *Maistre Venuer et Maistre des Eaues et des Forests*.[34] This particular late medieval job description set down the areas of responsibility of a *Maistre Venuer* and clearly indicates the close ties between hunt and Forest establishments. Were Masters of Game, *de facto*, accountable for the successful administration of both organisations? This appears a likely arrangement, at least in some forests, solving the issues of liaison and administration by a single appointment. The repetition of skills and knowledge required makes such appointments seem inevitable to modern business total quality management. The fortunate few who reached the highest ranks appear to have had the added possibility of ennoblement for their services, particularly in France. Certainly, these high achievers in their chosen profession attained great status and, in addition, enjoyed the respect of their social superiors.

Poaching is illegal hunting and it is the grey area of hunting as regards attempting to define social parameters in the later Middle Ages. Folk memory, reinforced by populist literature, folksongs, cinema and the media, has created an enduring, simplistic image: peasants poached because they were hungry and oppressed; lords hunted on horseback and repressed honest peasants. Indeed, the themes of the contemporary outlaw ballads always seem to include the taking of the king's deer, and these perennial themes accord well with the established historical attitude of popular discontent,[35] particularly that of the peasants and the rest of the commons. To the outlaws in the rhymes of Robin Hood and Gamelyn, the Greenwood was their home, its beasts their food.[36]

Deer were obvious targets for peasant poachers. It has been said that Englishmen below the rank of gentleman were not much interested in poaching deer and would much rather take wildfowl, hares, rabbits and fish.[37] This is probably true in part; the risks and penalties for poaching venison could be severe, so a considerable degree of courage was necessary to take a deer. However, the records of the Forest courts indicate that peasants were often prosecuted for poaching venison. In addition to those indicted are the unknown numbers of peasant poachers who escaped apprehension, so the real figure is likely to be very high. Deer had two great attractions for peasant poachers. Firstly, a red or fallow deer carcass of either sex furnished a large amount of meat which would keep a family in much-needed protein for many meals. Even a roe deer, buck or doe, produced a respectable poundage of tender meat. The carcass could be quickly broken up on the spot, or perhaps later in a concealed place, then covertly transported to the poacher's house. Perhaps it was secretly sold, peasants ignoring the unwritten taboo of the gentry and aristocracy on selling venison.[38] The trade in venison, with a considerable cash return, was an obvious incentive to peasant deer poaching. Secondly, the nature of deer meat had advantages to poachers. Venison can be eaten fresh if necessary, and doubtless it often was, providing a hearty meal and also getting rid of the evidence, but it can be tough and rather tasteless. Venison is game; hanging tenderises the flesh and the slow controlled breakdown of the muscle fibres produces the characteristic 'gamy' taste. A carcass hangs well for ten to fourteen days or more, the speed of decline thereafter depending upon the air temperature and location of hanging. It can also be smoked or salted and remains edible for months. The food return on a single poaching expedition was thus high and must often have been considered well worth the risks involved. In a study which is based upon the records of the Forest courts of the thirteenth and fourteenth centuries, Jean Birrell asserts that, despite the dangers of encounters with forest officials and the severity of penalties, 'the peasantry of forest villages continued to take deer in the royal forests'.[39] Her evidence, taken from the Forest eyre rolls, proves that there was indeed a rich tradition of peasant deer poaching, much of it carefully planned and performed. Some peasants were regular hunter-poachers, using a range of appropriate methods, many of which were exclusive to their class. These men were, of necessity, skilled hunters, who were 'lerned' in their own fashion, their knowledge the familial accumulation of centuries of living close to nature. Birrell clearly makes the point:

> These were methods which often demanded a knowledge of the habits and movements of the different types of deer and a degree of self-discipline and manual dexterity . . . which might be thought to fit ill with the disdain for them which pervades the hunting treatises, and even to compare favourably with the aristocratic methods which these same treatises extol.[40]

The records indicate that the commonest method used by peasants to hunt deer, and also lesser beasts, was the trap or snare. Local men were accused at virtually every eyre of taking deer *cum laqueis*, with snares, or of being in possession. It is inevitable that such devices were home-made and of cheap, easily obtainable materials including horsehair, withies and, especially, cord. Snares were small, light and easily concealed so were ideal for poaching. A trap, *trappa*, was more complex, having wooden parts such as a frame, and a snare. These were ingenious devices; some snares and traps entangled the antlers, others the feet. 'Engines' are also specified and the commonest consisted of sharpened stakes to impale the deer. Two types of projectile were used. The sling, hurling a stone, was a deadly weapon and in the right hands could kill a stag, as the Sherwood Forest eyre for September 1280 records.[41] Bows and arrows were also used but were not particularly favoured by peasant poachers, probably because they were too noticeable in the forest and also owing to the risk of a wounded deer escaping. This reality seems very much at odds with the popular legend of the outlaw-poacher, invariably using his skill with the longbow to shoot the king's deer. In reality, a single arrow seldom dropped a large beast such as a deer.[42] Forest peasants also did not favour the use of large nets to catch deer, probably as these were bulky, heavy, difficult to conceal, tedious to make, expensive to buy and were confiscated if the deer poacher was apprehended.[43]

Equally, much peasant poaching was opportunistic, reaping the wounded or unpicked products of legitimate and aristocratic hunters, as well as the odd stray deer and the victims of dogs or wolves. Taking advantage of such opportunities must have been second nature to the peasant men and women living and working in the holdings and villages of Forest environments.[44] It is not too broad a generalisation to comment that such opportunist hunting is still a feature of rural areas, particularly those which include woods or forests. It is debateable whether scavenging the ungathered and lost quarry of the aristocratic hunt is 'true hunting', although this surely depended upon whether the deer was wounded, followed up, then killed, or found badly injured or dead and simply picked up. However, in the eyes of the law any situation involving taking deer was certainly poaching as the end product was venison. The scale of peasant deer poaching, as Birrell remarks, can only be guessed at, but it is very significant that peasant poachers appear in every Forest eyre she examined,[45] a good indication of the universality of such illegal hunting in English forests. It would, of course, be very useful if these often detailed records of the Forest courts mentioned peasants hunting and poaching beasts other than deer, but unfortunately they do not. The laws and records reflect the prevailing preoccupations of the upper classes with the dominant culture of deer hunting. Jean Birrell comments realistically on whether peasants poached other birds and beasts: 'It seems highly likely that they did and that the activities revealed by the forest eyre were only a small part of a wider picture.'[46]

However, not all poaching was the work of peasants or those who lived outside the law. Evidence from the Forest courts, particularly the main courts of jurisdiction, the Forest eyres, indicates that medieval man (and, on occasion, woman), whatever his rank or class, found opportunities to hunt, whether legally or illegally. Poaching by all classes upon the 'woody Grounds and fruitful Pastures, privileged for wild Beasts and Fowls of the Forest Chase, and Warren'[47] was widespread and must be included within the generic term of hunting, whether legitimate or not.

The opening sequence of *The Parlement of the Thre Ages* epitomises the romantic poaching ideal; the lawless hunter and dreamer in all the pride of his manhood[48] ventures into the forest on a May dawn:

> my werdes to dreghe,/ In'to þe schawes my-selfe a schotte me to gete/ At ane hert or ane hynde, happen as it myghte.[49]

Fanciful though the image first appears to the audience or reader, it soon becomes evident that the anonymous poet must himself have been a hunter, as the information he provides on the technique of lone stalking is fascinatingly realistic and accurate. First he camouflages himself, 'Bothe my body and my bowe I buskede with leues';[50] then he hides. He tests the wind after a hart has appeared and got wind of his scent:

> I waitted wiesly the wynde by waggynge of leues,/ Stalkede full stilly no stikkes to breke,/ And crepite to a crabtre and couerede me ther-vndere:/ Then I bende vp my bowe and bownede me to schote,/ Tighte vp my tylere and taysede at the hert.[51]

The discomfort of remaining quiet and absolutely motionless while being bitten by gnats is vividly evoked:

Then I maste stonde als I stode, and stirre no fote ferrere,/ For had
I my [n] tid or mouede or mode any synys,/ Alle my layke hade
bene loste þat I hade longe wayttede,/ But gnattes gretely me
greuded and gnewen myn eghne . . . .[52]

Having shot the hart, the hunter breaks it correctly, rewards his
hound, 'Brayde [out] his bowells my berselett to fede',[53] and following
the established custom, 'Cuttede corbyns bone and kest it a-waye'[54]
for the crows and ravens. The poet is specific in his term for the illegal
hunter's dog, a barcelet (or bercelet) which was a hunting dog trained
to follow up wounded game, the ideal dog for a poacher. The Forest
records of Cannock Forest (1270s) and Sherwood Forest (1329) both
mention deer poachers possessing bercelets.[55]

Now the hunter abandons gentlemanly procedures. Knowing that
the slaying was a lawless act, he carefully conceals the pieces of
carcass in a hole and a hollow oak, safe from both foresters and
hunters who, doubtless, patrol this fee or section of the forest:

And heuede alle in-to ane hole and hidde it with ferne,/ With
hethe and with hore masse hilde it about,/ Pat no fostere of the fee
scholde fynde it ther-aftir;/ Hid the hornes and the hede in ane
hologhe oke,/ Pat no hunte scholde it hent ne haue it in sighte.[56]

The poet skilfully combines the 'lernedness' of the gentle hunter
with the wily woodcraft of the experienced poacher, thus subtly
recruiting the whole audience's sympathy for the 'gome alle in
grene'. It is interesting and significant that 'gentle blood' or
references thereto, such as the correct breaking of the hart, was
esteemed by most members of medieval society, even by criminals.[57]
As has been discussed in a previous chapter, lone stalking was a
popular form of hunting by all classes, and by its nature was a
method ideally suited to poaching. James I of Scotland had it
banned in 1424,[58] though doubtless the effect of this legislation on
poachers and poaching was minimal. Laws are only effective if they
can be properly enforced and lone poaching was, and is, most
difficult to control.

Rights to hunt and to warren, and royal licences to hunt and take game, were privileges almost entirely restricted to members of the ruling classes. Game-stocked parks were the preserve of wealthy individuals and institutions. Yet, there was much poaching by the upper classes, whether intentional or not. Although members of the ruling classes tended to hunt in the forests which were nearest their homes, as men who were always on the move visiting their properties and friends, they also hunted, legally or illegally, wherever they happened to be. In a sense, they regarded the whole countryside as a place where they had a right to hunt.[59] Also, during the excitement of the mounted chase, when hounds were on to a strong hart and the field was spread out, boundaries must have been crossed and re-crossed many times without thought of ownership and rights. However, doubtless this was often used as an excuse for deliberate trespass and killing of the king's deer. Undoubtedly, a title was an asset in such dubious situations if one was apprehended. In 1482 Queen Elizabeth Woodville wrote accusingly and peevishly to Sir William Stonor, a country gentleman of good estate, the Member of Parliament for Oxford and Knight of the Bath:[60]

> that ye have taken upon yow now of late to make maistries withynne our fforest and Chace of Barnewod and Exsille, and þat in contempt of us uncourteisly to hunt and slee our deer withynne þe same to our grete mervaille and displeasir.[61]

Sir William was forgiven and later appointed one of the Knights of the King's Body.[62] The Forest Proceedings of the Duchy of Lancaster record that the Earl of Derby was prosecuted under the Forest Law for taking more than two thousand deer in the Forest of High Peak over a period of six years.[63] The inordinate time-span before justice was enacted was no doubt due to the infrequent meetings of the Duchy of Lancaster Forest eyre. The eyre was the supreme Forest court and dealt with major offences, such as the Earl of Derby's, and reviewed everything since the previous eyre. Officially, an eyre was held in each forest every seven years, but in practice meetings became increasingly irregular, an extreme instance being fifty years.[64] Some sixteenth-century poaching by gentry was apparently a surrogate for war, hunting and fighting containing similar elements of excitement, danger, violence and death. Around 1550, Sir William St Lo, accompanied by perhaps thirty others, poached thirty deer from a park in Somerset belonging to the Bishop of Bath and Wells. As a defiant gesture to the bishop and his keepers, he set up the deer heads upon pales in the same park, apparently encouraging others to hunt illegally in the game preserve.[65] The examples of aristocrats and gentry poaching venison are endless. Given the social context, aristocratic poaching is an unsurprising feature of the period. Hunting was an integral part of aristocratic culture and was encouraged, not only as a rehearsal for war but also as a symbolic substitute for combat in an England which was increasingly under the king's rule. It enabled warrior-gentlemen to display feats of daring in the hunting field akin to those of war.[66] Whether the hunting was lawful or unlawful was, one suspects, often irrelevant to the deed. The punishment, at worst a stiff fine, was worth the risk and probably added to the kudos of the action. Illegal hunting also attracted those gentlemen of questionable rank as it helped affirm their professed gentility and gallantry.[67]

Abbots and lesser ranks of the Church were frequently convicted of poaching, but were liberally treated regarding licences to hunt the lesser game (not deer) legally in the king's Forests. The question of the clergy hunting was never really clarified and it remained ambiguous throughout the later Middle Ages. The Patent Rolls of Edward II record that Godfrey, Abbot of Peterborough, was convicted of trespass for hunting without licence in the king's Forest of Huntingdon, and of taking a doe. Thus in spite of his cloth, he was convicted like a layman although duly pardoned, perhaps owing to his high social status. The more exalted members of the Church were obviously legally hunting deer as they were allowed deer-leaps to ensure that their parks within the king's Forest were kept well stocked.[68] The function of these man-made sloping structures was to allow tenants of parks to drive deer from the unenclosed Forest into their own fenced reserves. They also allowed access by hunters in the surrounding Forest who were pursuing wounded deer taking shelter in the park. This sensible arrangement suited both the owner of the game rights and his tenant.[69]

Hunting and poaching by monks was widely practised and this is hardly surprising, given the noble background and upbringing of many monks and the rural setting of most monasteries. Monasteries such as Fountains, Rievaulx and Jervaulx lay at the centre of great estates which included good hunting country. The hunting field brought the lay gentry and their monastic neighbours together and the *Leicester Abbey Chronicle* states that in the mid-fourteenth century, the influence of Abbot Clowne with the local gentry was based upon his knowledge of hounds and venery.[70] There were attempts from within the Church to curb illegal hunting and hawking by monks. For example, one of *The Ordinances of the Prior and Chapter of Ely* for 1314 states:

> Likewise, it is decreed that none among the brothers may keep for his own use, or for another on his behalf, greyhounds or birds of prey within the precinct of the monastery or elsewhere on the estate, without having obtained the permission of the prior; and this ordinance likewise must be observed everywhere within the jurisdiction of the monastery and by all manner of servants.[71]

This was at least an effort to control sports officially disapproved of by the Church by the simple remedy of internal licensing. In this particular case, much depended upon the attitude and pre-dilections of the prior. He may have been a hunting man himself who was wise enough not to attempt to ban hunting and hawking by the brotherhood but rather to limit these sports by his own authority.

Chaucer introduces his audience to the hunting cleric with his Monk in *The Prologue* to the *Canterbury Tales*:

> A MONK ther was, a fair for the maistrye,/ An out-rydere, that lovede venerye;/ A manly man, to been an abbot able./ Ful many a deyntee hors hadde he in stable.[72]

He is thus a hard-rider to hounds with a stable full of hunters, the stereotypical hearty hunting cleric recognised by all, ignoring the ancient dictums of the Church. However, Chaucer is presenting a more complex picture, one which comments not only on clerics who broke the rules but also challenges the outmoded attitudes of the Medieval Church towards its own members. Although from a priory governed by the archaic and strict rules of St Maur and St Benedict, Chaucer's Monk is one of the new men, behaving in modern ways:

> Ther as this lord was keeper of the celle,/ The reule of seint Maure or of seint Beneit,/By-cause that it was old and som-del streit,/ This ilke monk leet olde thinges pace,/ And held after the newe world the space.[73]

Chaucer then makes it very clear that his Monk despises and indeed cares nothing for the old-fashioned regulations of the Church Fathers and would not waste his time reading or labouring. Let others, exemplified by Augustine, do that.

> He yaf nat of that text a pulled hen,/ That seith, that hunters been nat holy men;/ Ne that a monk, when he is recchelees,/Is lykned til a fish that is waterlees;/ This is to seyn, a monk out of his cloister./ But thilke text held he nat worth an oistre;/ And I seyde, his opinioun was good./ What sholde he studie, and make him-selven wood,/ Upon a book in cloistre alwey to poure,/ Or swinken with his handes, and laboure,/ As Austin [Augustine] bit? How shal the world be served?/ Lat Austin have his swink to him reserved.[74]

This is why he has become a hard-riding hunter, sparing no expense:

> Therfore he was a pricasour aright;/ Grehoundes he hadde, as swifte as fowel in flight;/ Of priking and of hunting for the hare/ Was al his lust, for no cost wolde he spare.[75]

Forest officials were not guiltless of poaching and abuse of their office during the fourteenth century. Some foresters were involved in illegal hunting on their own account and in permitting illegal hunting by others within their bailiwicks. Giles Beauchamp, the warden of the Forest of Groveley and keeper of Clarendon Park, was accused of various abuses and corruption over the twenty-three years he held office. These included hunting in the forest himself, and allowing the Bishop of Salisbury, and on another occasion a knight, illegally to take does. Two of his predecessors were charged with similar offences in the conduct of their office.[76] As mentioned in chapter six within the context of town residents' hunting, students were also known to be poachers, hence the 1421 Statute of Henry V relating to problems of discipline at the University of Oxford. These poachers included clerks and scholars who took deer, hares and conies with dogs and greyhounds in many warrens, parks and forests in Oxfordshire, Berkshire and Buckinghamshire.[77]

In Scotland, officials called currors were the backbone of Forest administration before 1499, being responsible for protecting the timber and deer. A statute of 1499 gave the responsibility for vert and venison to the forester-tenants. When a calf, fawn, roe-kid or any other deer was killed on his stead, the forester-tenant had to find the slayer or else pay the penalty himself.[78] In the fifteenth century, the fine for the death of a hart was £10, and for killing a hind the fine was raised from £5 to £10 in the 1470s. In the early years of the sixteenth-century, the illegal hunter faced the escheat of his dogs and weapons (the reversion of private property to the Crown), followed by a trial and fine, presumably still of £10.[79] These huge fines were clearly fixed to be beyond the means of common people, so perhaps their real purpose was to deter the ruling classes from poaching. Their poaching was not only more serious in terms of quantities of venison taken; it also set a bad example to the commons and encouraged flouting of the law, an important consideration in maintaining the king's peace. These were obviously factors which also applied to England and Wales, as well as Scotland.

At the other end of the scale from poaching venison and other game was the illegal taking of rabbits. Skilled warreners were much sought after and were among the highest paid manorial officials.

Mark Bailey quotes a salary of over £5 per annum for an Ely Abbey warrener of 1411; this surprisingly high pay was to compensate for the danger and isolation of a warrener's occupation rather than the amount of labour the job entailed.[80] The main purpose of a warren to its owner was economic, not sporting, and lay in the value of meat and rabbit skins produced.[81] Warrens were profitable targets for poaching, which was conducted on all scales from random opportunism to multiple habitual offenders. The dedicated poacher reared lurchers (crossbred dogs trained to hunt silently) and greyhounds which were released into the warren to pick off and retrieve conies one by one. Bailey makes the point that the large number of poaching cases in the court rolls of the East Anglian Breckland reflects the importance of illegal hunting as a source of income to the local peasants. Rabbit poaching was so lucrative that, inevitably, highly organised gangs were formed, operating on a large scale in the bigger warrens of the Breckland.[82] Their valuable products were no doubt distributed in the larger towns and particularly in London, where a well-organised market catered for illicit venison and game.[83]

The Forest court records from the thirteenth and fourteenth centuries show that small gangs of peasant poachers, made up of men from neighbouring villages within a Forest, were stealing venison, often on a regular basis. The evidence is not always clear, but it appears that many were led by men from a higher social station,[84] a significant point which also emerges from an earlier study of criminal gangs operating in the fourteenth century. Poaching was only one of the many crimes committed by criminal gangs in the first third of the fourteenth century[85] and in later centuries. In *Crime and Public Order in England in the Later Middle Ages*, John Bellamy examines this phenomenon of criminality and violence. Stealing farm stock, as well as game, on a large scale was common. The poachers' motives were various: filling the larder, settling scores and exacting revenge, making a profit, even the thrill of the chase. In many cases of raids on parks and chases there was collusion by keepers and their underlings,[86] who were presumably bribed or pressurised in some way. It is likely that

135

some poachers may have had kinship ties with estate workers, foresters or hunt employees. Records show that the leaders of such gangs were drawn for the most part from the gentry, the knights and esquires, often the younger sons.[87] One of the most notorious gangs was that of James and John Coterel who were raiding estates and parks in the late 1320s. They were the younger sons of a Derbyshire gentleman.[88] The Folville brothers, leaders of another highly successful gang, were the sons of John de Folville, lord of Ashby-Folville in Leicestershire and Teigh in Rutland. Lord John Fitzwalter, another aristocrat, was an Essex gang leader during the 1340s. The rank-and-file members of the gangs appear to have had more humble origins,[89] however, and thus possibly more excuse for poaching. In support of this, Bellamy quotes several cases in which convicted poachers were proved to be suffering from shortages of food.[90] Gang raiding and poaching as a distinct phenomenon continued into the first third of the fifteenth century, culminating with Richard Stafford , called 'Frere Tuk', a gang leader and Sussex knight, making peace with the law around 1429.[91] There was also much poaching with violence by armed men during the reigns of Richard II, Henry IV and Henry V in chases, parks and warrens. Some of those who were apprehended claimed rights of chase within these areas, possibly with justification.[92] An interesting point to emerge from Bellamy's research is that even within the context of lawless hunting by gangs, social status and division of labour according to class remain paramount. It seems likely that the education of the upper classes, with its emphasis upon leadership, is a key element in poaching-gang structure.

Although large-scale poaching of game by gangs and groups of men can hardly be termed 'sporting', the methods which must have been employed, those 'villainous techniques' known to, and remarked upon by, Fébus and the Duke of York, mean it has to be included within the wider parameters of hunting.

In a deer-hunting culture, most references to the serious crime of 'poaching' relate to stealing venison. It is well known that there were severe penalties for poaching in the twelfth century. In *Policraticus*, John of Salisbury notes that 'the punishment prescribed is confiscation of goods or loss of life or limb'.[93] These punitive penalties were based upon the 1016 *Charta de Foresta* of King Canute, a possibly fictitious piece of pre-Conquest legislation adopted and enforced by the Normans. The statutes were heavily biased in favour of the king, and stipulated that poaching deer was a capital offence.[94] William the Conqueror loved hunting, particularly the 'great deer', and established the *Nova Foresta* in 1079 as a preserve in which he could hunt deer. The Anglo-Saxon Chronicle, written *sub anno* 1087, makes scathing comment on William and his punitive Forest Laws:

> He made many deer-parks, and he established laws therewith; so that whosoever slew a hart, or a hind, should be deprived of his eyesight. As he forbad men to kill the harts, so also the boars; and he loved the tall deer as if he were their father. Likewise he decreed respecting the hares that they should go free. His rich men bemoaned it, and the poor men shuddered at it. But he was so stern that he recked not the hatred of them all; for they must follow withal the king's will, if they would live or have land, or possessions, or even his peace.[95]

However, the 1217 *Carta de Foresta* of Henry III confirmed the liberties obtained in Magna Carta of 1215.[96] A seminal section in the latter favouring a more just system, particularly for the commons, reads:

> 48. All evil customs connected with forests and warrens, foresters and warreners, sheriffs and their officials, river-banks and their wardens shall immediately be inquired into by twelve sworn knights of the same county . . . and shall be utterly abolished by them so as never to be restored . . .[97]

Henry's Charter also stipulates that

> No man from henceforth shall lose either life or limb for killing our deer; but if any man shall be taken and convicted for taking our venison, he shall make a grievous fine if he hath anything

whereof, and if he hath nothing to lose, he shall be imprisoned a year and a day; and after the year and day expired, if he can find sufficient sureties he shall be delivered, and if not he shall adjure [entreat] the Realm of England.[98]

A new *Carta de Foresta* was enacted in 1224 by Henry III and this was almost identical to his first charter. Henry's Forest Laws apparently show a concern to shield the English public from suspicion and oppression by the officials protecting the king's game.[99] A new leniency had, in certain important areas such as the mutilation and execution of convicted deer poachers, replaced the harsher attitudes of the Norman kings. The penalty meted out in the Forest court for most offences was a fine. The accused, if found guilty, was in mercy or amerced a sum of money commensurate with the crime committed. The administering of this more proportionate justice, and the modification of it according to the rank of the convicted poacher, is, however, open to allegations of corruption, as the cases quoted in the earlier part of this chapter demonstrate. It must be said, though, that modification cut both ways. As regards fining, the matching of monetary punishment to status was no bad thing and a sensible *modus operandi* by the Forest eyres. On the other hand, the records indicate that poachers of high or ecclesiastical rank appear to have been forgiven or discharged without payment more often than humble illegal hunters. The seminal fact is that members of all classes were undoubtedly involved in poaching and the alternatives cited in lines five and six of the Henrician Charter concerning the convicted poacher's estate, imply that in the early thirteenth century rich and poor were expected by the authorities to partake in illegal hunting and were to be treated accordingly. Perhaps the new Angevin legislation owed less to reasons of justice and more to political and social expediency. Importantly, the sovereign continued to benefit from fines imposed for infringements of Forest Law.

It is self-evident that the Forest Charters were aimed at preserving and protecting the vert and venison for the king, and also any fortunate men or women who were licensed by the king to hunt in the royal Forests. These laws potentially affected all other persons in England, including members of the nobility and the Church. The Ricardian statute of 1390, the first 'game law' to be passed which came under the jurisdiction of the Common Law courts, not the Forest courts (increasingly the Forest eyres), restricted the rights of hunting to those with an income from land of at least 40s per year. This effectively excluded the majority of the population, so was socially restrictive. Sir William Blackstone, in his *Commentaries on the Laws of England* (1765–9), summed up the situation very succinctly:

> Though the forest laws are now mitigated, and by degrees grown entirely obsolete, yet from this root has sprung a *bastard slip*, known by the name of *Game Law*, now arrived to, and wantoning in its highest vigour: both founded upon the same unreasonable notion of permanent property in wild creatures; and both productive of the same tyranny to the Commons: but with this difference; that the forest law established only one mighty hunter throughout the land, *the game laws have raised a little Nimrod in every manor*.[100]

After 1340 the Forest eyres met less and less often, so the courts became increasingly ineffective in controlling the sovereign's vert and venison. At the same time, it appears that the licences to impark and the grants of free warren increased. These grants from the Crown extended the exclusive nature of hunting.[101] The Forest Laws further declined into semi-abeyance during the fifteenth century.

However, the new Tudor monarch, Henry VII, was a dedicated and enthusiastic hunter, determined at the outset to redress this decline of royal authority. Politically, he also regarded unrestricted hunting as a likely cover for conspiracies. In consequence, the game laws were revived at the outset of the Tudor monarchy. The Game Act of 1485 was the first legislation to make hunting at night or in disguise a felony.[102] The mid-Tudor period brought outbreaks of popular unrest and each one resulted in new and more restrictive legislation. The northern Pilgrimage of Grace and other lesser disturbances resulted in the Game Acts of 1539–40, consisting of punishments for new categories of hunting offences, including hunting in disguise or at night in royal parks and Forests, and stealing eggs or fledglings of falcons or hawks from the king's manors. These were enforced under Common Law by the local assizes and quarter sessions. By the early sixteenth century, poaching offences appear more and more often in records for the Court of Star Chamber and the Duchy Court of Lancaster.[103] In 1547, Edward VI repealed all of the capital game offences enacted in 1539–40. However, the great destruction of deer parks and game, the result of widespread riots and rebellions in 1549, led to a three-year revival of the capital penalty for those game offences specified in the 1539–40 Game Acts. A further act of 1549–50 was passed to try and counter large-scale deer poaching in the king's parks but these were made felonious offences. Elizabeth was more practical and realistic than her predecessors, making game offences misdemeanours which were punishable by three months' imprisonment, treble damages caused and seven year sureties for good behaviour.[104]

By the early seventeenth century game legislation and enforcement were vehicles of royal prerogative and aristocratic privilege. Even the common lands and wastes, places where commoners secretly hunted, were affected by restrictive legislation and by game preservation schemes, such as enclosures, implemented by the landowners. The game laws of later centuries highlight the doctrine of the absolute and unqualified rights of private property,[105] which embraced the ownership of specified wild animals, including rabbits, on one's own land. These laws became the foundation for the notoriously draconian enactments of Georgian and Victorian England, which together with the harsh Norman game laws, appear to have shaped popular public opinion on game legislation. As a matter of interest, Forest Law in the New Forest, neglected and almost forgotten except by Forest freeholders, formally ended in 1964.

In the northern Italian city states during the later Middle Ages game laws were also a feature of hunting. For example, restrictive laws were introduced in Verona, a city controlled by the Republic of Venice, concerning game seasons and the rights of various classes of person to hunt different types of game. By the fifteenth century, the rulers of Milan (the Visconti), Ferrara (the Este) and Mantua (the Gonzaga) had enclosed huge areas as hunting parks from which the commonalty were excluded. These hunting reserves were an important representation of the prince's or noble's power, and the grounds and game were accordingly protected and preserved by their feudal authorities. There were stiff fines for trespass and harsher penalties for poaching. In the park at Pavia, for example, night trespassers were fined the huge sum of 50 florins or would have a foot amputated. In the same park there was a sliding scale of fines for poaching game, apparently based upon size, ranging from an immense 100 florins for taking a hart or fallow buck to 2 florins for a quail.[106] These penalties were intended to be punitive and punished not only the crimes of trespass and poaching but, perhaps more significantly, the act of defying the power and influence of the recently established princes and nobles. Their intention was thus very different to the game laws in England where a poacher was punished for his crime of poaching and fined according to his status and ability to pay.

In Saxony at the beginning of the fifteenth century game laws still allowed peasants to hunt small game and predators, but this right was removed after 1500 when hunting became the privilege of the ruling classes. This created great bitterness as the peasants could no longer protect their crops, orchards and stock. Restrictions affecting the rural peasantry included limiting the height of fences, prohibiting the use of pointed fence posts to prevent deer injuring themselves, collaring dogs with wooden bars or clubs to prevent them hunting game, and taking away the ancient right of pannage (turning out pigs to pasture, particularly to eat acorns in the autumn) in the forests. However, villagers were still required by feudal law to provide the labour needed for big hunting days, particularly driving game to the hunters at their stands. These restrictions and obligations fuelled popular discontent and resulted in uprisings such as the Peasants' War of 1524–5.[107] Such legal restrictions on peasant hunting were politically self-destructive as they denied men not only their personal freedom but also one of

141

their few important sources of protein. An increase in unlawful hunting was an inevitable consequence, in addition to the more serious problems of peasant discontent and rebellion.

The underlying problem was that many people enjoyed poaching. Perhaps the deep-seated instinct and psychological need to hunt, whatever one's station in society, is one of the more valid reasons why poaching was so widespread during the later Middle Ages. Certainly, it appears that in England the problem of illegal hunting was difficult to contain under the system of the Forest courts and required some measure of reform from the late fourteenth century onwards. The infrequent number of prosecutions after 1400 under the 1390 act suggests that this attempt to control poaching by Common Law was also ineffective. Reforms to the game laws during the late fifteenth and sixteenth centuries demonstrate the growing importance of class privilege in establishing a rigid structure of hunting legislation. What is also demonstrated by such ubiquitous and determined illegal hunting over several hundred years is the mistake of equating poaching with class. Sources clearly show that members of all levels of society were involved in illegal hunting; to them their position in society was either of no consequence or, at most, marginal, to the act of poaching. This activity not only crossed social barriers; in some more extreme cases, such as outlawry and poaching gangs, it actually united men from varied backgrounds in another common cause, outwitting the law.

SIX

Medieval Dianas

The previous chapters have shown the economic and social importance of hunting and hawking in the late medieval European world and how these activities provided sport, exercise, preparation and training for war, social contact, food and subsistence, and also pleasure. Although hunting and falconry were extensively written about in the instructional manuals and treatises and commonly figure in romantic literature, virtually all late medieval contemporary writings ignore the role and practical involvement of women in any form of hunting. There is, however, a disparate and considerable corpus of evidence, particularly in illustrative sources, which indicates that women at all levels of society were involved in hunting in its broadest sense, ranging from deer hunting by aristocratic ladies to food collection by peasant women.

Recent research indicates that women were actively involved in virtually every aspect of medieval life at all social levels, although in many cases only exceptionally. For example, Jeremy Goldberg's work has demonstrated the active participation of women in a wide variety of trades and even guilds in fifteenth-century towns.[1] Townswomen, hitherto largely unresearched because of a dearth of direct written evidence, achieved roles and status within late medieval urban society which earlier historians had not considered likely or even possible. Compton Reeves points out that women were exempted from that part of the Sumptuary Statute of 1363 ordaining that artisans were to confine themselves to one craft, as women were 'often engaged in multiple craft labours such as brewing, baking, and spinning as part of their normal activities'.[2] However, no evidence has emerged, as yet, of women being employed at any level as professionals in royal, or noble, hunt establishments. Hopefully future research may produce many examples. In spite of this exception, and given the tidal wave of interest in medieval women and their functions and status, it is surprising that the subject of women and hunting has been neglected by modern researchers and writers.

The general impression gleaned from late medieval art and literature, almost entirely produced and written by men for men, is that high-ranking women were usually limited to the passive function of decorative audience, admiring, applauding and occasionally receiving symbolic parts of the carcass, but only rarely participating in the dangerous and unseemly excitement of the stalk or chase. John Cummins endorses this view when he remarks that 'for women to take part in the rigours of classic "par force" hunting, as opposed to its social preliminaries and aftermath, must have been a rarity'.[3] This remark is based upon his extensive studies of the illustrations in practical manuals and manuscripts. Illustrations of women as active participators in hunting activities have long been interpreted by most historians as being part of the 'world upside-down' tradition. There is much persuasive evidence for this viewpoint of female involvement in masculine activities. Veronica Sekules comments, 'Scenes of women hunting are quite common . . . but they do not always document known practice'. She points out that the *Taymouth Hours* is prefaced by the inscription, 'Cy comence jeu de dames' ('Here begins the sport of ladies') and continues that the pictures may have been intended to be amusing, in the 'world upside-down' tradition, or to be allegorical, referring to the pursuit of men by women and vice versa.[4] Some of the illustrations in *Queen Mary's Psalter* showing women engaged in jousting, fighting and other male occupations are quite probably of figurative and metaphoric, rather than literal, significance. The two damsels tilting with lances but dressed in elegant robes provide a good example of this humorous reversal of roles.[5] However, even with what at first sight appears to be the obvious satirisation of women, care in interpretation must be exercised. It is common knowledge that in the case of warfare there were notable exceptions to such generalisations of 'world upside-down' reading, such as the female warriors Jeanne d'Arc and Jeanne Hachette, as well as several cases of female Orders of Knighthood. The Orden de la Hacha in Catalonia was founded in 1149 by Raymond Berenger, Count of Barcelona, to honour the women of Tortosa who helped defend the town against Moorish attack. The Order of the Glorious Saint Mary was founded by Loderigo d'Andalo, a noble of Bologna, in 1233. There is also evidence of women serving in the established military orders of the Teutonic Knights, Knights Hospitaller and Order of Saint John, providing more than the simple provision of aid, and undertaking other menial and Hospitaller functions.[6] These functions may have included some kind of armed role as female warriors.

Like the hare which, as discussed in chapter three, often appears in 'world upside-down' scenes in marginal pictures, particularly in an opposite role such as the hunter instead of the quarry,[7] women seem to have been a favourite target for male satire in medieval manuscript margins and other pictorial sources. Again like hares, women often feature in 'world upside-down' misericords, having the characteristics of Eve and being represented as rebellious, vain, lustful and gossiping. Misericords frequently present a general picture of domestic strife between the sexes with women depicted as the winners.[8] They are also commonly shown indulging in male pursuits such as hunting, jousting and fighting. Hares were also, like women, regarded as ambiguous creatures, characterised by craftiness and foolishness, the ability to appear and disappear mysteriously and having the power of transformation into and from a witch.[9] To the medieval male mind, the close connection between women and hares was an established fact and this traditional association is continued by modern hare hunters who always refer to the quarry as 'she', irrespective of its sex.[10] Another hunting personification term for the hare is 'puss', both an informal term for a girl or young woman, and an archaic word probably derived from the Middle Low German *pus*, meaning a hare.[11] The perceived similarities between women and hares in the Middle Ages may be the reason why the hare is perhaps the commonest of animals to figure in the margins of medieval illuminated manuscripts, although its satirical guise varies from hare-hunter and falconer, to hare-knight, cleric, judge and hare-witch.[12] Men, it seems, were preoccupied with the representation of women in forms other than those which they deserved or were entitled to.

Of course, there is a temptation to accept illustrative evidence too readily as being a true record of reality and actual practice. No doubt many, if not most, illustrations are idealised by intent. However, there is also a danger of interpreting all such evidence, particularly women hunting, as symbolic and without practical significance. It seems more reasonable to take a middle view, conceding that some illustrative evidence may, and in a lesser number of cases probably does, reflect real practices. This notion is not revolutionary but in the face of the 'world upside-down' school is certainly radical, and it is supported by three significant points. Firstly, there are many short, often indirect, textual references to women hunting. Secondly, it is accepted that women were active participators in the sport of falconry; why not hunting? Thirdly, evidence from other periods is completely positive as regards women of rank hunting[13] and to suggest that hunting was an exclusively male preserve at any level of medieval society is ludicrous and exhibits a complete lack of understanding of female human nature.

The enduring historical lack of reference to women and hunting seems likely to be the continuation of a long-established tradition based upon male expertise, education and authorship. The apparent lack of physical involvement by women in hunting wild quarry – apart from hawking for which there is a mass of evidence – has been perpetuated by male writers on the subject for centuries. Of course, there were relatively few women writers generally, so the lack of female narrative in hunting is hardly surprising.

Four of the most influential medieval manuals on the techniques and practical methods of hunting, already used extensively in this study, provide examples of this overt gender exclusiveness. In chronological order these canonical manuscripts are:

The Art of Hunting, written by William Twiti, *c.* 1330;
Les Livres du roy Modus et de la royne Ratio, written by Henri de Ferieres, c.1376/7;
Livre de chasse, by Gaston Fébus, begun in 1387;
The Master of Game, produced by Edward, Duke of York, *c.* 1406/13.

All four texts are, seemingly, completely male-oriented books of instruction, written by men for men. Women, as a separate gender, are not mentioned or acknowledged. Or are they? The concluding passage of the Shirley Manuscript of *The Master of Game*[14] provides an exception to this apparent rule. Edward of Norwich concludes with the hope that all his readers, 'that hathe herde or rude this lytell tretys', have approved of it and corrected it as necessary according to their own knowledge. He then continues:

> And in my simple manner as best I could and as might be learned of old and many diverse gentle hunters, I did my business in this rude manner to put the craft and the terms and the exercise of this said game more in remembrance and openly to the knowledge of all lords, *ladies*, gentlemen and *women*, according to the customs and manners used in the high noble court of this Realm of England [my italics].[15]

Although Edward specifies only courtly women, 'ladyes' and 'wymmen', he does acknowledge that they had heard or read his book of instruction. Not only were women hunting but, more significantly, they too had specialised knowledge and were 'lerned' in the art of hunting, in the same manner as their men folk. This does make sense; people cannot participate in any sport or pastime without acquiring skills and knowledge. In reality, then, we can conclude that one of the major gender divisions, the 'learnedness' much prized and vaunted by men, did not exist.

Mention must be made also of the *Boke of Saint Albans*, a treatise covering the male preserves of hawking, hunting and heraldry, whose authorship is traditionally credited to a female writer, Dame

Juliana Berners. Nicholas Orme comments that this female authorship is an unusual indication that women might possess, or be thought to possess, a detailed knowledge of hunting techniques and be able to pass them on.[16] There is, however, a long-standing controversy regarding the authenticity of the author's gender. Whoever the author was, the *Boke of Saint Albans* was probably compiled in the early 1480s from other earlier sources, certain indicative fragments being recognisable. The complete manual was printed by the London printer Wynken de Worde in 1486.[17]

The fact that Dame Juliana is also credited with a *Treatise on Fishing*[18] makes her authorship of the *Boke of Saint Albans* questionable, as at this time fishing was a very popular pastime with a consequently, low status compared to the 'gentil' sports of hunting and hawking. A significant part of the reason for this attitude was that real gentlemen regarded fishing as a 'tame pursuit' lacking the dangers of hunting.[19] Fishing was also cheap, requiring little specialised equipment, unlike hawking, so was not restricted by cost to the wealthy, an important element in aristocratic pastimes. Until the preparation for war aspect lost its importance, 'fishing with an angle' remained a poor second to pursuing quarry upon horseback or on foot. It thus seems questionable, though not impossible, that the same author would have written sporting manuals of instruction for both aristocratic and commonalty readers. The *Boke of Saint Albans* does make a clear distinction between netting and trapping fish, an occupation of 'crafty men', and 'of fishing with an angle . . . one of the disports that gentlemen use'. Maurice Keen points out that it is fly-fishing that is referred to here as the *Boke* contains several patterns for tying artificial flies. He continues to explain that a 'disport' is 'a stylish, "gentle art", fit for the pursuit of gentlemen in their free time'.[20] However, the hunting and hawking manuals stress practical methodology and procedures within socially acceptable sporting boundaries, tacitly ignoring the provision of meat aspect, whereas fishing books are essentially practical texts lacking ritual, concerned with filling the bag in the most effective manner. In spite of favourable inclusion in the *Boke*, fishing at that time was thus analogous with pragmatic commonalty methods of hunting for subsistence and therefore, perhaps, with overtones of poaching. It must be realised that in the Middle Ages the status of a sport partly rested upon its necessity function. For the aristocracy, hunting was a leisure pursuit that emphasised both social superiority and masculine notions of military service. Thus if hunting was generally conceived of as a 'masculine' pastime, then perhaps medieval authors could not accept the active participation of women, so they took the least controversial route and did not acknowledge them in their books.

Literary sources frequently mention women hunting in classical antiquity, such as Theseus's Queen Hippolyta and her younger sister Emily in Chaucer's *Knight's Tale*[21] and in Arthurian legend there is the lady who hunts accompanied only by women. This great huntress 'overshotte the hynde, and so by myssefortune the arow smote sir Launcelot in the thyke of the buttok over the barbys'.[22] A significant accident regarding gender roles and where the arrow hit; also an extremely painful incident bearing in mind the wide splayed barbs of the type of hunting arrow typically used for large game. There are also many medieval German sources in which ladies accompany or actually participate in the hunt, but again, most of these are motivated by an established plot or love allegory. References to contemporary medieval women taking an active part in hunting remain conspicuously absent and only one fifteenth-century German professional manual refers to female participation.[23]

The occasional references in textual sources to women and hunting can be tantalisingly brief. Thus, one of the earliest references to English fox hunting dates from 1221, when Henry III gave the Abbess of Barking permission to chase the fox in Havering Park, Essex.[24] This reference is interesting for a variety of reasons: the 'verminous' nature of the quarry being hunted, and the gender and pious occupation of the person to whom the permit was granted. As earlier stated, the Church officially disapproved of its members hunting and hawking, although one or both activities were practised by many members of all levels of the First Estate. It is tempting to assume that the abbess hunted the foxes in Havering Park herself on horseback with hounds, and to link the low status of

149

the fox, a 'non-noble' beast, to that of women, but there is no evidence to elucidate either of these intriguing points. It is more likely that the male servants of the abbey carried out the necessary control of the park foxes, which had probably been worrying sheep, by some effective but non-sporting commonalty hunting methods such as netting or trapping. If that were the case, then it can hardly be cited, as it has been on several occasions, as the first recorded example of English women being actively engaged in fox hunting.

Ladies of the nobility had several roles to play, which were presumably approved by their men folk, within the aristocratic field of hunting. As audience they were allowed to watch the fine spectacle of the hunt streaming across the fields and lawns of an enclosed park, but from a safe viewing point, such as a hill top, castle tower or roof.[25] In 1452, the Emperor Frederick III visited King Alfonso of Aragon. To commemorate the visit, Frederick was taken hunting on the plain of Palma and the grand finale to the day was a staged hunt in the royal park of Astroni. Here, the ladies were spectators and were accommodated on a dais, protected from the sun by an awning and surrounded by a wooden palisade.[26] One of the colourful illustrations in the early sixteenth-century *Thuerdank* of Emperor Maximilian I shows the ladies of his court sitting at ease by the Plansee in the Tyrol, enjoying the spectacle of Maximilian hunting red deer in the forests and chamois in the mountains, and fishing in the lake.[27] The illustrations in this book are composite pictures, the artist employing the oft-used painting technique of representing two or more separate activities as happening simultaneously, rather than painting a sequence of events with an identical, or similar, background. This method was ideal for showing progressive sporting activities such as hunting and hawking.

Much of the illustrative evidence shows ladies in this passive role of admiring onlookers, and there appears to be little doubt that female approval, applause and even adoration, were important to the aristocratic medieval hunter and sportsman, just as they were to the tourneying knight. The four hunting tapestries in the Victoria and Albert Museum, known as *The Devonshire Hunts*, illustrate this point clearly. Probably made to celebrate the occasion of the marriage of John, Lord Talbot, to Margaret Beauchamp in 1424, the tapestries contain many vignette scenes of aristocratic ladies watching and admiring the various hunting activities of their husbands and lovers.[28] As John Cummins comments: 'It is difficult to assess which of these are hunters and which spectators, but clearly the ladies . . . have not been charging through river and thicket in pursuit of boar, bear or deer.'[29]

Admiring ladies are also conspicuous in the April and September tapestries of *Les Chasses de Maximilien* cycle in the Louvre, although these ladies are mounted.[30] Again, it is unclear whether they have just ridden up from a safe view-point to coo and flirt with their men during a lull, or if they are active participants in the chase. In the tapestry for April, one girl is sitting coyly behind her man whereas another lady looks more workmanlike, apparently riding side-saddle. The vexing question of whether and when women rode astride or side-saddle is difficult to answer from medieval and early Renaissance illustrative sources. When women travelled, they sat either 'pillion' behind a man, or, according to the Anglo-Norman historian Odericus Vitalis, 'in female fashion on women's saddles'. When they hunted, they usually rode astride their mounts. Probably the earliest illustration of a lady riding astride in clothing designed for that specific purpose is an etching by Antonio Tempesta, (1565–1630).[31] A *bas de page* illustration from *The Trinity* of *The Hours of Marguerite D'Orléans*, made shortly after her marriage in 1426 to Richard, Count of Etampes,[32] does show the involvement of some aristocratic women. The *par force* hunt is in full cry, pursuing a fine hart along a streamside beside a forest, and two elaborately dressed ladies are near the front of the field sitting up behind their men folk. No ambiguity or symbolism here, everybody is clearly enjoying a good day out together.

If ladies were fortunate enough to be present at the ceremony of the unmaking of the hart or buck, they were liable to be presented with a foot, or occasionally the head, of the beast.[33] This symbolic bestowal of a special titbit to the fair sex, the meaning of which may be erotic but is not clear from the sources, continued in English fox hunting well into recent times by the presentation of a fox's pad to lady hunters attending the kill. It may well be that the hart's foot was regarded by aristocratic medieval hunters, both male and female, as a 'secret' and erotic symbol. Deer are ungulates and have cloven feet, each of which is referred to as a 'slot'. Prints of deer in soft ground are still called slot-marks. The appearance of a deer's foot, when viewed from beneath, bears a distinct resemblance to the vulva, 'slit' or 'slot'. On the other hand, the foot is the least useful part of the carcass, its only function being as a decorative trophy. On another level, perhaps this also symbolised the male notion of a noblewoman's place, not only in the medieval hunt but also in upper-class society.

The death at the end of the hunt provided the necessary closure to the sporting part of the aristocratic chase. It was not intentionally prolonged, as the earlier descriptions in chapter three make clear. The life-blood of the quarry was regarded as significant too, and not only in the *curée* ceremony of feeding the hounds. 'Blooding', the ancient ritual of daubing the faces of young stag hunters present at the kill for the first time, continued as a tradition in fox hunting well into the middle of the twentieth century and, covertly, probably much later. Here, the huntsman would daub each cheek of novice young hunters with the blood of the newly killed fox, applied with its brush. The 'anointing' of novice hunters with animal blood was a rite of passage, an initiation into the 'mysteries' of adult hunting, which probably had its origins in pagan times. Some regard these ceremonies as profane, appearing to be travesties of Christian baptism.[34] However, blood was regarded as one of the four humours of the body and as such was thought to have remarkable, even magical, properties. The hart was a 'noble warrior', the premier beast of the chase, so it is hardly surprising that his life-blood was regarded with some superstition. Thus, medieval ladies-in-waiting smeared their hands in stag's blood after the breaking ceremony, believing it would whiten the skin. On one occasion, Queen Elizabeth I was said to be 'gratified', meaning 'pleased', personally to despatch a stag by slitting its throat.[35] This was undoubtedly an unusual action by a woman, its success demonstrating both the

33 A peasant netting a small bird using a draw-cord net on a pole. (*British Library, London,* The Luttrell Psalter, *fol. 63*)

34 A concealed peasant plays his whistle to attract songbirds. (*Bibliothèque nationale*, Paris, Les Livres du Roy Modus et de la Royne Ratio, *MS fr. 12399, fol. 95*)

35 Conies at their warren, unaware of the ferret or pole-cat about to enter a burrow. (*British Library, London*, The Luttrell Psalter, *fol. 176v*)

36 Peasants with ferrets and purse-nets working a warren. (*Burrell Collection, Glasgow, Peasants Ferreting, Burgundian Tapestry*)

37 Contrasts in hunting quarry and methodology carved on a misericord: the central theme is the stag hunt but to the left a rabbit peeps from its burrow. (*King's Lynn Museum, King's Lynn*)

38 In the bleak mid-winter: peasants returning from an unsuccessful hunt. *The Hunters in the Snow*, by Pieter Bruegel the Elder, 1565. (*Bridgeman/Kunsthistorisches Museum, Vienna*)

39 Ladies flirting with their lovers during a pause in the hunt. (*Musée du Louvre, Paris*, Les Chasses de Maximilien, *tapestry for September (right detail)*)

40 A dismounted hunter caresses his female companion. (*Musée du Louvre, Paris, Les Chasses de Maximilien*, tapestry for May (*left detail*))

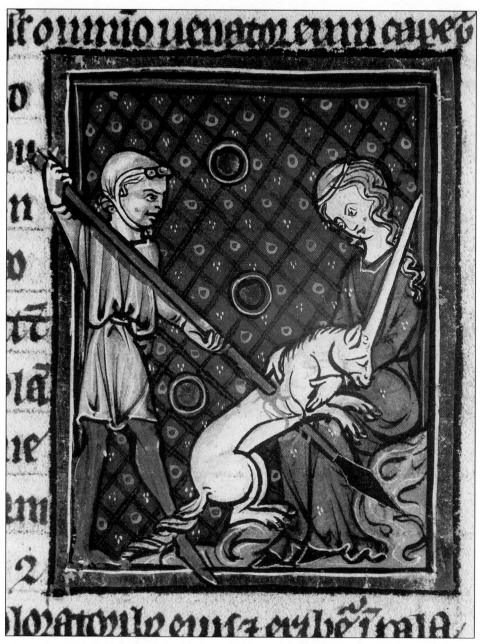

41 The wily hunter slays the unicorn sleeping in the virgin's lap. (*Trinity College, Cambridge, The Wren Library, MS R. 14. 9. fol. 90v*)

42 (above) and **43** (overleaf) Ladies hawking, aided by bercelets. (*British Library, London, Queen Mary's Psalter, MS Royal 2B VII, fols 177v and 178*)

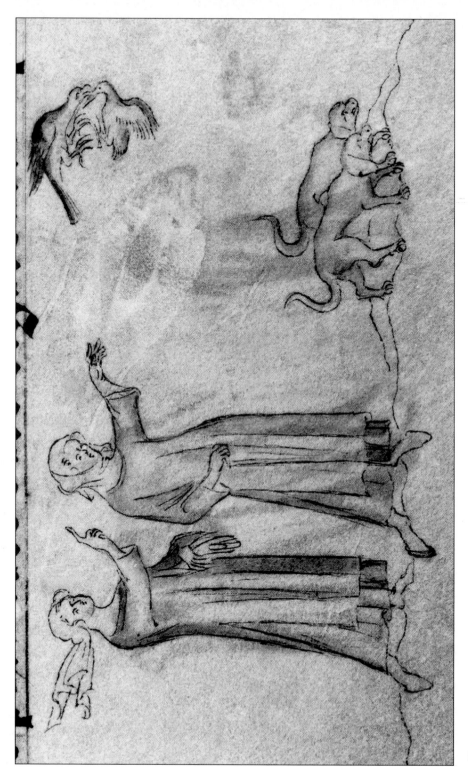

44 A lady wearing a veil flying her peregrine at a mallard. (*British Library, London, Taymouth Hours, MS Yates Thompson 13, fol. 73*)

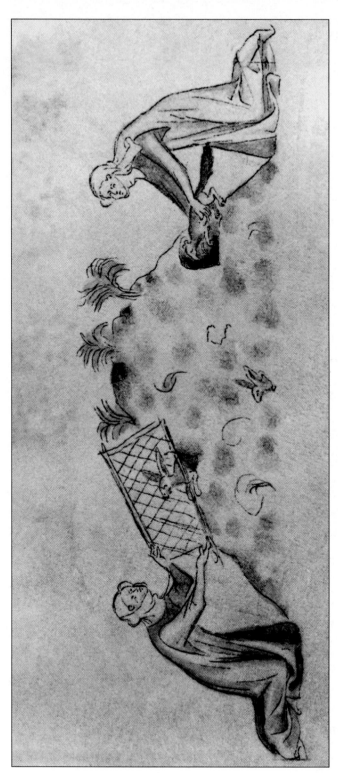

45 Women using ferrets and nets to take rabbits at an artificial warren. (*British Library, London,* Queen Mary's Psalter, *MS Royal 2B VII, fol. 155v*)

46 Noble and commonalty hunting methodology both shown in the same aristocratic manuscript illumination. (*Bridgeman/Bibliothèque nationale, Paris*, The Hours of Marguerite d'Orléans, *MS Lat. 1156B, The Trinity, fol. 163*)

47 The main and marginal worlds of medieval hunting: the mounted noble hunts a hare with hounds in the forest while the poor man with a cross-bow poaches a rabbit at a warren on the field boundary. (*British Library, London, MS Egerton 1146*, Calendar for June, *fol. 7v*)

courage and anatomical knowledge possessed by the queen. This latter 'lernedness' is further illustrated in a woodcut in George Gascoigne's treatise *The Noble Arte of Venerie or Hunting*. The royal huntsman presents a knife to Elizabeth in order for her to slit open the belly of a stag,[36] the first process in the ritual of undoing the hart. Elizabeth apparently had no repugnance to fresh, warm blood in quantity and did not consider her sex a barrier to full participation in the post-chase sanguinary rituals.

What is significant about this varied corpus of evidence is that some women of royal, noble or gentle birth were actually present at the climactic ritual of unmaking and therefore qualified for a specific piece of the carcass to which no other group was entitled. What is not clear, and is almost impossible to substantiate, is whether these ladies had followed the hunt on horseback as part of the field and been present at the death, or had been summoned to the unmaking from a convenient viewing point by their lords. It seems most reasonable to suppose that both situations occurred, perhaps the former event being rather more unusual at the end of a Forest hunt, whereas the latter was more likely and convenient in a park hunt.

The female roles of spectator, admirer and participator in end-rituals, also include an erotic function, lust being for some participants a natural result of the excitement and heat experienced during a fast and successful hunt. The alternative word for hunting, 'venery', has a dual meaning, derived on the one hand from the Latin *venari*, meaning 'to hunt'; on the other from *venereus*, meaning 'pertaining to Venus'.[37] In the minds of many writers and artists the two were inextricably entwined and it is therefore unsurprising that sex features in some sources. A cameo scene from *The Devonshire Hunting Tapestries* makes public this private eroticism between hunters and their consorts. While watching the breaking-up of the hind, and the *curée* or ceremonial feeding of the hounds by the hunt servants, the gentle hunters and their ladies are caught indulging in enjoyable love-play.[38] In the poem *Guillaume de Dole*, the hunters return to camp to wash before supper. There are no towels so, quite naturally, 'They borrow the ladies' white chemises, /And take their chance to put their hand /On many a white thigh.'[39] This erotic element was not always restricted to the hot, sweaty aftermath of the hunt, when adrenalin was still pumping through the veins. In the May tapestry of *Les Chasses de Maximilien*, one dismounted hunter takes time off eagerly to caress the breasts of his coy but compliant female companion while the pre-hunt feast is being set up by busy servants.[40] May was traditionally regarded as the month of love so perhaps this lustful cameo at the margin of the main scene is appropriate. Hunting had several physical levels and Veronica Sekules comments, 'The image of the hunt often does refer quite evidently to lustful relationships between men and women'.[41] Before or after the chase was a natural and opportunist occasion for lovers to consummate their passion so at one level these erotic scenes can be read quite literally. It is also possible that the covert message from the artist is an illustration of the parallel between hunting and the pursuit of love, comparable to the imagery employed by poets and writers.

Hunting imagery developed into perplexing allegory in some late medieval sources. The theme of morality is illustrated by *The Pursuit of Fidelity*, a fifteenth-century tapestry from the upper Rhineland in the Burrell Collection.[42] Here, a fine hart of ten is being driven into a fixed net by three hounds while the hunter, mounted on a dapple-grey with his lady up behind, winds his horn. Above the hunter, a scroll is inscribed with the Middle German words, '*uf iag nach triuwen Frau*', meaning, 'in pursuit of a faithful woman'. A scroll over the lady reads, '*ich die kein Lieber zu gelebt*', her rejoinder meaning, 'I with whom no lover has lived'. The '*die*' of her reply is feminine gender and clearly indicates that this is a dialogue between the young noble and his love: he states his quest or hunt for a faithful wife; she avers her innocence and virginity, hence her suitability and enduring fidelity as his future wife. The source, like all medieval allegories, can be read in several ways, however. John Cummins's interpretation is that the lovers are in pursuit of the elusive quarry fidelity, represented by the hart, which is on the verge of capture in their net.[43] Another level may be warning against the deceit of women of uncertain virtue looking for a well-bred but gullible husband. In this case, the hart may represent the hunter (and his 'heart') being driven into the net of marriage by the hounds of his lady's protestations and wishes. In addition, the hart can be seen as symbolic of the maid, hunted by her lover and being moved into the net of fulfilment by his hounds which represent his desires and good qualities. It became conventional to give hounds allegorical names in later hunting allegories, particularly in German poetry. These often represented the characteristics and qualities of the male lover and included Courtesy, Kindness, Bliss, Longing, Daring, Delight and Grace.[44] Such pointed and appropriate naming of hounds assisted the audience in the complex and sometimes ambiguous interpretation of a literary or pictorial source, as well as often giving, no doubt, wry amusement.

The most peculiar role in hunting played by noble women involved that fabulous single-horned beast, the unicorn. It was supposed to be the fiercest of beasts, able to fight and defeat an elephant using its single horn, as illustrated in *Queen Mary's Psalter*.[45] Literate European hunters with a knowledge of bestiaries and hunting manuals seriously believed in unicorns. The main reason for this was that much of the information used by the writers of bestiaries and hunting books was taken from the Greek collection of animal legends called the *Physiologus*, compiled between the second and fourth centuries. This book describes the unicorn as small, fierce and impossible to capture by conventional means. The only successful method known used a young virgin as bait, placing her in a passive and apparently vulnerable situation. She was taken by the hunter into a remote piece of forest which the quarry was known to frequent. The hunter then concealed himself nearby. When the evasive unicorn scented the demure virgin, it approached silently and then laid its head upon her lap, before falling into a deep slumber. This enabled the wily hunter to steal up and quickly despatch the beast, before cutting off its magical horn.[46] These are quite extraordinary instructions, totally unlike any other hunting methodology, and it seems absurd that practical and educated hunters should take such directions seriously. However, there was a genuine precedent for their belief.

In the late thirteenth century, Marco Polo described unicorns he had seen in Sumatra, probably rhinoceroses, and he too, mentions this technique of capturing the beast.[47] Europe lacked the rhino and it is almost certain that this exotic Asian animal became the reality of the legendary fairy beast. Therefore, as it apparently existed, it could be hunted and slain, like any other forest animal. A number of late medieval sources illustrate the traditional hunting technique, including MS Royal 12 F xiii in the British Library[48] and the fifteenth-century *Unicorn Tapestries*. The fifth tapestry of the cycle shows a maiden taming the unicorn within a paling enclosure, the *hortus conclusus*; the sixth is of male hunters on foot slaying the unfortunate beast with spears.[49] The classic unicorn tableau can be seen in a perfect and charming tiny manuscript miniature in the Wren Library, Trinity College, Cambridge.[50] The allegorical and religious symbolism of the unicorn surrendering to a young virgin, and the increasing complexity of this relationship in the texts of the later Middle Ages, is a separate subject and dealt with in other studies. However, the role of the maiden within the context of hunting is interesting in its ambiguity. As bait, she is vital to the success of the hunt, yet her role could be said to be passive as she plays no part in physically killing the unicorn. But she has performed the most dangerous part of the hunt, taming a fierce, magical animal by a combination of her sexual purity and feminine courage. This is hardly 'passivity' in modern eyes but to medieval minds the gender relations in the unicorn hunt must have been clear; 'slaying' defines the masculine role of the hunter, whereas other activities, whatever the qualities necessary, are subsidiary.

To be fair to the medieval authors, starved of accurate and scientific information, it must be remembered that bestiaries contained depictions and descriptions of all manner of birds and beasts, most real but some imaginary. These texts were attempts to make sense of the natural world by classifying all birds and beasts. Educated people looked at bestiaries and believed and marvelled at the information they contained because, owing to the lack of accurate evidence in their restricted world, they had no choice. The unicorn and its stories appealed to medieval people, whether hard-headed hunters or not. It is thus perhaps understandable that the unicorn was one of the few fabulous fictitious creatures, the reptilian basilisk was another, to survive the Renaissance and remain credible for several centuries.[51]

In spite of all the sources which present these so-called passive feminine roles, there is some literary and illustrative evidence that women of noble birth did take both a real and an active part in certain types of hunt. A twelfth-century Scottish poem called *The Enchanted Stag* describes a 'tinchell', or deer drive, in which 120 'fian' or hunters, with 1,000 hounds, and 100 women and 1,000 men in attendance, killed 100 deer and 100 stags. The tinchell of beaters drove the deer towards an 'elrick' or barrier, behind which stood the hunters armed with bows and spears, their hounds ready to pull down wounded beasts.[52] The fact that only a small number of women are specified in this poem may indicate the presence of a noble female élite of active participators. As described in chapter three, classic bow and stably hunting in the later Middle Ages and early Renaissance involved hunters waiting on foot at stands or stations for the driven quarry to appear within bowshot. Wooden 'standings' were often available for the comfort of important guests and their ladies. These constructions, often called stable-stands, could be raised platforms built next to a drive or ride, or on a boundary of the section driven. Sometimes they were erected between the branches of a large tree, providing effective and safe cover for the hunter.[53] In George Gascoigne's book, *The Noble Arte of Venerie or Hunting*, published in 1575 and originally attributed to George Turbervile, a woodcut depicts Queen Elizabeth standing upon such a structure, receiving her kneeling huntsman's report.[54] He is presenting her with a 'dish' of leaves containing the fewmets, or droppings, of the hart which he proposes will be hunted that day. He waits for her approval of his estimation of the warrantability or huntability of the beast which is based upon the size, shape and consistency of the fewmets. As a keen huntress, Elizabeth would have had the knowledge to comment with authority on her huntsman's evaluation and advice.

On a larger scale, Lucas Cranach the Younger's painting of the hunting party given by Elector John Frederick of Saxony for Emperor Charles V at the castle of Torgau, 1544, includes an elaborately attired lady armed with a loaded crossbow waiting at a hidden stand by a lake into which red deer are being driven.[55] She is John Frederick's wife, Electress Sybille. Admittedly, she is the exception in this painting as an active representative of her sex and has been allocated little picture space, yet she is fulfilling the same hunting function as her male counterparts. She is probably using a relatively light crossbow called a German spring-bolt, whereas the key huntsmen in the foreground, including her husband and the Emperor, are using heavy crossbows, or arbalests.[56] Three male assistants have two more crossbows ready loaded to quickly hand her, an indication, perhaps, of her skill with this weapon. She is not the only woman visible but is accompanied by six similarly attired ladies-in-waiting who provide her with company and support. In this cameo scene, Cranach has made a clear distinction between Sybille, the active royal huntress, and her passive courtly female audience. In addition, she is looking directly out of the picture at the viewer, not at where she is shooting; she thus arrests one's attention and this emphasises her importance as the lone woman hunter. Cranach paid much knowledgeable attention to the details of this hunt and to its personages, yet it recorded a political illusion as Charles V and John Frederick never hunted together at Torgau. The panorama illustrates the Elector's hope that the quarrel between the Catholic monarch and the Protestants was over.[57]

No doubt then, as now, some royal or noble sportsmen appreciated a female partner who could shoot skilfully or ride to hounds with courage. Mary of Burgundy, the first wife of the future Holy Roman Emperor Maximilian I, was the personification of this type of woman. She was acknowledged as a fine horsewoman who excelled at most sports. This formed an important link of affection and respect between the royal pair, and in 1477 her husband wrote with much obvious pleasure, 'My wife is thoroughly at home with falcons or hounds; she has a greyhound of great pace'.[58] Anne de Beaujeu, sister of Louis XI and Regent of France, was also a celebrated huntress and lady of great courage. Her prowess is clear in the poem by Jacques de Brézé who says, 'She was always among the first' and 'she got through where never a lady got through before'. She even presided in person over the *curée*,[59] a rare event for a woman and not mentioned in the hunting manual. It could be argued that Mary and Anne were perhaps unusual in their skills and reckless bravery in the hunting field, and in addition had royal status, so were deemed worthy of recording for posterity. This is probably true, but it seems inevitable that other ladies of rank hunted as part of their social obligations, and for pleasure too, and that female icons such as Mary and Anne were regarded with adulation and as outstanding role models by other women.

The only active sporting role in which women are commonly portrayed in illustrations of the period is as falconers. Possibly hawking was seen as a more proper activity for ladies of rank, lacking the fast pace and bloodier aspects of hunting but involving the aristocratic skills of horsemanship and the pursuit of game. Learning the skills of hawking was certainly part of an aristocratic young woman's education. Two long French poems from the thirteenth century by Robert de Blois and Jacques d'Amiens specify that hawking, together with chess, telling stories, being witty and playing musical instruments, was part of 'the notion of polished manners required of society ladies'.[60] Robert de Blois lists some of the qualities of a heroine thus:

She could carry and fly falcon, tercel and hawk, /She knew well how to play chess and tables, /how to read romances, tell tales and sing songs. All the things a well-bred /lady ought to know she knew and lacked none.[61]

'Flying at the brook', a method in which falcons were flown at herons or wild duck, flushed and put up by pointers or spaniels, was popular with lady falconers. A miniature from a French or Italian manuscript at the Musée Condé shows three men and a woman indulging in this riverside sport.[62] Two early fourteenth-century prayer books contain scenes of women hawking. *Queen Mary's*

Psalter has three such illustrations, all line drawings, showing ladies on horseback and on foot, flying their falcons at wild duck and herons which have been flushed from cover by small hounds.[63] *The Taymouth Hours* contains a sequence of scenes illustrating falconry practice, as follows: a lady of rank putting up duck from a fountain by beating a gong; flying a peregrine at duck; her bird striking the prey; using a lure of feathers to bring in her falcon after an unsuccessful flight; rewarding the bird with a gobbet of meat;[64] perching the falcon; and finally, proudly showing off the quarry, a duck, to another lady.[65] A late fourteenth-century illustration from the *Tacuinum Sanitatis in Medicina*, probably a product of Verona, northern Italy, depicts a sensibly apparelled lady riding astride, about to fly her bird at partridge, the quarry having been flushed by what appear to be a pair of pointers.[66] The late fifteenth-century *Hours of Engelbert of Nassau* contains a charming variation on the active part played by women in the two previous examples. The sequence portrays a male falconer flying his pair of falcons at winged quarry and then presenting the prey to his lady. Two other ladies, apparently of lower rank, pluck the bird and the knight's lady uses the feathers to manufacture a crest for her lover's jousting helmet.[67]

Aristocratic women were certainly involved in falconry, but their public participation, recorded in many sources, is an important indicator of gender relations within aristocratic society. Men must have approved of this active role; otherwise artists would not have considered producing the many examples of manuscript and tapestry illustrations featuring female falconers. Men were in fact conceding that falconry was not an exclusively masculine preserve, unlike hunting where women were perhaps regarded at best as 'guests' and at worst as 'intruders'. However, it is reasonable to assume that this male attitude probably did not reflect whether women hunted or not, merely current notions on masculine and feminine roles. Importantly, women did not kill their prey in hawking; this was performed for them by the hawk or falcon. Women facilitated the kill, as the virgin does in trapping the unicorn. Lady falconers were, in this way, subservient to their falcons, the birds, as hunters and killers, acting as gender replacements for their men folk. There is a certain gender irony in this as it was the bigger and fiercer falcon or female bird of raptor species, not the tiercel or male, which was almost invariably used to fly at prey. There is a further paradoxical aspect to this point in that kings and nobles commonly identified with the falcon, admiring her 'warrior' qualities. Male acceptance of women falconers in their own right, though within the parameters of marriage, is no better indicated than by the collection of seals belonging to nobles' wives, housed in the Archives Nationale, Paris, in which the predominant motif is that of a mounted lady bearing a falcon on her wrist.[68] Here we have the feudal authority of the noble on horseback, derived from marriage to a knight, together with the symbol of an exclusive pastime denoting female empowerment.

Illustrative evidence for women hunting game other than wild birds is more restricted, sequences or cycles of venery being particularly unusual. However, there are two sources which contain this type of information in the form of marginal drawings accompanying religious texts. Both sources are persuasive in their content, with regard to known contemporary aristocratic hunting methods, and in their reality, given that the participants are all female.

The first source has already been extensively quoted from in previous chapters: *Queen Mary's Psalter* is a book of psalms dating from the beginning of the fourteenth century but deriving its title from its presentation to Queen Mary in the middle of the sixteenth century. The prayer book is English in origin, of the common Sarum type with some variations, and includes a Calendar and litany of saints.[69] In his introduction to the book of the manuscript, the editor, Sir George Warner, remarks, ' Many of the female figures . . . have a tender grace and sweetness which says much for the artist's ideal of womanhood',[70] suggesting that the artist was probably idealising reality (which of course, artists do and always have done, when it suited them). However, this comment may be misleading, given the date of editing, 1912, and the subjectivity of Sir George's observation.

The Psalter contains numerous marginal tinted drawings, many of which refer to hunting, including the following four: two ladies riding astride, one of whom winds her hunting horn; a lady on foot shooting a stag in the back of the head; two women using a ferret and framed net to take conies from a warren; and two women putting up hares from their forms or lies.[71] In all four drawings the women are dressed in simple nobles' gowns. This is particularly interesting with regard to the women netting rabbits, a distinctly commonalty pastime, usually carried out by servants for their lord or the owner with rights of warren. It has already been established that the hunting of conies was regarded with distaste by the nobility and confined to common fur hunters. Why, then, has the artist idealised these female figures by giving them standard ladies' gowns? It may be that in the masculine world of venery, the taking of rabbits could be considered as 'women's work'. The rabbit was of low status and husbanded in artificial or natural warrens, not hunted in aristocratic fashion. This is not to say that the creature was not highly regarded as an economic asset, bred for its fur and meat. The possession of a warren conferred financial status and often considerable income on its owner.[72] That is a different question altogether and does not involve notions of gender roles and status.

The second important source is MS Yates Thompson 13, a personal prayer book known as *The Taymouth Hours*, dating from between 1325 and 1335. The book is so called as it was in the library of Lord Breadalbane of Taymouth Castle in the eighteenth century.[73] In addition to the Calendar with its occupational pictures and signs of the zodiac, the first half of the *Hours of the Virgin* contains scenes of country life from the first third of the fourteenth century. It was probably produced in London for a female member of the Neville family.[74] She may be seen in folio 7, kneeling under a canopy with her hands joined in prayer, while a priest elevates the host. If the subjects of the manuscript were, as is likely, specified by the patron, then they clearly indicate the first owner's love of sport and her fondness for romantic stories.[75]

The *Hours of the Virgin* includes over thirty marginal coloured illustrations of women, dressed in the conventional robes of high rank, actively participating in hawking and hunting. These could be interpreted as being illustrative of female skills and include women flying a peregrine at wild duck; boar hunting on foot; and stag hunting, both on horseback and dismounted, with hounds. In addition, the traditional and gory *après chasse* rituals are shown being carried out by the lady hunters, including feeding rabbit guts to a hound (perhaps a low status parody of the *curée*); displaying the boar's head on a spear; and breaking-up the hart in time-honoured fashion, including hoisting the head on a spear.[76]

It has been observed that these pictures are unrealistic since only women are portrayed, yet this Book of Hours was intended for a young woman who probably loved sports. Why should the presence of males be acknowledged, particularly if they are only the professional hunters or servants necessary in an aristocratic stag or boar hunt? Also, there is no practical reason why properly trained and skilled women could not hunt alone or in small groups, despite male prejudice or masculine concerns for safety. Of course hunting potentially dangerous beasts over rough country was much more likely to be a male, rather than a female, pastime, and there were always going to be exceptions to the general axioms of gender roles, Mary of Burgundy providing the outstanding example in the late medieval period.

South of the Alps, hunting was a privileged activity in which the ladies of the Renaissance courts, as well as the men of the patrician and signorial classes, frequently indulged. A set of lost hunting frescoes situated in a loggia at Belfiore, dated to shortly after 1391, and described a century later, makes this active participation clear:

> One sees represented the illustrious memory of the much loved prince Alberto d'Este, with many gentlemen and ladies on horseback, hunting with leopards and hounds after hares, bucks, stags and bears, where one sees the fierce kill of the animals hunted and the arrows leaving the Syrian bows drawn by the hands of the ladies with worthy and strong gestures.[77]

The frescos show mounted women taking part in the pursuit of not only the hare and fallow buck, but also the far more dangerous red deer stag and bear, the latter animal long extinct in Britain. The description of ladies using bows suggests that at the climax of the hunt, they were standing at stations or trysts, shooting at game which was driven within range. The Syrian bow mentioned was probably the English or Turkish bow, as described by Gaston Fébus in *Livre de chasse*.[78] There are thus two familiar types of aristocratic hunting described here, *par force de chiens* and bow and stably. The Italian practice of using leopards as animals of pursuit, together with hounds, is very odd, and to northern European hunters must have appeared an outlandish custom. Although leopards were sometimes kept as pets by monarchs, it is more likely that the hunting felines referred to were in fact cheetahs, as in their natural habitat of the open plains, or savannah, they stalk prey then run it down. Cheetahs would undoubtedly have provided superior sport as animals for coursing swift quarry.[79] It is possibly significant that the Latin term for greyhound is *leporarius*, a reference to the main function of these hounds which was coursing the hare or *lepus*.[80] Perhaps north European medieval commentators confused *leporarius* with leopard and so established the notion of a fabulous and exotic hunting beast.

There is a wealth of post-medieval evidence testifying to the active participation of royal and aristocratic women in the chase. The future Queen Elizabeth I spent much of her time hunting when she was residing at Hatfield as a young princess and she continued to enjoy bow and stably hunting as a mature woman. Many of the ladies of the dazzling seventeenth-century court of Louis XIV regularly rode to hounds with the king. Princess Elizabeth-Charlotte, Liselotte or 'Madam' as she was known and the second wife of the Duc d'Orléans, the king's brother, often hunted with the Dauphin, frequently spending eight hours, or even more, in the saddle.[81] Hunting to hounds continued to be an expected part of court activity, including the participation of women if they so desired. In the 1860s, Elizabeth of Austria, the beautiful wife of Emperor Franz Joseph, rode to hounds in England and Ireland with a reckless bravery, gaining herself the nickname of 'The Queen of the Chase'.[82] During much of the nineteenth century, Dame Marie Cécile

Charlotte de Lauretan, Baroness de Dracek, hunted stag, wild boar and fox on what is now the modern Franco-Belgian border. However, her preferred quarry was the wolf, and in her time this formidable huntress alone accounted for 670.[83]

The real amount of active involvement of women in hunting is unknown and probably impossible to quantify. What appears clear is that there were gender-specific roles and rituals associated with the noble hunt, reflecting a demarcation between male and female spheres in late medieval aristocratic society. Unfortunately, owing to the almost complete lack of textual and pictorial evidence, it is difficult to apply this sort of conclusion to commonalty women and their roles in hunting. It seems likely that in European peasant communities, traditionally conservative in attitude, the gender roles as regards hunting and food gathering were even more defined than in aristocratic circles. Hunting and killing quarry probably carried with it notions of masculinity, similar to those in present-day isolated ethnic communities. 'Assisting' was more likely the female peasant role. A fifteenth-century Burgundian tapestry of peasants ferreting rabbits clearly shows this demarcation of roles based upon gender: the men net and despatch rabbits while their women serve as able assistants.[84] However, this was still very definitely an active role for the peasant women. They were at the warren, taking an essential part, although one which was (no doubt) regarded by both sexes as subordinate to that of the male hunters, whose gender-defining main role, like that of their noble counterparts, was in killing the quarry. Taking life was the male prerogative, paralleled in the inescapable function of warriors, whatever their period or station in society. Women, as the earthly inheritors of the Blessed Virgin Mary, could not be expected to take life because of their 'sacred' child-bearing function.

In her study of Forest court records, Jean Birrell has found very few records of peasant women being involved in poaching and these were under particular opportunistic circumstances. At night, deer habitually moved out from forest covert into the fields, orchards and even gardens of peasant communities, in search of provender. They were still protected by Forest Law, however, and this sort of damage was naturally much resented by cultivators. The obvious solution, plus the attraction of fresh venison, was to take such trespassing beasts as best one could. Thus, a husband and wife from Sowerby despatched a (possibly wounded) hart in their garden within Inglewood Forest in 1280. A group of five men and women took a young deer in the village of Carlton which had strayed from Rockingham Forest. This occurred in February 1287 when fodder may have been particularly short in the Forest at this time.[85] It is difficult to be certain, but here again, it appears likely these peasant women were assisting their men folk in killing isolated deer, rather than being the active takers of life.

It is interesting that some peasant women were involved in hunting in another way and that was as receivers of poached venison, a 'passive' crime and a marginal element of peasant hunting. Rose Glade of Arnold was convicted of supplying a man caught in possession of venison in Sherwood Forest in 1272. Gillian, daughter of Roger le Dunte, of Minstead, was described as a receiver of John Salandryn and 'others' in 1315.[86] Why were peasant women involved in a criminal activity which carried the probability of severe penalties if the perpetrators were apprehended? The obvious answers are the considerable cash return and the fact that they were on the spot, but perhaps also their gender made them less likely to be suspected by the Forest authorities. Certainly, these village women and the other 'fences' fulfilled a valuable role in the lucrative trade of distributing stolen venison.

SEVEN

Conclusions

The general picture which emerges is that hunting was universal and widely practised by members of all classes, and both sexes, within the hierarchy of late medieval society. It is fair to say that the practical and imaginative literature of the time is, by its nature and origins, élitist, and therefore almost entirely ignores hunting by the commonalty. This observation applies even more particularly to pictorial evidence and surely this is to be expected. The ruling classes did not patronise artists to commemorate the commons and peasantry at play. Naturally, nobles were interested in being featured at their own élitist pastimes and in how they spent their leisure. The commons, in contrast, worked for their living and did not have the privilege of leisure. The medieval Church supported the status quo, mollifying the toiling peasantry with the convenient teaching comment of St Benedict, '*Laborare est orare*', meaning 'To work is to pray'. The hunting manuals, written by gentle authors for the nobility and gentry, clearly demonstrate this preoccupation with élitism too. A very few hunting books contain evidence for more widespread practices, and these, together with other evidence, such as statutes, Forest court records, hunt establishment records and a very limited amount of illustrative material, support the view that the rest of society was also heavily involved in hunting. It is not that commonalty methods were any less effective than aristocratic practices. The chapters in *Livre de chasse* by Gaston Fébus on commonalty hunting methods clearly show that he considered them to be not only ingenious but also useful and instructive to gentle hunters. He was thus using these methods to teach gentlemen who otherwise might not have known about such practices. Fébus was not writing for common men, even though his treatise indicates a certain empathy with lesser hunters. Common men would not have had access to such books and were, in any case, largely illiterate. However, his awareness and acknowledgement of humble men hunting, and of the effectiveness of their pragmatic methodology, are important within the social context of late medieval society. Jean Birrell points out that though lower-class methods of deer hunting were scorned by gentlemen, peasant skills and knowledge were recognised when peasants were employed as *ductores* or guides, by hunting parties unfamiliar with the country and local deer population.[1] Naturally, the people who lived in the Forests and in the unenclosed areas, knew all about taking game, their habitats, habits and movements. It was an everyday part of their life and must have provided a considerable part of their conversation. They did not need to read about the eating habits of the hart, wild boar or hare; they could observe them at close quarters in their own fields, orchards and gardens, and covertly in preserves. Hunting was a common feature of everyday life on the great estate. The marginal hunting pictures in *The Luttrell Psalter* indicate this and the few illustrations of peasant hunting show that Sir Geoffrey Luttrell acknowledged not only its occurrence but also its place within the structure of medieval rural society. Although all classes had some reasons in common for taking wild quarry (food and sport being the most obvious ones), social factors and gender relations, both related to rank and status, were also key elements. These latter factors are also directly responsible for the difficulties in elucidating the universality of hunting.

Examination of the textual and pictorial sources clearly demonstrates that there was a class structure within hunting indicated by dress, equipment, quarry type, and especially by language, methods and techniques. All men hunted, but in different ways, according to their rank. Each class perception of what constituted hunting must have been limited, and therefore biased, by these socio-economic and gender factors. However, there is much evidence that the common interest of hunting united the classes under certain conditions of dependence, enabling men to cross social barriers and even rise in rank and status. The legitimate vehicle for this was the royal and noble hunt establishment, with its social mix of trained and employed professional men and aristocratic hunters. Stealing venison and other game was the illicit vehicle of social equality, as anyone who poached, be they noble, priest, peasant or woman, committed the same heinous crime within the legislative strictures of an aristocratic deer-hunting culture. The Forest Laws were the social levellers in this particular way, although punishment appears to have been related to class and the ability to pay an appropriate fine. Ironically, game legislation united the classes in another, more lasting way. Those outlaws of myth and legend who poached the king's deer, particularly Robin Hood and his Greenwood band of merry men, became folk heroes, the admired icons of rich and poor alike. That all classes identified with these law-breakers is the real triumph of the anonymous fifteenth-century poets.

However, the 1390 Game Law spelled the end to commonalty hunting on unenclosed land and initiated an establishment policy, basically one of increased cooperation between Crown and great and small nobility, to restrict hunting to persons of 'gentle' rank. This legal measure naturally added to the hardening of class divisions already apparent during the second half of the fourteenth century. The act was in fact seldom invoked or enforced over the next century, probably the result of the decline in population and the easing of pressure on resources, including game meat. However, Henry VII reissued the 1390 Game Law, revived the Forest eyres, targeted poaching and re-established royal authority in his Forests. Successive restrictive game acts passed by Tudor governments confirmed the sport and pastime of hunting as a privilege of the nobility and gentry.[2]

Both the social dichotomy and universality of hunting are perfectly demonstrated by two manuscript pictures. The first is part of 'The Trinity', an illustration from *The Hours of Marguerite D'Orléans*, made soon after her marriage to Richard, Count of Étampes in 1426.[3] The *bas de page* is of the standard hart hunt, the mounted field of both men and women, with professionals on foot, pursuing the quarry with hounds along a stream valley by the edge of a forest. Horns are being winded and the leading hunter steadies a cross-hilted spear to thrust at the hart. A hunt servant with his spear is waiting ahead in cover, his sturdy alaunt ready to seize hold of and bring down the quarry when it is wounded by the hunter. However, if we follow the stream up its course to the top right, we suddenly come on the tiny figure of a hunter, dressed in blue with red leggings and a red hat with a wickerwork game-bag strapped to his waist. He is concealed in a clump of Greater Reedmace, a plant often but incorrectly called 'bulrush', beside the water's edge. This small but deadly figure is taking, quite literally, a pot-shot with his crossbow at a duck struggling to rise from the water, an 'unsporting' action on his part, while other birds circle overhead in panic. This hunter is physically marginal to the main hunting scene, though still a part of it. He is also, in medieval eyes, marginal to the theme of hunting and yet an acknowledged, though lesser, element. The nobles hunt in aristocratic style, legitimately and in public, while he, a common hunter and almost certainly a poacher, is hunting unsportingly and covertly. The audience's eye is immediately caught by the exciting, colourful depiction of the glorious stag hunt; it is easy to overlook the lone insignificant figure. He is skilfully hidden from us, the audience, by the artist. This too mirrors reality; the illegal hunter lurks in hiding, far from the public gaze and unseen, but still a recognised feature of medieval hunting.

The second example is in the same tradition of dual depiction and is the June *bas de page* illustration in the Calendar of MS Egerton 1146, made around 1500.[4] At first glance, the scene is of classic hare hunting. The noble hunter, mounted on a splendid horse and accompanied by his hounds, pursues a hare through thick woodland. His companion has clearly been unhorsed, perhaps an indication of the danger of hunting at speed in the forest. However, this is not the whole story. Nearby, a poor man with a crossbow, probably a poacher, is also hunting, and he is taking a pot-shot at a rabbit on the field boundary, outside the forest. Here we have many of the ingredients of legitimate aristocratic hunting: the hare as the noble quarry; hunting on horseback with hounds; the elaborate but practical and tidy dress of the hunter; his expensive equipment, including whip and spurs (his sword is hidden as it is carried on the left hip, as is the case in seven of the other Egerton Calendar pictures); the fine tack of the horses; the environment of the forest; the danger and excitement of the mounted chase. There are also the elements of commonalty hunting: the rabbit, despised as true quarry but forbidden to men without rights of warren; hunting on foot; the green but ragged dress of the peasant; his lack of edged weaponry; the agrarian nature of the ground hunted, the field showing ridge and furrow cultivation with a growing green crop, presumably a variety of cereal; and a rabbit warren in the foreground. Importantly, this commonalty hunting, perhaps of the illegal variety, takes place outside the enclosed forest, the hunting preserve of the nobility, but next to a warren. In addition, the face of the noble hunter is clearly depicted in profile in what is virtually miniaturist detail; he is a recognisable individual, as a medieval noble would be. In contrast, the face of the peasant is obscured by his crossbow. He is thus anonymous, just one of the rural masses; he could be anyone, it is not important. This was, of course, an age when individuality was still largely one of the prerogatives of the gently born but, increasingly, identification was a feature also being applied to, and used by, wealthier townsfolk, scholars and artists. The miniaturist is very cleverly giving an aristocratic audience the stereotypical picture of feudal social division, based upon certain signals they all would understand, and yet, at the same time, he is clearly indicating the universality of hunting. 'Everybody does it but in different ways and for different quarry' is the sub-text to this miniature masterpiece. A tacit sympathy and acknowledgement can be detected in this picture by the patron, and/or the artist, for the common hunter, even the poor poacher. Moreover, it is the only picture from the cycle of twelve hunting scenes in the Calendar of MS Egerton 1146 which depicts a poor man hunting. The other eleven miniatures are, significantly, of aristocratic quarry and methodology.

This particular picture can additionally be read at another level, and that is in a very personal way. The *bas de page* is such a strange montage of untypical elements that it should perhaps be interpreted in a correspondingly unusual manner. It appears entirely possible

171

that it commemorates, or 'freeze-frames', a real hunting incident in the Germanic forest of five hundred years ago. The mounted hunter, who features as the central figure in the other Calendar pictures, is the patron of the Book of Hours, and the hunter thrown from his horse is his hunting companion and friend. It is a pleasant thought that the patron may have instructed the artist to include, and thus record forever, this highly memorable incident, this special day, in his personal prayer book. No doubt he afterwards took great pleasure in looking at this superb miniature during long and possibly tedious services in his private chapel.

Medieval and Renaissance man and, to an extent impossible to quantify, woman also, was fascinated by hunting and by the image of the chase. In an age when natural resources probably appeared infinite and the wilderness of nature close at hand, the pursuit of wild quarry must have fulfilled many of the needs of body and mind. For the nobility, hunting cleansed the spirit and counteracted the artificiality and sinfulness of court life. It created the Catholic guilt of pleasure then relieved it by hard exercise and the excitement of the chase. Perhaps the ritualistic procedures at the end of the hunt were a replacement for established religious practice, fulfilling some deep spiritual need to communicate with nature. Some of these instinctive needs and their solutions hold true for modern hunters, but they are seldom expressed in rhyme, song or verse any more, more often in prose form. How-to-do-it books or instructive manuals are, however, a feature of all modern sports and pastimes, including hunting and other field sports. Contemporary instructional literature stresses the 'right way to do things', and people accept this sensible notion. How can it be otherwise? What keen and interested newcomer to hunting, fishing or shooting would go out without reading at least some literature on practices, dress and equipment? In addition, those of us who are already 'lerned', gain much continued pleasure from reading and re-reading such texts. Books on field sports, whose modern wisdom is regarded with so much respect are, no more nor less, the equivalents of the medieval hunting books. Modern procedures are now based upon 'good practice' rather than élitist ritual, and ceremony, still an important element, is now termed 'tradition'. So, are modern hunters much different from our hunter-ancestors? It seems clear that in respect to the written word they differ but little from those remote aristocratic hunters of the medieval world. The real difference is that most of European society is now literate; therefore all who can read have access to textual information, which is reinforced by the many thousands of hunting, fishing and shooting websites to be found on the Internet. Being conversant with 'the right way' is no longer an exclusive class and aristocratic prerogative. Over a period of five and a half centuries, the printed word has gradually, but inexorably, eroded and removed that particular bastion of social division. The big difference in methodology is that most hunting is now done on foot with the aid of a rifle or shotgun. Hunting live quarry on horseback with hounds is still practised but it is now the exception, rather than the rule. Indeed in some countries, hunting on horseback is no longer allowed. The development of reasonably priced and accurate firearms has democratised hunting, bringing the pursuit of almost all types of game within reach of most Europeans. Millions of people in Europe are now legitimate hunters. However, it is significant that in spite of the wide availability of hunting, poaching is still a problem in every European country.

Throughout the ensuing centuries, man has continued to hunt, in spite of the shrinkage of wild places, loss of habitat, growth of urban areas, restrictive legislation, party politics and, very importantly, changes in quarry type and populations. In some favoured areas of the world, hunting generates much-needed currency from abroad, and this includes the grouse-moors of Yorkshire and Scotland as well as the more exotic and remote hunting grounds of Africa, Asia and Russia. In most countries of the world, the right to hunt depends not upon rank and status but upon a valid permit and the ability to pay a fee or subscription. In many countries, the bag is not only limited but, particularly with larger game, is specific as to how many individuals of each quarry type may be taken on one permit. Today, there is much national and international control, and hunting is widely recognised as a vital factor in conservation policies of maintaining habitat together with the complex interdependent eco-systems of animal and bird species. It seems ironic that attitudes have come full circle. We now recognise what was obvious to our European ancestors a millennium ago: our own oneness with nature and the irreplaceable functions of hunting in the maintenance and preservation of the planet.

Hunting may be out of fashion in the British Isles at the moment, but there is nothing any individual, or political party, can do to take away man's inbuilt thrill of the chase. For that is the factor that has remained unchanged, *the chase*, the pursuit of a living, wild creature which possesses all the advantages of its wildness. Whether on horseback with hounds, on foot with dog and gun, or wading the stream with rod in hand, the hunt is all, or almost so. The climactic kill is, in a way, immaterial, though sadly, the necessary full-stop to the chase. There are few true hunters who do not experience a momentary pang of regret when coming upon the fallen quarry, be it stag, pheasant, hare or woodcock. It is strange but true that releasing caught quarry, whether fish, feather or fur, does not satisfy the inward hunter. It is peculiarly unfulfilling. There is also the simple but ancient pleasure of putting your quarry in the game-bag and taking it home, being aware that you are providing delicious food for yourself, family and friends. There are exceptions to this kill-and-keep factor, particularly in fishing, such as the necessary release of salmon and sea-trout, caught in some hard-hit British or foreign river, for conservation or re-stocking purposes. However, this does not affect the point regarding the deep atavistic traits of man and the fulfilment of some of those needs by hunting. The medieval authors and hunters perceived the great moral question and ambiguity of hunting. Man needs to hunt to release the pressures of being human, to appreciate the countryside, the seasons, to be aware of the beauty and brevity of life, and the inevitability and sadness of death. He needs to be barbaric in order to be civilised, cruel to be cultured. Many people are still fascinated by hunting and most Europeans have strong feelings either for or against this most ancient of man's pastimes. Not to allow hunting would be a gross, perhaps far reaching, miscalculation of the possible damage to our

174

innermost psyche. We are all the inheritors of hunter-gatherers from not so long ago and the stream of consciousness of our ancient ancestors still runs deep and powerful. As that great hunter and big-game fisher Ernest Hemingway puts it in his terse but beautifully direct and perceptive way:

We were all hunters and it was the start of that wonderful thing, the hunt.[5]

Notes

The following abbreviations have been used:

Birrell: Jean Birrell, 'Peasant deer poachers in the medieval forest', in Richard Britnell and John Hatcher (eds), *Progress and Problems in Medieval England* (Cambridge, 1996), pp. 68–88.

BSA facsimile edn: Dame Juliana Berners, *The Boke of Saint Albans, 1486,* facsimile edition (London, 1899).

Dalby: David Dalby, *Lexicon of the Mediaeval German Hunt* (Berlin, 1965).

H & H: John Cummins, *The Hound and the Hawk, The Art of Medieval Hunting* (London, 1988).

Ldc, 616: Paris, Bibliothèque nationale, *Livre de chasse*, MS fr. 616.

Ldc, Tilander: Gaston Phébus, *Livre de chasse*, ed. Gunnar Tilander, *Cynegetica,* XVIII (Karlshamn, 1971).

MG, 1904: Edward, Duke of York, *The Master of Game*, ed. W.A. and F. Baillie-Grohman (London, 1904).

MG, 1909: Edward, Duke of York, *The Master of Game*, ed. W.A. and F. Baillie-Grohman (London, 1909).

Modus: Gunnar Tilander, (ed.), *Les Livres du roy Modus et de la royne Ratio,* Vol. 1, Société des Anciens Textes Français (Paris, 1932).

Pisanello: Luke Syson and Dillian Gordon, *Pisanello, Painter to the Renaissance Court* (London, 2002).

PTA: M.Y. Offord, (ed.), *The Parlement of the Thre Ages*, Early English Text Society No. 246 (London, 1959; repr. 1967).

Tristan: Gottfried von Strassburg *Tristan*, trans. and ed. A.T. Hatto (London, 1960; repr. 1967).

Introduction

1.   Nicholas Orme, *Medieval Children* (New Haven and London, 2001; repr. 2002), pp. 133 and 155.

Notes

2. Linda Colley, *Britons, Forging the Nation 1707–1837* (New Haven and London, 1992), pp. 170–1.
3. Marcel Thomas and François Avril, *The Hunting Book of Gaston Phébus*, Commentary by Wilhelm Schlag (London, 1998), p. 18.
4. Roger B. Manning, *Hunters and Poachers* (Oxford, 1993), p. 116.
5. Ralph Whitlock, *Historic Forests* (Bradford-on-Avon, 1979), pp.18 and 21.
6. H & H, pp. 57–9.
7. The author is grateful to Professor Anthony J. Pollard for access to, and use of, his unpublished conference paper 'The 1390 Game Law'.
8. Manning, *Hunters and Poachers*, forests and chases maps, pp. 118 and 119.
9. Whitlock, *Historic Forests*, p. 21.
10. Anne Rooney, 'Hunting in Middle English Literature, 1300–1500' (Ph.D. dissertation, Trinity College, Cambridge, 1985), p. 3.
11. Richard, Almond, and A.J. Pollard, 'The Yeomanry of Robin Hood and Social Terminology in Fifteenth-Century England', *Past & Present*, No. 170, February 2001, pp. 52–77.
12. J.N. Bartlett, 'The Expansion and Decline of York in the Later Middle Ages', *Economic History Review*, 2nd Series, Vol. XII, 1959–60.
13. H & H, p. 2.
14. Ldc, Tilander, p. 55, fol. 4v. ll. 35–7.
15. PTA, Prologue, p. 1, ll. 7–14.
16. Ldc, Tilander, p. 51, fol. 3, ll. 3–6.
17. William Langland, *Piers Plowman*, the C-text, ed. Derek Pearsall (London, 1978), Passus IX, p. 170, l. 223.
18. MG, 1904, p. 161.
19. Marcelle Thiébaux, *The Stag of Love: The Chase in Medieval Literature* (Ithaca and London, 1974), p. 22.

Chapter One

1. Marcel Thomas and François, Avril, *The Hunting Book of Gaston Phébus* (London, 1998), p. 5.
2. Ldc, Tilander, p. 51, fol. 3, ll. 3–6.
3. John of Salisbury, *Policraticus*, Bk 1, trans. Joseph B. Pike (London, 1938), pp. 22–5.
4. *Ibid.*, p. 18.
5. MG, 1904, p. 4.
6. *Ibid.*, p. 5.
7. *Ibid.*, p. 69.
8. Nicholas Orme, *From Childhood to Chivalry* (London, 1984), p. 82.
9. *Tristan*, pp. 68–71.

10. Orme, *From Childhood to Chivalry*, p. 84.

11. *Ibid.*, p. 84.

12. *Ibid.*, p. 191.

13. *Ibid.*, p. 193.

14. Marion Wynne-Davies, *Bloomsbury Guide to English Literature* (London, 1989; repr. 1992), pp. 399–400.

15. Ldc, 616: Reading and learning the names of hounds from scrolls, Ch. 22, fol. 51v. and Practising blowing horns and holloaing, Ch. 26, fol. 54.

16. Orme, *From Childhood to Chivalry*, p. 41.

17. Nicholas, Orme, *Medieval Children* (New Haven and London, 2001; repr. 2002), p. 280.

18. Orme, *From Childhood to Chivalry*, pp. 118 and 191.

19. H & H, p. 176; A.C., Spearing, *The Gawain Poet: A Critical Study* (Cambridge, 1970), p. 10.

20. William, Langland, *Piers Plowman*, the C-text, ed. Derek Pearsall (London, 1978), Passus VIII, p. 147, l. 24.

21. *Ibid.*, p. 147, ll. 28–31.

22. Robert P. Miller, (ed.), *Chaucer: Sources and Backgrounds* (Oxford, 1977), pp. 180 and 182.

23. Philippe Contamine, *War in the Middle Ages*, trans. Michael Jones (Oxford, 1984), p. 215.

24. Pisanello, p. 85.

25. Spearing, *The Gawain Poet: A Critical Study*, p. 9.

26. Langland, *Piers Plowman*, ed. Derek Pearsall, Passus IX, p. 172, l. 264.

27. London, British Library, *The Luttrell Psalter*, Add. MS 42130, fol. 31.

28. Derek Brewer, *Chaucer in his Time* (London, 1963), p. 187.

29. William Twiti, *The Art of Hunting, 1327*, ed. Bror Danielsson (Stockholm, 1977), p. 21.

30. MG, 1904, pp. 202–3.

31. London, British Library, MS Egerton 1146, Calendar for April, fol. 5v.

32. Ldc, 616: Making nets and snares from cord with the aid of a ropemaker's spinning wheel, Ch. 25, fol. 53v. and Hunting *par maistrise*, by cunning and skill; catching deer, wild boar and wolves with nets, Ch. 60, fol. 103.

33. MG, 1909, p. 30.

34. Anne Rooney, *Hunting in Middle English Literature* (Cambridge, 1993), p. 194.

35. Charles Lethbridge Kingsford, (ed.), *The Stonor Letters and Papers, 1290–1483*, Camden Society, 3rd Series, Vol. XXX, Vol. II, (London, 1919), p. 106 269 and p. 110 274.

36. H & H, pp. 63, 260–5.

37. Roger B. Manning, *Hunters and Poachers* (Oxford, 1993), p. 10.

38. MG, 1904, p. 142.

39. J.A. Burrow (ed.), *Sir Gawain and the Green Knight* (Harmondsworth and London, 1972), p. 55, l. 1378.

40. Anne Rooney (ed.), *The Tretyse off Huntyng*, Scripta 19 (Brussels, 1987), p. 53, l. 183 and p. 77.

41. Twiti, *The Art of Hunting, 1327*, ed. Bror Danielsson, p. 40, fol. 37, ll. 13, 14, 15.

42. *Ibid.*, p. 42, fol. 37, ll. 57–8.

43. MG, 1904, p. 137.

44. H & H, p. 204: Herons and bitterns were thought to have restorative properties; according to the *Tacuinum Sanitatis*, cranes were first hung and then eaten by people who performed physical labour.

45. PTA, p. 8, vi, ll. 220–5.

46. H & H, pp. 192–3.

47. *Ibid.*, p. 241.

48. Ldc, 616: Trapping wolves: Ch. 63, fol. 107, Ch. 66, fol. 108v., Ch. 67, fol. 109, Ch. 68, fol. 110, Ch. 69, fol. 110v. Trapping bears: Ch. 62, fol. 106v. Trapping wild boar: Ch. 61, fol. 105v, Ch. 64, fol. 107v.

49. H & H, p. 242.

50. R.E. Latham, *Revised Latin Word-List from British and Irish Sources* (Oxford, 1965; repr. 1989), p. 125.

51. Bible, King James's Version, Proverbs 30: 24, 26.

52. Mark Bailey, *A Marginal Economy? East Anglian Breckland in the Later Middle Ages* (Cambridge, 1989), pp. 129–31.

53. MG, 1904, p. 125.

54. *Ibid.*, p. 41.

55. London, British Library, *Queen Mary's Psalter*, Royal MS 2 B. VII, fol. 155v. In contrast, fol. 156 shows female beaters putting up hares from their forms (lies). These animals are easily differentiated from conies by their larger size and longer ears.

56. MG, 1909, pp. 63 and 261.

57. Grant Uden, *A Dictionary of Chivalry* (Harmondsworth, 1968; repr. 1977), p. 82.

58. Compton Reeves, 'The Sumptuary Statute of 1363: A look at the aims and effectiveness of English legislation on diet and clothing', *Medieval Life, The Magazine of the Middle Ages*, Issue 16, Winter 2001/2, (Gilling East, York), p. 17.

59. *Ibid.*, p. 17.

60. Bailey, *A Marginal Economy?*, p. 186.

61. Reeves, 'The Sumptuary Statute of 1363' p. 17.

62. Charles MacKinnon, *The Observer's Book of Heraldry* (London and New York, 1966; repr. 1975), p. 40.

63. Oliver Rackham, *The History of the Countryside* (London, 1986; repr. 1993), p. 35.
64. MG, 1909, p. 67.
65. Reeves, 'The Sumptuary Statute of 1363', p. 17.
66. Marcelle, Thiébaux, *The Stag of Love* (Ithaca and London, 1974), p. 22.
67. Rackham, *History of the Countryside* (London, 1986; repr. 1993), p. 34.
68. Manning, *Hunters and Poachers*, p. 11.
69. Birrell, p. 81.
70. MG, 1909, p. 261.
71. Manning, *Hunters and Poachers*, p. 11.
72. Kurt G. Blüchel, *Game and Hunting* (Cologne, 1997; English version, 2000), p. 216, pl. p. 217.
73. Colin McKelvie, *Snipe and Woodcock, Sport and Conservation* (Shrewsbury, 1996), p. 190.
74. François Villon, *Selected Poems*, trans. Peter Dale (London, 1978, repr. 1988); 'The Testament', stanza 68, p. 91.
75. Ldc, Tilander, p. 55, fol. 4v, ll. 35–7:

Ore te proveray comme veneurs vivent en cest monde plus joyeusement que autre gent, quar, quant le veneur se lieve au matin, il voit la tres doulce et belle matinee et le temps cler et seri et le chant de ces oyselez, qui chantent doulcement, melodieusement et amoure usement, chascun en son langage, du mieulz qu'il peut, selon ce que nature li aprent. Et, quant le solleill sera leve, il verra celle doublce rousee sur les raincelez et herbetes, et le soleill par sa vertu les fera reluire; c'est grant plaisance et joye au euer du veneur.

76. PTA, Prologue, p. 1, ll. 7–14.
77. *Ibid.*, pp. 17–20.
78. Ldc, Tilander, p. 251, fol. 83, l. 9–11:

C'est bonne chasce que du cerf, quar c'est belle
chose bien quester un cerf, et belle chose le
destourner, et belle chose le laissier courre et
belle chose le chacier, et belle chose le
rachacier, et belle chose les abais, soient en
yaue ou en terre, et belle chose la cuirie, et
belle chose bien l'escorchier et bien le deffere
et lever les droiz, et belle chose et bonne la venaison.

79. MG, 1904, pp. 7–8.
80. Ldc, Tilander, p. 251, fol. 83, ll. 9–11:

Et comme j'ay dit au commencement de mon livre que bons veneurs vivent longuement et joyeusement, et, quant ilz muerent, ilz vont en paradis, je veuill ensigner a tout homme d'estre veneur, ou en une maniere ou en autre, mes je di bien que, s'il n'est bon veneur, il n'entrera ja en paradis.

81. Birrell, pp. 84–5.
82. Maurice Keen, *English Society in the Later Middle Ages 1348–1500* (London, 1990), p. 186.

Chapter Two

1. Dalby, p. v.
2. *Tristan*, p. 11.
3. *Ibid.*, p. 11.
4. Pisanello, p. 80.
5. *Ibid.*, p. ix.
6. Roger B. Manning, *Hunters and Poachers* (Oxford, 1993), pp. 4 and 5.
7. *The Paston Letters*, ed. Norman Davis (Oxford, 1963, 1983; reissued 1999), p. xiii.
8. *Ibid.*, p. xx.
9. *Ibid.*, pp. 215 and 217.
10. Marcelle Thiébaux, *The Stag of Love* (Ithaca and London, 1974), p. 21.
11. Frederick II of Hohenstaufen, *The Art of Falconry, being the De Arte Venandi cum Avibus*, trans. and ed. Casey A. Wood and F. Marjorie Fyfe (Stanford, 1943; repr. 1955), p. 476.
12. Modus: Tilander, p. liii.
13. Ldc, 616, fol. 5.
14. MG, 1909, p. xi.
15. Dr Franz Neiderwolfsgruber, *Kaiser Maximilians I. Jagd und Fischereibücher* (Innsbruck, 1965; ed. 1992), pp. 5–12. *Der gross Weidmann* means 'the great sportsman'.
16. *Tristan*, p. 11.
17. Gaston Phébus, *Le Livre de la chasse*, presentation et commentaries de Marcel Thomas (Paris, 1986), p. 19.
18. MG, 1909, Ch. 1, The Prologue, p. 1.
19. MG, 1904, p. 113.
20. MG, 1909, pp. 2 and 1.
21. BSA, facsimile edn, p. 5.
22. *Ibid.*, aii, *The Boke of Hawking*.
23. *Ibid.*, ei, *The Boke of Hunting*.
24. Manning, *Hunters and Poachers*, p. 12.

25. George Turbervile, *The Booke of Faulconrie or Hauking, London, 1575*, facsimile edn, (Amsterdam and New York, 1969), frontispiece. It is now generally accepted that *The Noble Arte of Venerie or Hunting, 1575*, was written by George Gascoigne, rather than George Turbervile. See Manning, *Hunters and Poachers*, p. 148, pl. 4. This may or may not also apply to *The Booke of Faulconrie or Hauking*.
26. *Ibid.*, Dedication.
27. *Ibid.*, p. 372.
28. H & H, p. 234.
29. Anne Rooney (ed.), *The Tretyse off Huntyng*, Scripta 19, Mediaeval and Renaissance Texts and Studies (Brussels, 1987), p. 39.
30. A.R. Myers (ed.), *English Historical Documents, 1327–1485* (London, 1969). See *569*, 'The lower orders are not to be allowed to hunt, 1390', p. 1004.
31. Manning, *Hunters and Poachers* (Oxford, 1993), anonymous quote, p. 4.
32. Izaak Walton and Charles Cotton, *The Complete Angler*, Vol. 1 (Chiswick, 1826), p. 89.
33. Royal Commission on Historical Monuments, England, MCMLXVIII, *An Inventory of Historical Monuments in the County of Cambridge*, Vol. 1, *West Cambridgeshire*, pp. 185 and 181.
34. Anne Rooney, *Hunting in Middle English Literature* (Cambridge, 1993), pp. 194–6.
35. Pisanello, p. 159.
36. Ramsgate, The Benedictine Monks of St Augustine's Abbey, *The Book of Saints* (London, 1942, repr. 1989), p. 101.
37. *Ibid.*, p. 138.
38. Pisanello, p. 160.
39. Ldc, 616, Ch. 52, fol. 93 and Ch. 8, fol. 27v.
40. Pisanello, pp. 160 and 85.
41. *Ibid.*, pp. 160 and 163.
42. *Ibid.*, pp. 159 and 160.
43. *Ibid.*, p. 156.
44. H & H, p. 70.
45. Michael Camille, *The Medieval Art of Love* (London, 1998), p. 98.
46. *Ibid.*, p.101.
47. *Ibid.*
48. Derek Brewer, *Chaucer in his Time* (London, 1963), p. 187.
49. *Ibid.*, p. 9.
50. *Ibid.*, p. 10.
51. H.L. Savage, 'The Significance of the Hunting Scenes in Sir Gawain and the Green Knight', *Journal of English and Germanic Philology*, Vol. 27 (1928), p. 1.

52. Rooney, *Hunting in Middle English Literature,* p. 198.
53. Orme, *From Childhood to Chivalry* (London, 1984), p. 191.
54. *Ibid.*, pp. 191–2.
55. Thiébaux, *The Stag of Love*, p. 21.
56. H & H, p. 189.
57. Frederick II of Hohenstaufen, *The Art of Falconry*, p. xxv.
58. H & H, p. 9.
59. MG, 1909, p. 2.
60. Frederick II of Hohenstaufen, *The Art of Falconry*, p. xxxv.
61. Phillip Glasier, *As the Falcon her Bells* (London, 1963), p. 65.
62. H & H, pp. 196–7.
63. Alison Hanham (ed.), *The Cely Letters 1472–1488* (London, 1975), p. 29 33, p. 30 33, p. 33 37, p. 36 39.
64. *Ibid.*, p. 57 63, p. 58 63, p. 59 65.
65. H & H, p. 195.
66. Glasier, *As the Falcon her Bells*, p. 219.
67. H.W.C. Davis (ed.), *Mediaeval England* (Oxford, 1924), p. 338.
68. Glasier, *As the Falcon her Bells*, p. 65.
69. H & H, p. 187.
70. Davis (ed.), *Mediaeval England*, p. 338.
71. H & H, p. 189; Modus, pp. 173–4.
72. Glasier, *As the Falcon her Bells*, p. 217.
73. *Ibid.*, pp. 219 and 222.
74. William Twiti, *The Art of Hunting: 1327*, ed. Bror Danielsson (Stockholm, 1977), p. 16.
75. BSA, facsimile edn, two unnumbered folios at end of *The Boke of Hawking*.
76. Davis, (ed.), *Mediaeval England*, p. 338; H & H, pp. 188 and 189.
77. H & H, p. 189.
78. John of Salisbury, *Policraticus*, Bk I, trans. Joseph B. Pike (London, 1938), p. 25. The Church's opposition to hunting and hawking is also mentioned in Anne Rooney's Ph. D. dissertation, p. 9.
79. H & H, p. 193.
80. T.H. White, *The Goshawk* (London, 1953), p. 13.
81. For a discussion on the differing categories of yeoman, see Richard Almond, and A.J. Pollard, 'The Yeomanry of Robin Hood and Social Terminology in Fifteenth-Century England', *Past* and *Present*, No. 170, February 2001, pp. 54–8.
82. See T.H. White's *The Goshawk* for the dedicated task of caring for and flying a male goshawk.
83. H & H, p. 190–94.
84. Turbervile, *The Booke of Faulconrie or Hauking, London 1575*, pp. 25–6.
85. *The Complete Works of William Shakespeare* (London, 1944), p. 348.

썼ちがnew

86. Ldc, 616, fol. 68; New York, Pierpont Morgan Library, *Le Livre du roy Modus et de la royne Ratio*, fol. 12, stag hunt.
87. Frederick II of Hohenstaufen, *The Art of Falconry*, p. 280.
88. *Ibid.*, p. 281.
89. Chantilly, Musée Condé, *Très Riches Heures du Duc de Berri*, MS 65, Calendar for August, fol. 8v.
90. New York, Pierpont Morgan Library, *Livre de la chasse*, MS M. 1044, fol. 59: How the hart should be sought and hunted.
91. London, British Library, MS Egerton 1146: Calendar for November, fol. 12v, and December, fol. 13v.
92. Vienna, Kunsthistorisches Museum, *The Hunters in the Snow*.
93. Arnout Balis, Krista De Jonge, Guy Delmarcel, and Amaury Lefébure, *Les Chasses de Maximilien* (Paris, 1993), p. 10.
94. Paris, Musée du Louvre, *Les Chasses de Maximilien*, tapestry for December.
95. Twiti, *The Art of Hunting: 1327*, p. 23.
96. *Ibid.*, plates after p. 116, nos 1, 2, 3, 6, 9, 12, 14, 17, 18, 19; text pp. 22–3. See also: Sir George Warner (ed.), *Queen Mary's Psalter* (London, 1912).
97. *Ibid.*, plates after p. 116, nos 1, 2, 7 and 11; text, p. 23.
98. Ldc, 616, Ch. 28, fol. 56v.
99. *Ibid.*, Ch. 26, fol. 54.
100. *Ibid.*, Ch. 55, fol. 96v.
101. Grant Uden, *A Dictionary of Chivalry* (Harmondsworth, 1968), p. 157.
102. Twiti, *The Art of Hunting: 1327*, p. 23.
103. Maurice Keen, *Chivalry* (New Haven and London, 1984), p. 249.
104. MG, 1904, p. 118.
105. *Ibid.*, p. 123.
106. Paris, Musée du Louvre, *Les Chasses de Maximilien*, tapestry for December.
107. Puma, *Messe für Jagd, Sport und Freizeit* (Solingen, 2002), p. 12.
108. Ldc, Tilander, p. 269, fol. 20, ll. 2–4:

Aussi puet on prendre les bestes a traire aux arcs, a l'arbaleste et a l'arc de main, que on apelle angloys ou turquoys. Et, se le veneur veult aler trayre aux bestes, et il veult avoir arc de main, l'arc doit estre de yf ou de boix, et doit avoir de long, de l'une ousche, ou la corde se met, jusques á l'autre, vint poigniees.

109. Twiti, *The Art of Hunting: 1327* text, p. 24; p. 56, fol. 40, ll. 11–12.
110. *Ibid.*, text p. 24, plates 11 and 12; text, p. 24, plates 5 and 22.
111. H & H, p. 41.
112. Keen, *Chivalry*, p. 154.
113. *Ibid.*, p. 249.
114. H & H, p. 173.

115. MG, 1904, p. 151.

116. *Ibid.*, p. 143.

117. Ann Hyland, *The Medieval Warhorse, From Byzantium to the Crusades* (London, 1994), p. 85.

118. *Ibid.*, p. 34.

119. *Ibid.*, pp. 86–7.

120. Frederick II of Hohenstaufen, *The Art of Falconry*, p. 281.

121. London, British Library, *The Luttrell Psalter*, Add. MS 42130, fols 43v, 159 and 87v.

122. Twiti, *The Art of Hunting: 1327*, text, p. 23, plates 1, 2, 6, 7, 11.

123. H.L. Savage, 'Hunting in the Middle Ages', *Speculum*, Vol. 8 (1933).

124. BSA, facsimile edn, unpaginated opp. fol. iiii (r).

125. R.S. Summerhays, *Summerhays' Encyclopaedia for Horsemen* (London, 1962), p. 160.

126. London, National Gallery, *The Vision of Saint Eustace*.

127. MG, 1904, p. 143.

128. Nigel Saul, *Knights and Esquires: The Gloucestershire Gentry in the Fourteenth Century* (Oxford, 1981), pp. 26–9.

129. BSA, facsimile edn., fol. iiii (r).

130. H & H, pp. 71–2.

131. London, British Library, MS Egerton 1146, fol. 16r.

132. John Harthan, *Books of Hours and their Owners* (London, 1977; repr. 1988), p. 95.

133. Oxford, Bodleian Library, MS Douce 62, fol. 31v.

134. MG, 1909, p. 216.

135. Nancy Heaton, *The Language of Hunting* (Knutsford, 1985), p. 8.

136. Ldc, Ch. 20, fol. 50; Marcel Thomas, and François Avril, *The Hunting Book of Gaston Phébus* (London, 1998), p. 35.

137. *Ibid.*, p. 35.

138. MG, 1909, p. 119.

139. *Ibid.*, pp. 120–1.

Chapter Three

1. Julians Barnes, *Boke of Huntyng*, ed. Gunnar Tilander, *Cynegetica*, XI (Karlshamn, 1964), p. 22.

2. *Ibid.*, p. 22 for 'rascal'; see also MG, 1909, p. 294, 'any lean deer; any deer under ten [tines] was usually called rascal'. *Ibid.*, p. 287, for 'folly', meaning 'lesser deer, not hart or buck'. For 'vermin', see *The Tretyse off Huntyng*, p. 55, ll. 220–40, including 'to speke & blow to all maner vermyn þat worchyth or hideth hym in gresse'.

3. Anne Rooney (ed.), *The Tretyse off Huntyng*, Scripta 19, Mediaeval and Renaissance Texts and Studies (Brussels, 1987), p. 39.
4. Barnes, *Boke of Huntyng*, ed. Tilander, p. 22.
5. *Ibid.*, p. 24.
6. Dalby, p. xv.
7. Oliver Rackham, *The History of the Countryside* (London, 1986; repr. 1993), pp. 33–4.
8. Pisanello, p. 80.
9. Ldc, Tilander, p. 84, Ch. 8, l. 5; Franz *Neiderwolfsgruber, Kaiser Maximilians I. Jagd und Fischereibücher*, Ch. 'Bärenjagd' (bear hunting), pp. 34–6.
10. Dalby, p. xv.
11. *Ibid.*, p. xvi.
12. Kurt Lindner (ed.), *Die Lehre von den Zeichen des Hirsches*, Quellen und Studien zur Geschichter der Jagd, III (Berlin, 1956).
13. Neuenstein, Hohenloheschen Zentral-Archivs, *Die Hohenloheschen Handschrift*, Nr. W. 5, fol. 15r.
14. MG, 1909, p. 225.
15. *Ibid.*, p. 226: 'Until he was a hart of ten . . . he was not considered a chaseable or warrantable deer.' See also Dalby, p. 102, 'jage-baere = warrantable', old enough to be chased (of a stag).
16. MG, 1909, p. 29.
17. *Ibid.*, pp. 224–5.
18. Rooney (ed.), *The Tretyse off Huntyng*, pp. 16–17.
19. MG, 1909, p. 23.
20. *Ibid.*, p. 23. See also fn., p. 23: a springole was 'an engine of war used for throwing stones'.
21. Roger B. Manning, *Hunters and Poachers* (Oxford, 1993), p. 111.
22. *Ibid.*, p. 117.
23. Ralph Whitlock, *Historic Forests of England* (Bradford-on-Avon, 1979), p. 38.
24. H & H, p. 61.
25. Dalby, p. xvi.
26. Ldc, 616, fols 11–12: Ldc, Tilander, table, pp. 48–50.
27. Ldc, 616, fols 29–30:

C'est une orguilleuse et fiere beste et perilleuse, quar j'en ay veu aucunne foiz moult de maulz avenir et l'ay veu ferir homme, des le genoill jusques au piz tout fendre et tuer tout mort en un coup sanz parler a homme, et moy meismes a il porte a terre moult de fois, moy et mon coursier, et mort le coursier.

28. MG, 1909, p. 264.
29. Rackham, *History of the Countryside* (London, 1986: repr. 1993), pp. 36–7.

30. London, British Library, *The Luttrell Psalter*, Add. MS 42130, fol. 19v.
31. Cambridge, Fitzwilliam Museum, *Wild Boar*.
32. Rooney (ed.), *The Tretyse off Huntyng*, p. 29.
33. H & H, p. 97.
34. William Twiti, *The Art of Hunting: 1327*, ed. Bror Danielsson (Stockholm, 1977), p. 40, fol. 37, ll. 13–15.
35. MG, 1909, p. 221.
36. *Ibid.*, p. 181.
37. H & H, p. 111.
38. Dalby, p. xviii.
39. *Ibid.*, p. xviii.
40. Oxford, Bodleian Library, MS Bodley 264, fol. 81v.
41. Madrid, Museo del Prado, *Garden of Earthly Delights*.
42. Madrid, Museo del Prado and Madrid, Monasterio de san Lorenzo, El Escorial: *Haywain*.
43. Christa Grössinger, *The World Upside-Down, English Misericords* (London, 1997), text, p. 85 and plate p. 66.
44. Rackham, *History of the Countryside*, p. 34.
45. MG, 1909, p. xxi.
46. Ldc, Tilander, p. 83, fol. 15v, ll. 2–3; p. 85, fol. 15v, l. 5.
47. *Ibid.*, p. 23.
48. H & H, p. 121.
49. Neiderwolfsgruber, *Kaiser Maximilians I. Jagd und Fischereibücher* pp. 35–6.
50. W.A. Baillie-Grohman, 'Ancient Weapons of the Chase', *Burlington Magazine*, 1904, Vol. IV, p. 158.
51. Dalby, p. xvii.
52. London, British Library, MS Egerton 1146: Calendar for October, fol. 11v; fol. 20r.
53. H & H, pp. 136–7.
54. Ldc, 616, Ch. 10, fol. 31v.
55. H & H, pp. 132 and 135.
56. *Ibid.*, p. 138.
57. Barnes, *The Boke of Huntyng*, ed. Tilander, p. 22, l. 8.
58. H & H, p. 136 and pp. 138–40.
59. Dalby, p. xviii.
60. London, British Library, MS Egerton 1146, Calendar for February, fol. 3v.
61. H.W.C. Davis, *Mediaeval England* (Oxford, 1924), p. 339.
62. Rackham, *History of the Countryside*, p. 35.
63. Edmund Bogg, *Regal Richmond, and the Land of the Swale* (Leeds, 1909), pp. 234 and 233.

64. Rackham, *History of the Countryside*, pp. 35–6.
65. Davis, *Mediaeval England*, p. 339.
66. Nicholas Orme, *From Childhood to Chivalry* (London, 1984), p. 194. See *Sir Gawain and the Green Knight* trans. Brian Stone (Harmondsworth, 1959; repr. 1974), ll. 1133–1923, passim. Stag: pp. 48, 49, 53 and 54. Boar: pp. 56, 57, 60, 61 and 62. Fox: pp. 64, 65 and 70. Also see M.Y. Offord (ed.), *The Parlement of the Thre Ages*, Early English Text Society, No. 246 (London, 1959; repr. 1967), ll. 21–96.
67. A.C. Spearing, *The Gawain-Poet, A Critical Study* (Cambridge, 1970), p. 9.
68. *Ibid.*, p. 10.
69. Dalby, p. x.
70. Ldc, 616: Hart: Ch. 45, fol. 77; Hare: Ch. 50, fol. 89v.
71. Modus, Tilander, pp. 67, 69 and 72; cf. Ldc, Tilander, pp. 193, 216 and 221.
72. Dalby, p. xi.
73. Marcelle Thiébaux, *The Stag of Love: The Chase in Medieval Literature* (Ithaca and London, 1974), pp. 28–40; Dalby, pp. x–xv.
74. MG, 1909, pp. 209–10. Fumes and fewmets are obsolete terms for the droppings of deer, the terms being derived from the French word *fumées*. Gaston de Foix and Edward of York differ in their nomenclature for the droppings of different quarry.
75. Twiti, *The Art of Hunting: 1327*, p. 48, fol. 38v, ll. 17–21 and 23.
76. A similar practice is employed by matadors to despatch bulls in modern bullfighting.
77. *Tristan*, p. 78.
78. *Ibid.*, pp. 79–80.
79. H & H, p. 43.
80. Rooney (ed.), *The Tretyse off Huntyng*, p. 16.
81. Reader's Digest, *Universal Dictionary* (London, 1987), p. 536.
82. *Tristan*, pp. 79 and 80.
83. Richard Almond and A.J. Pollard, 'The Yeomanry of Robin Hood and Social Terminology in Fifteenth-Century England', *Past & Present*, No. 171, February 2001.
84. Ldc, 616, Ch. 40, fol. 70.
85. Rooney (ed.), *The Tretyse off Huntyng*, p. 56, ll. 237–43.
86. *Tristan*, p. 81.
87. BSA, facsimile edn, fol. iiir.
88. Rooney (ed.), *The Tretyse off Huntyng*, p. 50, ll. 106–16.
89. *Ibid.*, p. 55, ll. 225–34.
90. MG, 1909, p. 208.
91. H & H, p. 44: also Dalby, p. 12 (iii) 'feeding hounds with bread, mixed with the blood and flesh of the quarry they were to hunt'.

92. Ldc, Tilander, pp. 181–3, fol. 54v., ll. 1–20; MG, 1909, pp. 196–7.
93. MG, 1909, p. 209.
94. Ldc, 616, C. 41, fol. 72; London, British Library, MS Egerton 1146, Calendar for August, fol. 9v.
95. *Tristan*, p. 81.
96. Dalby, pp. xiv–xv.
97. *Tristan*, p. 11.
98. MG, 1909, pp. 176–7.
99. *Ibid.*, pp. 175 and 197.
100. Rooney (ed.), *The Tretyse off Huntyng*, pp. 15 and 16.
101. MG, 1904, pp. 110–11.
102. For a splendid fictional account of drift-hunting in the New Forest, firmly based upon sound research, see Edward Rutherfurd, *The Forest* (London, 2000), pp. 5–92.
103. Twiti, *The Art of Hunting: 1327*, p. 48, fol. 38v, ll. 29–31.
104. *Ibid.*, p. 50, fol. 38v, ll. 34–7.
105. *Ibid.*, p. 51.
106. MG, 1909, p. 197.
107. *Ibid.*, p. 263.
108. A.R. Myers (ed.), *The Household of Edward IV* (Manchester, 1959), p. 113. Both the *Black Book* and *The Master of Game* use the word 'yeoman' in English and the fifteenth-century hunting books use this term consistently to mean the professional hunt and Forest officials.
109. MG, 1909, pp. 188–9 and p. 259.
110. *Ibid.*, p. 263.
111. *Sir Gawain and the Green Knight*, trans. Brian Stone (Harmondsworth, 1959; 2nd edn, 1974), Fit III, 46, p. 64.
112. *Ibid.*, 47, p. 65.
113. 'The Book of the Duchesse', in *The Complete Works of Geoffrey Chaucer*, 2nd edn, ed. Walter W. Skeat, 7 vols (Oxford, 1894–1900), I, 287–93, II. 291–475.
114. Vienna, Kunsthistorisches Museum, *The Stag Hunt of the Elector Frederick the Wise; The Stag Hunt for the Emperor Charles V at the Castle of Torgau*.
115. Pisanello, p. 83.
116. Italy, Siena, Collezione Monte dei Paschi, *Bullfighting and Other Games in the Piazza del Campo, Siena*.
117. BSA, facsimile edn. fol. ii(r).
118. MG, 1909, p. 210.
119. C.J. Cornish, *Wild England of Today* (London, 1895), p. 157.
120. MG, 1909, pp. 253–7.
121. Dalby, p. xliii.

122. London, British Library, MS Egerton 1146, Calendar for May, fol. 6v.
123. Birrell, pp. 71–4.

Chapter Four

1. H & H, p. 234.
2. Kurt G. Blüchel, *Game and Hunting* (Cologne, 1997), p. 118.
3. Janet Backhouse, *The Luttrell Psalter* (London, 1989), p. 48.
4. *Ibid.*, p. 14.
5. Birrell, p. 87.
6. Nicholas Orme, *Medieval Children* (New Haven and London, 2001 repr. 2002), p. 182.
7. MG, 1904, p. 14.
8. Ldc, Tilander, p. 259, fol. 87, !. 9.
9. *Ibid.*, p. 251, fol. 83, ll. 18–19:

   et est droitement deduit d'omme gros ou d'omme vieill ou d'un prelat ou d'omme qui ne veult travaillier . . . mes non pas pour homme qui veult chascier par mestrise et par droyte venerie.

10. Edith Rickert, *The Babees' Book: Medieval Manners for the Young: Done into Modern English from Dr. Furnivall's Texts* (London, 1923).
11. H & H, p. 234.
12. Maurice Keen, *The Outlaws of Medieval Legend* (London, 1977), p. 166; extract from *Knighton's Chronicle*.
13. *Ibid.*, p. 166.
14. Roger B. Manning, *Hunters and Poachers* (Oxford, 1993), p. 17.
15. A.R. Myers (ed.), *English Historical Documents, 1327–1485* (London, 1969), p. 1004 569, 'The lower orders are not to be allowed to hunt, 1390'.
16. Nicholas Orme, *From Childhood to Chivalry* (London, 1984), pp. 191–2.
17. A.R. Myers (ed.), *English Historical Documents, 1327–1485* p. 1004 569.
18. A.J. Pollard, *Late Medieval England 1399–1509* (Harlow, 2000), p. 186.
19. The author is grateful to Professor Anthony J. Pollard for access to, and use of, his unpublished conference paper 'The 1390 Game Law'.
20. Myers (ed.), *English Historical Documents, 1327–1485* (London, 1969), pp. 1153 and 1178.
21. Pollard, *Late Medieval England 1399–1509*, p. 189.
22. Maurice Keen, *English Society in the Later Middle Ages 1348–1500* (London, 1990), p. 15.
23. R. Trevor Davies, *Documents Illustrating the History of Civilisation in Medieval England (1066–1500)* (New York and London, 1926; repr. 1969), p. 147.

24. H & H, p. 234.
25. Rose-Marie and Rainer Hagen, *15th Century Paintings* (Cologne, 2001), p. 25.
26. Compton Reeves, 'The Sumptuary Statute of 1363: A look at the aims and effectiveness of English legislation on diet and clothing', *Medieval Life*, Issue 16, Winter 2001/2 (Gilling East, York), p. 18.
27. Frederick II of Hohenstaufen, *The Art of Falconry*, trans. and ed. Casey A. Wood and F. Marjorie Fyfe (Stanford, 1943; repr. 1955), p. 280.
28. H & H, p. 178.
29. William Twiti, *The Art of Hunting, 1327*, ed. Bror Danielsson (Stockholm, 1977), text, p. 22; see plates 1, 2, 3, 5, 10, 11, 15, 17, 21, 22 after p. 116.
30. London, British Library, *Queen Mary's Psalter*, MS Royal 2. B. VII, fol. 112.
31. Blüchel, *Game and Hunting*, p. 220.
32. Maurice Keen, *The Outlaws of Medieval Legend* (London, 1977), p. 2.
33. Ldc, 616, Ch. 40, fol. 70.
34. Richard Almond and A.J. Pollard, 'The Yeomanry of Robin Hood and Social Terminology in Fifteenth-Century England', *Past & Present*, No. 170, February 2001, pp. 63–4.
35. PTA, p. 5, I, l. 122.
36. *Ibid.*, p. 7, VI, l. 194.
37. John Spiers, *Medieval English Poetry, The Non-Chaucerian Tradition* (London, 1957), p. 290; Marcelle Thiébaux, *The Stag of Love*, (Ithaca and London, 1974), p. 22.
38. PTA, p. 1, Prologue, l. 22.
39. Ldc, 616, Ch. 73, fol. 114.
40. *Ibid.*, Ch. 76, fol. 115v; Marcel Thomas, and François Avril, *The Hunting Book of Gaston Phébus* (London, 1998), p. 70.
41. Manning, *Hunters and Poachers*, p. 26.
42. H & H, p. 179.
43. *Ibid.*, p. 136.
44. MG, 1909, pp. 64–7.
45. London, British Library, *The Luttrell Psalter*, Add. MS 42130, fol. 64v.
46. Modus, Tilander: pp. 69–71; pp. 162–3.
47. MG, 1904, p. 148.
48. *Ibid.*
49. MG, 1909, p. 222.
50. François Villon, *Selected Poems*, trans. Peter Dale (London, 1978; repr. 1988), 'The Testament', stanza 110, p. 125.
51. Ldc, 616, Ch. 81.
52. *Ibid.*, Hare driving with bells, Ch. 82, fol. 119; Netting hares in their muses, Ch. 81, fol. 118v.
53. Modus, Tilander, fol. 51v.

54. Ldc, 616: making nets and snares, Ch. 25, fol. 53v; netting large game, Ch. 60, fol. 103; netting rabbits, Ch. 51, fol. 92.
55. London, British Library, MS Egerton 1146, Calendar for April, fol. 5v.
56. Dalby, p. xiii.
57. *Ibid.*
58. Manning, *Hunters and Poachers*, p. 25.
59. Modus, Tilander, fol. 53.
60. London, British Library, *Queen Mary's Psalter*, Royal MS 2. B. VII, fol. 112.
61. Modus, Tilander, fol. 97.
62. J.E. Hodgson (ed.), *Percy Bailiff's Rolls of the Fifteenth Century*, Surtees Society, 134 (Durham, 1921), p. 115.
63. *Ibid.*, p. 69.
64. Modus, Tilander, fol. 93; H & H, p. 245.
65. London, British Library, *The Luttrell Psalter*, Add. MS 42130, fol. 63.
66. Modus, Tilander, fol. 93v.
67. *Ibid.*, fol. 96v.
68. John of Salisbury, *Policraticus*, ed. Joseph B. Pike (London, 1938), p. 22.
69. Modus, Tilander, fol. 95.
70. New York, Pierpont Morgan Library, MS M 945, fol. 107r.
71. John of Salisbury, *Policraticus*, ed. Joseph B. Pike (London, 1938), p. 22.
72. Manning, *Hunters and Poachers*, p. 76.
73. P.R. Coss, 'Aspects of Cultural Diffusion in Medieval England: The Early Romances, Local Society and Robin Hood', *Past & Present*, No. 108, August 1985, pp. 75–6.
74. Rose-Marie and Rainer Hagen, *16th Century Paintings* (Cologne, 2001), p. 82.
75. Modus, Tilander, fol. 90v.
76. H & H, p. 244.
77. Modus, Tilander, fol. 85.
78. Oliver Rackham, *The History of the Countryside* (London, 1986; repr. 1993), p. 50.
79. London, British Library, MS Egerton 1146, fol. 23v.
80. *Ibid.*, fol. 161v.
81. Thomas and Avril, *The Hunting Book of Gaston Phébus*, p. 65.
82. Ldc, 616, Ch. 67, fol. 109.
83. H & H, p. 241.
84. Ldc, 616, Ch. 63, fol. 107.
85. *Ibid.*, Ch. 61, fol. 105v.
86. H & H, p. 241; Ldc, 616, Ch. 62, fol. 106v.
87. London, British Library, MS Egerton 1146, Calendar for November, fol. 12v.
88. London, British Library, *Queen Mary's Psalter*, Royal MS 2. B. VII, fol. 155v.

89. Mark Bailey, *A Marginal Economy? East Anglian Breckland in the Later Middle Ages* (Cambridge, 1989), pp. 185 and 18.
90. MG, 1904, pp. 125 and 41.
91. Bailey, *A Marginal Economy?*, pp. 130–1.
92. London, British Library, *The Luttrell Psalter*, Add. MS 42130, fol. 176v.
93. Glasgow, Burrell Collection, Burgundian tapestry, *Peasants Ferreting*.
94. Ldc, 616, Ch. 7, fol. 26v; also Thomas and Avril, *The Hunting Book of Gaston Phébus*, p. 25.
95. Ldc, 616, Ch. 52, fol. 92; also Thomas, and Avril, *The Hunting Book of Gaston Phébus*, pp. 55–6.
96. Christa Grössinger, *The World Upside-Down, English Misericords* (London, 1997), pp. 165 and 167.
97. *Ibid.*, p. 166.
98. *Ibid.*, p. 164.
99. *Ibid.*, p. 167.
100. *Ibid.*, p. 166.
101. Vienna, Kunsthistorisches Museum, *The Hunters in the Snow*.
102. Penelope Le Fanu Hughes, *Bruegel* (Royston, 2002), p. 44.
103. *Ibid.*
104. *Ibid.*, p. 54.
105. Ldc, Tilander, p. 258, fol. 85v, l. 11.
106. H & H, p. 247.
107. W.A. Baillie-Grohman, *The Land in the Mountains* (London, 1907), p. 249.

Chapter Five

1. P.R. Coss, 'Aspects of Cultural Diffusion in Medieval England: The Early Romances, Local Society and Robin Hood', *Past & Present*, No. 108, August 1985, p. 75.
2. Roger B. Manning, *Hunters and Poachers* (Oxford, 1993), p. 18.
3. Coss, 'Aspects of Cultural Diffusion in Medieval England', p. 75. Thanks to Professor A.J. Pollard for pointing out that this comment has a specific late fourteenth-century context.
4. London, British Library, MS Egerton 1146: Calendar pictures for April, fol. 5v; July, fol. 8v; August, fol. 9v; December, fol. 13v.
5. A.C. Spearing, *The Gawain Poet: A Critical Study* (Cambridge, 1970), pp. 9–10.
6. MG, 1904, p. 69.
7. MG, 1909, p. 176.
8. H & H, pp. 185 and 217.
9. Frederick II of Hohenstaufen, *The Art of Falconry*, trans. and ed. Casey A. Wood and F. Marjorie Fyfe (Stanford, 1943, repr. 1955), pp. 152–3.

10. *Ibid.*, p. xli.
11. *Ibid.*, p. xlii; also see H & H, p. 219.
12. H & H, p. 217.
13. H.W.C. Davis (ed.), *Mediaeval England* (Oxford, 1924), p. 338.
14. Phillip Glasier, *As the Falcon her Bells* (London, 1963), p. 217; also see H & H, pp. 193 and 194.
15. H & H, Appendix V, pp. 269–70.
16. *Ibid.*, p. 174.
17. MG, 1904, pp. 161–2.
18. Pisanello, p. 83.
19. H & H, pp. 218–19.
20. *Ibid.*, p. 173.
21. Pisanello, p. 163.
22. William Twiti, *The Art of Hunting, 1327*, ed. Bror Danielsson (Stockholm, 1977), pp. 33–4.
23. H & H, p. 185.
24. *Ibid.*, p. 270.
25. *Ibid.*, p. 185.
26. MG, 1904, p. 102.
27. Gervaise, Rosser, 'Going to the Fraternity Feast: Commensuality and Social Relations in Late Medieval England', *Journal of British Studies*, 33, 1994.
28. A.J. Pollard, 'Fellowship and Fraternity in the Early Stories of Robin Hood'. Seminar delivered to the Late Medieval Political Group, York Seminars, at the Centre for Medieval Studies, University of York, 3 December 2001. These ideas will be more fully set forward in Professor Pollard's forthcoming study of the Robin Hood stories, to be published by Routledge.
29. Manning, *Hunters and Poachers*, p. 235.
30. *Ibid.*, pp. 20–1.
31. Scotto Sisters [text by Annie Hubert-Bare], *The Heritage of French Cooking* (London, 1991, edn 1993), p. 19.
32. H & H, p. 218.
33. Chantilly, Musée Condé, *Très Riches Heures du Duc de Berri*, MS 65, Calendar for August, fol. 8v.
34. H & H, p. 172.
35. Maurice Keen, *The Outlaws of Medieval Legend* (London, 1977), p. 166.
36. *Ibid.*, p. 2.
37. Manning, *Hunters and Poachers*, p. 169.
38. Birrell, p. 85.
39. *Ibid.*, p. 68.
40. *Ibid.*, p. 69.
41. *Ibid.*, p. 74.

Notes

42. *Ibid.*, p. 75; H & H, p. 53. In practice, a longbow arrow or crossbow bolt would rarely kill a deer or other large beast outright. Such projectiles cause massive damage and bleeding which slows and eventually brings down the quarry, which is why a steady, trained dog was essential to legitimate hunters and poachers alike.
43. *Ibid.*, pp. 71–5.
44. *Ibid.*, p. 86.
45. *Ibid.*, p. 88.
46. *Ibid.*, p. 87.
47. Marcelle Thiébaux, *The Stag of Love* (Ithaca and London, 1974), p. 22.
48. John Spiers, *Medieval English Poetry, The Non-Chaucerian Tradition* (London, 1957), p. 290.
49. PTA, p. 1, Prologue, ll. 3–5.
50. *Ibid.*, p. 1, Prologue, l. 22.
51. *Ibid.*, p. 2, Prologue, ll. 40–4.
52. *Ibid.*, p. 2, Prologue, ll. 47–50.
53. *Ibid.*, p. 3, Prologue, ll. 66–89.
54. PTA, p. 3, Prologue, l. 80.
55. Barcelets: see Anne Rooney (ed.), *The Tretyse off Huntyng*, Scripta 19, Mediaeval and Renaissance Texts and Studies (Brussels, 1987), pp. 51–2, ll. 145–9, and p. 78. Forest records, see Birrell, p. 76.
56. PTA, p. 4, Prologue, ll. 92–6.
57. John Bellamy, *Crime and Public Order in England in the Later Middle Ages* (London and Toronto, 1973), p. 75.
58. John M. Gilbert, *Hunting and Hunting Reserves in Medieval Scotland* (Edinburgh, 1979), p. 57.
59. Birrell, p. 88.
60. Charles Lethbridge Kingsford (ed.), *The Stonor Letters and Papers 1290–1483*, Camden Society, 3rd series, Vol. XXIX, Vol. 1 (London, 1919), p. xxx.
61. *Ibid.*, Vol. XXX, Vol. II, pp. 150–51 319.
62. *Ibid.*, Vol. XXIX, Vol. 1 (London, 1919), p. xxx.
63. Charles R. Young, *The Royal Forests of Medieval England* (Leicester, 1979), p. 106.
64. Ralph Whitlock, *Historic Forests of England* (Bradford-on-Avon, 1979), p. 23.
65. Manning, *Hunters and Poachers*, pp. 36–7 and 41.
66. *Ibid.*, p. 35.
67. *Ibid.*, p. 235.
68. MG, 1904, pp. 203 and 204.
69. H & H, p. 61.

70. Maurice Keen, *English Society in the Later Middle Ages 1348–1500* (London, 1990), p. 14.

71. S.J.A. Evans, *Ely Chapter Ordinances and Visitation Record: 1241–1515*; *Ordinances of the Prior and Chapter 1314*, Camden Miscellany, 1940, p. 42:

Item ordinatum est quod nullus fratrum leporarios uel aues rapaces, infra scepta monasterii vel alibi in villa, absque licencia prioris optenta per se teneat, per aliumve aut presumat retinere; et hoc idem de quocumque infra curiam monasterii quoquomodo famulante statutum est obseruari.

72. Geoffrey Chaucer, *The Prologue to the Canterbury Tales*, ed. Stephen Coote (Harmondsworth, 1985; repr. 1986), p. 66, ll. 165–8.

73. *Ibid.*, p. 66, ll. 172–6.

74. *Ibid.*, p. 68, ll. 177–87.

75. *Ibid.*, p. 68, ll. 188–91.

76. Young, *Royal Forests of Medieval England*, pp. 166–7.

77. R. Trevor Davies, *Documents Illustrating the History of Civilisation in Medieval England (1066–1500)* (London, 1926; repr. 1969), p. 147.

78. Gilbert, *Hunting and Hunting Reserves in Medieval Scotland*, p. 142.

79. *Ibid.*, p. 99.

80. Mark Bailey, *A Marginal Economy? East Anglian Breckland in the Later Middle Ages* (Cambridge, 1989), p. 184.

81. Gilbert, *Hunting and Hunting Reserves in Medieval Scotland*, p. 213.

82. Bailey, *A Marginal Economy?*, pp. 185–6.

83. Manning, *Hunters and Poachers*, p. 163.

84. Birrell, p. 87.

85. Bellamy, *Crime and Public Order in England*, p. 78.

86. *Ibid.*, p. 80.

87. *Ibid.*, p. 72.

88. *Ibid.*, pp. 80 and 72.

89. *Ibid.*, p. 72.

90. *Ibid.*, p. 80.

91. *Ibid.*, pp. 80–1.

92. MG, 1904, p. 204.

93. John of Salisbury, *Policraticus*, Bk I, ed. Joseph B. Pike (London, 1938), p. 22.

94. MG, 1904, pp. 138 and 203.

95. Davies, *Documents Illustrating the History of Civilisation in Medieval England (1066–1500)*, p. 26.

96. MG, 1904, p. 138.

97. Harry Rothwell (ed.), *English Historical Documents 1189–1327* (London, 1975), pp. 321 48.

98. MG, 1904, pp. 203–4.

99. *Ibid.*, pp. 138 and 204.

100. Manning, *Hunters and Poachers*, p. 57.

101. The author is grateful to Professor Anthony J. Pollard for access to, and use of, his unpublished conference paper 'The 1390 Game Law'.

102. *Ibid.*, p. 64.

103. *Ibid.*, pp. 57–8.

104. *Ibid.*, p. 64.

105. *Ibid.*, p. 58.

106. Pisanello, p. 80.

107. Rose-Marie and Rainer Hagen, *16th Century Paintings* (Cologne, 2001), pp. 81–2.

Chapter Six

1. P.J.P. Goldberg, 'Women in fifteenth century town life', in J.A.F. Thomson (ed.), *Towns and Townspeople in the Fifteenth Century* (Gloucester, 1988).

2. Compton Reeves, 'The Sumptuary Statute of 1363: A look at the aims and effectiveness of English legislation on diet and clothing', *Medieval Life*, Issue 16, Winter 2001/2 (Gilling East, York), p. 17.

3. H & H, p. 8.

4. Veronica Sekules, 'Women and Art in England in the Thirteenth and Fourteenth Centuries', J. Alexander and Paul Binski (eds), *Age of Chivalry* (London, 1987), p. 47.

5. Sir George Warner, *Queen Mary's Psalter* (London, 1912), p. 39, plate 216a, fol. 197.

6. François R. Velde, 'Women Knights in the Middle Ages', http://128.220.1.164/heraldry/topics/orders//wom-kn.htm

7. Oxford, Bodleian Library, MS Bodley 264, fol. 81v.

8. Christa Grössinger, *The World Upside-Down, English Misericords* (London, 1997), pp. 85 and 93.

9. H & H, pp. 116–17.

10. For discussions on history and beliefs of hare gender, see MG, 1909, pp. 219–20, and H & H, pp. 110–11.

11. *Reader's Digest Universal Dictionary* (London, 1987), p. 1250.

12. H & H, p. 117.

13. Linda Colley, *Britons, Forging the Nation 1707–1837* (New Haven and London, 1992), p. 172.

14. London, British Library, Add. MS 16, fol. 165.

15. H & H, p. 249; MG, 1909, p. 200.

16. Nicholas Orme, *From Childhood to Chivalry* (London, 1984), p. 195.

17. BSA, facsimile edn, pp. 11, 14 and 7. Rachel Hands has cast doubt on the

authenticity of Juliana's authorship. See 'Juliana Berners and *The Boke of St. Albans*', *Review of English Studies* 18 (1967), pp. 373–86.

18. BSA, facsimile edn, p. 7.

19. *Ibid.*, p. 24.

20. Maurice Keen, *English Society in the Later Middle Ages 1348–1500* (London, 1990), p. 185.

21. Geoffrey Chaucer, *The Canterbury Tales*, trans. Nevill Coghill (London, 1951; repr. 1977), p. 64 ff.

22. Catherine Lafarge, 'The hand of the huntress: repetition and Malory's Morte Darthur', in Isobel Armstrong (ed.), *New Feminist Discourses* (London, 1995), p. 263.

23. Dalby, p. xix.

24. Oliver Rackham, *The History of the Countryside* (London, 1986, repr. 1993), p. 125.

25. H & H, p. 7.

26. Pisanello, p. 83.

27. Dr Franz Neiderwolfsgruber (text), *Kaiser Maximilians I. Jagd und Fischereibücher* (Innsbruck, 1965, edn. 1992), plate opp. p. 8.

28. Ann Claxton, 'The Sign of the Dog, an Examination of the Devonshire Hunting Tapestries', *Journal of Medieval History*, 14 (1988), pp. 127–79.

29. H & H, p. 7.

30. Paris, Musée de Louvre, *Les Chasses de Maximilien*, tapestries for April and September.

31. W.A. Baillie-Grohman, *Sport in Art* (London, 1913; reissued London and New York, 1969), pp. 163–4 and fig. 104, p. 167.

32. Paris, Bibliothèque nationale, *The Hours of Marguerite D'Orléans*, MS Lat. 1156B, 'The Trinity', fol. 163.

33. H & H, p. 180.

34. Roger B. Manning, *Hunters and Hunting* (Oxford, 1993), p. 40.

35. *Ibid.*, p. 27.

36. H.L. Blackmore, *Hunting Weapons* (New York, 1972), p. 59.

37. H & H, p. 81; see also R.E. Latham, *Revised Medieval Latin Word-List from British and Irish Sources* (Oxford, 1965; repr. 1989), pp. 506–7.

38. London, Victoria and Albert Museum, Tapestry 4, *The Deer Hunt*.

39. H & H, p. 8.

40. Paris, Musée du Louvre, *Les Chasses de Maximilien*, tapestry for May.

41. Sekules, 'Women and Art in England in the Thirteenth and Fourteenth Centuries', p. 47.

42. Glasgow, Burrell Collection, tapestry *The Pursuit of Fidelity*.

43. H & H, p. 79.

44. *Ibid.*, pp. 80–1.

45.   Anne Payne, *Medieval Beasts* (London, 1990), p. 27; London, British Library, *Queen Mary's Psalter*, MS Royal 2 B.VII, fol. 100v.

46.   H & H, p. 154.

47.   *Ibid.*, p. 153.

48.   London, British Library, MS Royal 12 F. xiii, fol. 10v.

49.   New York, Cloisters Museum, *The Unicorn Tapestries*, 5 and 6.

50.   Cambridge, Trinity College, Wren Library, R. 14. 9. fol. 90v.

51.   Anne Payne, *Medieval Beasts*, p. 27.

52.   John M. Gilbert, *Hunting and Hunting Reserves in Medieval Scotland* (Edinburgh, 1979), p. 52.

53.   MG, 1909, p. 260.

54.   Manning, *Hunters and Poachers*, plate 4, p. 148.

55.   Vienna, Kunsthistorisches Museum, *The Stag Hunt Given by the Elector John Frederick of Saxony for Emperor Charles V at the Castle of Torgau.*

56.   Rose-Marie and Rainer Hagen, *16th Century Paintings*, p. 81.

57.   *Ibid.*, p. 86.

58.   R.W. Seton-Watson, *Maximilian I* (London, 1902), p. 14.

59.   Jacques de Brézé, *La Chasse*, ed. Gunnar Tilander, Cynegetica VI (Lund 1959), pp. 36, 39, 43 and 45.

60.   Eileen Power, *Medieval Women* (Cambridge, 1975; repr. 1997), pp. 68–9.

61.   *Ibid.*, p. 70; notes p. 95.

62.   Chantilly, Musée Condé, MS XVI B, fol. 1v.

63.   London, British Library, *Queen Mary's Psalter*, Royal MS 2 B. VII, fols 151, 177v and 178.

64.   The archaic term 'gobbet' has recently been adopted by the IT profession to mean a small piece of electronic text.

65.   London, British Library, *The Taymouth Hours*, MS Yates Thompson 13, fols 72v–75v.

66.   Francisco Sauer and Joseph Stummvol (eds), *Tacuinum Sanitatis in Medicina. Codices Selecti,* Vol. VI–VI*, English transcription by Heide Saxer and Charles H. Talbot (Graz, 1967), fol. 67v.

67.   J.J.G. Alexander [text], *The Master of Mary of Burgundy. A Book of Hours for Engelbert of Nassau* (New York, 1970), pp. 41–58; Oxford, Bodleian Library, MS Douce 219–20, fols 47–68v.

68.   Paris, Archives Nationale.

69.   Warner (ed.), *Queen Mary's Psalter*, pp. 1 and 4.

70.   *Ibid.*, p. 8.

71.   London, British Library, *Queen Mary's Psalter*, Royal MS 2 B. VII, fols 152 and 153; fols 155v and 156.

72.   Mark Bailey, *A Marginal Economy? East Anglian Breckland in the Later Middle Ages* (Cambridge, 1989), pp. 129 and 131.

73. H.Y. Thompson, *Illustrations from One Hundred Manuscripts in the Library of Henry Yates Thompson*, Vol. 4 (London, 1914), p. 31.

74. Lucy Freeman Sandler, *Gothic Manuscripts 1285–1385* (London, 1986), pp. 107–9.

75. Thompson, *Illustrations from One Hundred Manuscripts*, p. 31.

76. London, British Library, *The Taymouth Hours*, MS Yates Thompson 13, fols 68–83v.

77. Pisanello, p. 80.

78. Ldc, Tilander, p. 269, fol. 20, ll. 2–4.

79. H & H, p. 31.

80. Latham, *Revised Medieval Latin Word-List*, p. 273.

81. Nancy Mitford, *The Sun King* (London, 1966), p. 50.

82. Andrew Wheatcroft, *The Habsburgs* (London, 1995; repr. 1996), p. 275.

83. *The Field*, March 1996, p. 114.

84. Glasgow, Burrell Collection, Burgundian Tapestry, *Peasants Ferreting*.

85. Birrell, p. 79.

86. *Ibid.*, p. 85.

Chapter Seven

1. Birrell, p. 76.

2. The author is grateful to Professor Anthony J. Pollard for access to, and use of, his unpublished conference paper 'The 1390 Game Law'.

3. Paris, Bibliothèque nationale, *The Hours of Marguerite D'Orléans*, MS Lat. 1156B, 'The Trinity', fol. 163.

4. London, British Library, MS Egerton 1146, Calendar for June, fol. 7v.

5. Ernest Hemingway, *True at First Light* (London, 1999), p. 156.

Bibliography

Manuscript Sources

Cambridge, Trinity College, Wren Library, R. 14. 9.
Chantilly, Musée Condé, MS XVI B.
Chantilly, Musée Condé, *Très Riches Heures du Duc de Berri*, MS 65.
London, British Library, Add. MS 16.
London, British Library, *The Luttrell Psalter*, Add. MS 42130.
London, British Library, MS Egerton 1146.
London, British Library, *Queen Mary's Psalter*, Royal MS 2 B. VII.
London, British Library, MS Royal 12 F. xiii.
London, British Library, *The Taymouth Hours*, MS Yates Thompson 13.
Neuenstein, Hohenloheschen Zentral-Archivs, *Die Hohenloheschen Handschrift*,
  Nr.W.5.
New York, Pierpont Morgan Library, MS M. 945.
New York, Pierpont Morgan Library, *Livre de la chasse*, MS M. 1044.
New York, Pierpont Morgan Library, *Le Livre du roy Modus et de la royne Ratio*.
Oxford, Bodleian Library, MS Bodley 264.
Oxford, Bodleian Library, MS Douce 62.
Oxford, Bodleian Library, MS Douce 219–220.
Paris, Bibliothèque nationale, *Livre de chasse*, MS fr. 616.
Paris, Bibliothèque nationale, *The Hours of Marguerite D'Orléans*, MS Lat. 1156B.

Printed Sources

Alexander, J.J.G. [text], *The Master of Mary of Burgundy. A Book of Hours for
  Engelbert of Nassau* (New York, 1970).
Almond, Richard, and Pollard, A.J., 'The Yeomanry of Robin Hood and Social
  Terminology in Fifteenth-Century England', *Past and Present*, No. 170, February
  2001.
Backhouse, Janet, *The Luttrell Psalter* (London, 1989).
Bailey, Mark, *A Marginal Economy? East Anglian Breckland in the Later Middle
  Ages* (Cambridge, 1989).
Baillie-Grohman, W.A., 'Ancient Weapons of the Chase', *Burlington Magazine*,
  1904, Vol. IV.
——, *The Land in the Mountains* (London, 1907).

——, *Sport in Art* (London, 1913; reissued London and New York, 1969).

Balis, Arnout, De Jonge, Krista, Delmarcel, Guy and Lefébure, Amaury, *Les Chasses de Maximilien* (Paris, 1993).

Barnes, Julians, *Boke of Huntyng*, ed. Gunnar Tilander, *Cynegetica* XI (Karlshamn, 1964).

Bartlett, J.N., 'The Expansion and Decline of York in the Later Middle Ages', *Economic History Review*, 2nd series, Vol. XII, 1959–60.

Bellamy, John, *Crime and Public Order in England in the Later Middle Ages* (London and Toronto, 1973).

Berners, Dame Juliana, *The Boke of Saint Albans, 1486*, facsimile edition (London, 1899).

Birrell, Jean, 'Peasant deer poachers in the medieval forest', in Richard Britnell and John Hatcher (eds), *Progress and Problems in Medieval England* (Cambridge, 1996).

Blackmore, H.L., *Hunting Weapon* (New York, 1972).

Blüchel, Kurt G., *Game and Hunting* (Cologne, 1997; English edn, 2000).

Bogg, Edmund, *Regal Richmond and the Land of the Swale* (Leeds, 1909).

Brewer, Derek, *Chaucer in his Time* (London, 1963).

Brézé, Jacques de, *La Chasse*, ed. Gunnar Tilander, *Cynegetica* VI (Lund 1959).

Burrow, J.A. (ed.)., *Sir Gawain and the Green Knight* (Harmondsworth and London, 1972).

Camille, Michael, *The Medieval Art of Love* (London, 1998).

Chaucer, Geoffrey, *The Canterbury Tales*, trans. Nevill Coghill (London, 1951; repr. 1977).

——. *The Prologue to the Canterbury Tales*, ed. Stephen Coote (Harmondsworth, 1985; repr. 1986).

Claxton, Ann, 'The Sign of the Dog, an Examination of the Devonshire Hunting Tapestries', *Journal of Medieval History* 14 (1988).

Colley, Linda, *Britons, Forging the Nation 1707–1837* (New Haven and London, 1992).

Complete Works of Geoffrey Chaucer, 2nd edn, ed. Walter W. Skeat, 7 vols (Oxford, 1894–1900).

Complete Works of William Shakespeare, Shakespeare Head Press edn (London, 1944).

Contamine, Philippe, *War in the Middle Ages*, trans. Michael Jones (Oxford, 1984).

Cornish, C.J., *Wild England of Today* (London, 1895).

Coss, P.R., 'Aspects of Cultural Diffusion in Medieval England: The Early Romances, Local Society and Robin Hood', *Past & Present*, No. 108, August 1985.

Cummins, John, *The Hound and the Hawk, The Art of Medieval Hunting* (London, 1988).

Dalby, David, *Lexicon of the Mediaeval German Hunt* (Berlin, 1965).

Davies, R. Trevor, *Documents Illustrating the History of Civilisation in Medieval England (1066–1500)* (New York and London, 1926; repr. 1969).

Davis, H.W.C. (ed.), *Mediaeval England* (Oxford, 1924).

Bibliography

Davis, Norman (ed.), *The Paston Letters* (Oxford, 1963, 1983; reissued 1999).

Edward, Duke of York, *The Master of Game*, ed. W.A. and F. Baillie-Grohman (London, 1904).

——, *The Master of Game*, ed. W.A. and F. Baillie-Grohman (London, 1909).

Evans, S.J.A., *Ely Chapter Ordinances and Visitation Record: 1241–1515; Ordinances of the Prior and Chapter 1314*, Camden Miscellany, 1940.

The Field, March 1996.

Frederick II of Hohenstaufen, *The Art of Falconry, being the De Arte Venandi cum Avibus*, trans. and ed. Casey A. Wood and F. Marjorie Fyfe (Stanford, 1943; repr. 1955).

Gilbert, John M., *Hunting and Hunting Reserves in Medieval Scotland* (Edinburgh, 1979).

Glasier, Phillip, *As the Falcon her Bells* (London, 1963).

Goldberg, P.J.P. 'Women in fifteenth-century town life', in J.A.F. Thomson (ed.), *Towns and Townspeople in the Fifteenth Century* (Gloucester, 1988).

Grössinger, Christa, *The World Upside-Down, English Misericords* (London, 1997).

Hagen, Rose-Marie, and Hagen, Rainer, *15th Century Paintings* (Cologne, 2001).

——, *16th Century Paintings* (Cologne, 2001).

Hanham, Alison (ed.), *The Cely Letters 1472–1488* (London, 1975).

Harthan, John, *Books of Hours and their Owners* (London, 1977; repr. 1988).

Heaton, Nancy, *The Language of Hunting* (Knutsford, 1985).

Hemingway, Ernest, *True at First Light* (London, 1999).

Hodgson, J.E. (ed.), 'Percy Bailiff's Rolls of the Fifteenth Century', *Surtees Society 134* (Durham, 1921).

Holy Bible, King James's version.

Hughes, Penelope le Fanu, *Bruegel* (Royston, 2002).

Hyland, Ann, *The Medieval Warhorse: From Byzantium to the Crusades* (London, 1994).

Keen, Maurice, *Chivalry* (New Haven and London, 1984).

——, *English Society in the Later Middle Ages 1348–1500* (London, 1990).

——, *The Outlaws of Medieval Legend* (London, 1977).

Kingsford, Charles Lethbridge (ed.), *The Stonor Letters and Papers, 1290–1483*, Camden Society, 3rd. Series, Vol. XXX, Vol. II, and Vol. XXIX, Vol. I (London, 1919).

Lafarge, Catherine, 'The hand of the huntress: repetition and Malory's Morte Darthur', in Isobel Armstrong (ed.), *New Feminist Discourses* (London, 1995).

Langland, William, *Piers Plowman*, the C-text, ed. Derek Pearsall (London, 1978).

Latham, R.E, *Revised Latin Word-List from British and Irish Sources* (Oxford, 1965; repr. 1989).

Lindner, Kurt (ed.), *Die Lehre von den Zeichen des Hirsches*, Quellen und Studien zur Geschichter der Jagd, III (Berlin, 1956).

MacKinnon, Charles, *The Observer's Book of Heraldry* (London and New York, 1966; repr. 1975).

McKelvie, Colin, *Snipe and Woodcock, Sport and Conservation* (Shrewsbury, 1996).

Manning, Roger B, *Hunters and Poachers* (Oxford, 1993).

Miller, Robert P. (ed.), *Chaucer, Sources and Backgrounds* (Oxford, 1977).

Mitford, Nancy, *The Sun King* (London, 1966).

Myers, A.R. (ed.), *English Historical Documents, 1327–1485* (London, 1969).

——, *The Household of Edward IV* (Manchester, 1959).

Neiderwolfsgruber, Franz, *Kaiser Maximilians I. Jagd und Fischereibücher* (Innsbruck, 1965, rev. edn, 1992).

Offord, M.Y. (ed.), *The Parlement of the Thre Ages*, Early English Text Society, No. 246 (London, 1959; repr. 1967).

Orme, Nicholas, *From Childhood to Chivalry* (London, 1984).

——, *Medieval Children* (New Haven and London, 2001).

Payne, Anne, *Medieval Beasts* (London, 1990).

Phébus, Gaston, *Le Livre de la chasse*, présentation et commentaires de Marcel Thomas (France, 1986).

——, *Livre de chasse*, ed. Gunnar Tilander, *Cynegetica* XVIII (Karlshamn, 1971).

Pollard, A.J., *Late Medieval England 1399–1509* (Harlow, 2000).

Power, Eileen, *Medieval Women* (Cambridge, 1975; repr. 1997).

Puma, *Messe für Jagd, Sport und Freizeit* (Solingen, 2002).

Rackham, Oliver, *The History of the Countryside* (London, 1986; repr. 1993).

Ramsgate, the Benedictine Monks of St Augustine's Abbey, *The Book of Saints* (London, 1942; repr. 1989).

Reader's Digest, *Universal Dictionary* (London, 1987).

Reeves, Compton, 'The Sumptuary Statute of 1363: A look at the aims and effectiveness of English legislation on diet and clothing', *Medieval Life, The Magazine of the Middle Ages*, Issue 16, Winter 2001/2 (Gilling West, York).

Rickert, Edith, *The Babees' Book: Medieval Manners for the Young: Done into Modern English from Dr. Furnivall's Texts* (London, 1923).

Rooney, Anne, 'Hunting in Middle English Literature, 1300–1500', PhD dissertation, Trinity College, Cambridge, 1985.

——, *Hunting in Middle English Literature* (Cambridge, 1993).

—— (ed.), *The Tretyse off Huntyng*, Scripta 19 (Brussels, 1987).

Rosser, Gervaise, 'Going to the Fraternity Feast: Commensuality and Social Relations in Late Medieval England', *Journal of British Studies* 33, 1994.

Rothwell, Harry (ed.), *English Historical Documents 1189–1327* (London, 1975).

Royal Commission on Historical Monuments, England, MCMLXVIII, *An Inventory of Historical Monuments in the County of Cambridge, Volume One: West Cambridgeshire*.

Salisbury, John of, *Policraticus*, Bk 1, trans. Joseph B. Pike (London, 1938).

Sandler, Lucy Freeman, *Gothic Manuscripts 1285–1385* (London, 1986).

Sauer, Francisco, and Stummvoll, Joseph (eds), *Tacuinum Sanitatis in Medicina. Codices Selecti, Vols VI–VI**, English transcription by Heide Saxer and Charles H. Talbot (Graz, 1967).

Saul, Nigel, *Knights and Esquires: The Gloucestershire Gentry in the Fourteenth Century* (Oxford, 1981).

Savage, H.L., 'Hunting in the Middle Ages', *Speculum*, Vol. 8 (1933).

Bibliography

——, 'The Significance of the Hunting Scenes in Sir Gawain and the Green Knight', *Journal of English and Germanic Philology*, Vol. 27 (1928).

Scotto Sisters [text by Annie Hubert-Bare], *The Heritage of French Cooking* (London, 1991; edn 1993).

Sekules, Veronica, 'Women and Art in England in the Thirteenth and Fourteenth Centuries', in J. Alexander and Paul Binski (eds), *Age of Chivalry* (London, 1987).

Seton-Watson, R.W., *Maximilian I* (London, 1902).

Sir Gawain and the Green Knight, trans. Brian Stone (Harmondsworth, 1959; 2nd edn, 1974).

Spearing, A.C., *The Gawain Poet: A Critical Study* (Cambridge, 1970).

Spiers, John, *Medieval English Poetry, The Non-Chaucerian Tradition* (London, 1957).

Strassburg, Gottfried von, *Tristan*, trans. and ed. A.T. Hatto (London, 1960; repr. 1967).

Summerhays, R.S., *Summerhays' Encyclopaedia for Horsemen* (London, 1962).

Syson, Luke and Gordon, Dillian, *Pisanello, Painter to the Renaissance Court* (London, 2002).

Tilander, Gunnar (ed.), *Les Livres du roy Modus et de la royne Ratio*, Vol. 1, Société des Anciens Textes Français (Paris, 1932).

Thiébaux, Marcelle, *The Stag of Love: The Chase in Medieval Literature* (Ithaca and London, 1974).

Thomas, Marcel and Avril, François, *The Hunting Book of Gaston Phébus*, Commentary by Wilhelm Schlag (London, 1998).

Thompson, H.Y., *Illustrations from One Hundred Manuscripts in the Library of Henry Yates Thompson*, Vol. 4 (London, 1914).

Turbervile, George, *The Booke of Faulconrie or Hauking, London, 1575*, facsimile edn (Amsterdam and New York, 1969).

Twiti, William, *The Art of Hunting, 1327*, ed. Bror Danielsson (Stockholm, 1977).

Uden, Grant, *A Dictionary of Chivalry* (Harmondsworth, 1968; repr. 1977).

Villon, François, *Selected Poems*, trans. Peter Dale (London, 1978; repr. 1988).

Walton, Izaak, and Cotton, Charles, *The Complete Angler*, Vol. 1 (Chiswick, 1826).

Warner, Sir George (ed.), *Queen Mary's Psalter* (London, 1912).

Wheatcroft, Andrew, *The Habsburgs* (London, 1995: repr. 1996).

White, T.H., *The Goshawk* (London, 1953).

Whitlock, Ralph, *Historic Forests* (Bradford-on-Avon, 1979).

Wynne-Davies, Marion, *Bloomsbury Guide to English Literature* (London, 1989; repr. 1992).

Young, Charles R., *The Royal Forests of Medieval England* (Leicester, 1979).

Electronic Sources

Velde, François R., 'Women Knights in the Middle Ages', http://128.220.1.164/heraldry/topics/orders//wom-kn.htm

Index

ad fustem, 83
Aitinger, Joseph Conrad 91
alaunts 36
Alexander III of Scotland 14
Alfonso V of Portugal, Hunting
  Ordinances of 120
Alfonso, King of Aragon 119, 150
Alphonso XI of Castile 16, 69
amerced 138
Angevin legislation 137–9
Anglicus, Walter and William, falconers
  118
angling 2, 3–4, 148–9; advantages of;
  148; disport of 148; fly-fishing 148;
  gentleman's pursuit 148; salmon and
  sea-trout 174; status of 148–9
Anglo-Saxon Chronicle 137
animal-baiting 34
Anne de Beaujeu 158–9
antelope 59
antler(s) 24, 63, 78
Aquitaine 36
argent, fat of hare 20
Arnold, Rose Glade of 166
art of venery 6
Arthurian legend 149
artificer 94
assemblée 74, 121
at bay 74
atavism 7, 8, 174
austringer 118, 124
authors, aristocratic 9–10, 30–1, 146–7

badger, as food 101; ham 24; hide 24;
  season 87
Baillie-Grohman, William A. and Florence

6, 10, 52, 63, 66, 85–6, 87, 101
Balliolo, William de, Master of
  Greyhounds 18
Barbarossa, Frederick 30
Barking, Abbess of 149
Baroncelli, Nicolo, sculptor 119
basset hounds 2
bast 77
Bath and Wells, Bishop of 131
Bayeux Tapestry 55
beagles 2
bear 36; baiting 34; in German sources
  69; hunting 34, 62, 73, 164; high status
  quarry 68; Iberia 69; low regard for 69;
  as personal challenge 69; spring-traps to
  catch 107
beasts of the chase 3, 61–2
beasts of venery 3, 61–2, 88
beaters 11
Beauchamp, Giles 134
Beauchamp, Margaret 151
beaver, fur and habitat 24
Becken-jeger 103
Belfiore, lost hunting frescoes 163
Berenger, Raymond, Count of Barcelona
  145
Berners, Dame Juliana 3, 32, 57, 58, 61,
  85, 147–8
bestiaries 155, 156
bevy-grease 20
Birrell, Jean 6
bison 88
bisshunters 22, 108, 162
Black Book 83
Blackstone, Sir William 139
Blades, William 31

206

Index

Index

German hart-hunting practice 79
German Peasants' War, 1524–5 93, 106, 142
German poetry 155
Germanic forest 172
Gest of Robin Hood, The 76
Giraldus Cambrensis 24
Gloucester 7
Golden Legend 35
good fellowship 122, 123, 124
goshawk 41, 45–6, 118
grandes battues 83
grease, grece, grease time 20, 67, 86, 88
great deer 137, *see* hart
Greek and Latin texts 81
green livery and hunting dress 98–100
Greenwood 84, 98, 99, 169
greyhound, gazehound 34, 36, 54, 58–9, 82, 94, 164; in Gothic manuscripts 58–9; hare coursing 67, 101; high status 58; low status 59; and Mary of Burgundy 158; Master of 18; poaching with 135; relays of 84
guaranteed sport 83, 84, 85, 117
Guicenna(n)s 63
Gutenberg, Johann 91
Guy of Warwick 14

habitat decline 64–5, 174
Hadamar 73
Hadrian 35
haggard 41, 47, *see* hawking terms
hair-pipes 94
hare 36, 67–8, 174; aristocratic hunting 67–8, 170–1; advantages for hunting 67; characteristics 145; classification 61; close season 85; commons hunting the 95, 101; driving with bells 102; excrements 67; hare-hunters, modern 145; high status 67, 68; hunting 73; in fields and vineyards 101; on misericords 68; in their muses 102; names for 145; in paintings 68; ruminant 67; satirical guises 146; season 87; snaring 92; students hunting the 96–7; women and 145; world upside-down imagery 68, 145

harriers 2, 18
hart: blood, blooding 152; breaking-up of 64, 72, 75–8, 80, 81, 98, 117, 129, 152; carcass, apportioning 77, 151–2; close season 85, 174; death of 152; dispatching of 74, 152; head of 78, 151; first and last of the season, special suppers 121; flaying 75; foot of 151–2; hunting 37, 62, 73–5, 82, 169; German sources 63; lone stalking 128–9; on misericords 111; post-death rituals 79; procedures 72; royal prerogative 63, 101; season 87; slot, slot-marks 152; symbolism of 37, 154–5; tines 36; warrantability 51, 63, 74, 112, 157; warrior-like characteristics 64, 152
Havering Park, Essex 149
hawk and falcon species 20–1, 42; classification 42–7; imagery 47; long-winged 42, 118; possession of 47; rank and status hierachy 42–6; short-winged 42, 118; stealing, birds, eggs 41, 140
hawking: aristocratic and élitist sport 39, 123; correct dress 48–51; knightly combat 39; mewing 40; provider of meat 20, 39, 45; terms of sport 48; value of hunting birds 40–1
hawks of the fist 42
hawks of the tower 42
hays, hayes 94, 108
Hemingway, Ernest 175
Henry III of England 137, 149
Henry IV of England 10, 120, 136; Royal Hunt Wages Account of 1470 123
Henry of Monmouth, Prince of Wales 31
Henry V of England 96, 134, 136
Henry VI of England 15
Henry VII of England 139, 169
herons 159–60
high deer, *see* hart
hind, red deer 36, 62; breaking-up 153; *curée* 153; hunting 62; season 87
Hippolyta and Emily 149
holds 75
Hood, Robin 7, 76, 98–9, 122, 125, 169
horn 116, 170; motes 83; prise 80
Horn 14

210

Index